MW00582405

IN SEARCH OF
AN OPEN MIND

IN SEARCH OF AN OPEN MIND

Speeches and Writings

LEE C. BOLLINGER

Columbia University Press

New York

Columbia University Press
Publishers Since 1893
New York Chichester, West Sussex
cup.columbia.edu
Copyright © 2025 Columbia University Press
All rights reserved

Cataloging-in-Publication Data is available from the Library of Congress.
ISBN 9780231217996 (hardback)
ISBN 9780231562010 (ebook)

Printed in the United States of America

Cover design: Julia Kushnirsky
Cover photo: Eileen Barroso

For Jean, always

CONTENTS

ACKNOWLEDGMENTS

Never in my life has it been truer to state that there are more people who have helped me with these speeches and writings—and the events surrounding them—than I can possibly recognize personally and thank here. While president of Columbia University, I had an extraordinarily supportive group of individuals who worked closely with me on nearly all of these pieces. Colleagues in my administration, provosts, deans, faculty, trustees, and so many others—all friends with whom I had the privilege of sharing a common and bold mission—I sincerely thank each one. Their presence is in these selections.

There are, however, a few individuals who had such a close hand in the composition process that they warrant special mention. Susan Glancy, my long-serving chief of staff, deserves the greatest credit for so thoroughly and gracefully being a wise advisor while organizing a superlative team. Christina Shelby was a superb assistant through much of the time represented here. And Evelyn Schwalb has followed and brought her own outstanding skills.

I have been fortunate to work with the most wonderful, talented executive vice presidents and senior advisors over the course of my presidency. The three who have been most involved in the crafting of these speeches and writings are David Stone, the former executive vice president for communications; Shailagh Murray, the current executive vice president for public affairs; and Jane Booth, chief legal officer. In the Communications Office, I would also like to recognize Scott Schell, the former vice president for public affairs, and Claire Levenson, the director of executive communications. Also, I want to especially acknowledge the more recent role David played in helping assemble this particular volume, which has been part of a larger project archiving the historical record of the period. He has been a true colleague and trusted friend.

Finally, I wish to pay tribute to my wife, Jean. When things matter most, fewer words are better. You will see several references to her throughout this book. Each one tries to express the reality that no one has played a larger and more positive role in my life than Jean. She has been the ideal audience I have always sought to impress.

PREFACE

I have spent most of my life in universities. After graduating from Columbia Law School in 1971, followed by a judicial clerkship with Judge Wilfred Feinberg on the U.S. Court of Appeals for the Second Circuit and then with Chief Justice Warren Burger on the U.S. Supreme Court, I immediately joined the University of Michigan Law School as an assistant professor. I soon began writing about First Amendment law—freedom of speech and press, specifically—and that became my scholarly focus, along with some other writing ventures. In 1987, I was invited by the faculty to become dean of the law school, which brought a whole new dimension to my academic career. It turned out that I liked doing this line of work and felt I was reasonably good at it. I was forty-one years old, deeply engaged with my research and writing, but also becoming aware that I was at risk of spending too much time immersed in my ideas with no prospect of additional insights beyond what I could summon in a few hours a day. It occurred to me that I could continue doing my intellectual work while adding something else to my life that might also be productive and rewarding; and being an academic leader seemed like the right path. As it happened, one opportunity followed another. Eventually, I became the president of the University of Michigan in 1997. Five years later, in 2002, I returned to Columbia as president, where I served (somewhat unexpectedly) for just over two decades.

This collection of speeches and writings spans that twenty-one-year period. The selections are representative of what I thought and did during this time. They are presented chronologically. Each speaks to the moment in which it happened, but together they tell a larger story about issues and matters that have concerned me over the course of my life. Of the myriad of subjects covered, four stand out. First and foremost, there are universities, and Columbia, of course—their role in society;

the sources of their strengths and contributions to the world as well as their limits and flaws; being a student or a professor; and how they should evolve. Next, and equally important to me, is the subject of freedom of speech and press—along with the idea of academic freedom—what it means at every level, from the U.S. Constitution to the personal, how it became what it is today and how it might evolve with new social conditions. Then, of prime importance to me too, is the rightness of affirmative action and its vital role in making ours a more just society. Lastly, and weaving its way through everything, are my attempts to think as deeply as I have been able to how to be a good person, to live a good life, and, more specifically, about how to develop the capacities of mind and intellect that yield the most we can gain from life. Having an open mind is at the core.

During my presidential tenure, in the opening quarter of the twenty-first century, Columbia, the nation, and the world underwent immense transformations. All were intertwined and affected everything I touch upon here. Wars and conflicts, economic bursts and crises,[1] revolutions in technologies (especially technologies of communication, which had a profound effect on journalism and media),[2] massive global trends in human movement and urbanization, democracy thriving and democracy threatened, new promises of breakthroughs in human health plus a life-crushing global pandemic, tectonic shifts in law, and intensifying climate change affecting our environment and even planetary well-being—all these developments and many others reverberated across the world and landed on a centuries-old leading research university in New York City.

Columbia has always been a great institution, but its real glory had occurred several decades earlier. In the 1950s and 1960s, there was no better university in the country or, indeed, the world. Department after department—from literature to the social sciences to the natural and biological sciences, as well as the graduate schools of medicine, law, and journalism—was widely acknowledged as a leader in its respective field. I always liked to point out this story as a telling example: If in, say, 1960, you had walked through the halls and faculty offices of the Physics Department, you would have found that more than half of the faculty had won or would win a Nobel Prize for their work. Financially, Columbia was in a strong position, with an endowment substantially equal to its peers, notably that of Harvard. Physically, the University had room to grow on its respective campuses, especially the glorious campus in Morningside Heights, designed by McKim, Mead and White, where Columbia moved at the end of the nineteenth century. All this began to unravel with the student protests of the latter half of the 1960s or, more

accurately, with the institutional responses to those protests. In 1968, tensions
with the surrounding communities of Harlem reached a breaking point when the
University proposed building a gym in an adjacent public park, which was in turn
jettisoned when both campus and community opposition to both the gym and
the Vietnam War led to widespread student protest, building takeovers and
clashes with police. Nearly every college and university in the United States was
buffeted by these events, but none took it harder than Columbia. It split the faculty
so deeply that many departed for other places, such as the University of Chicago
and the rising Stanford. It was to this Columbia that Jean and I arrived in the summer of 1968, young and newly married from Eugene, Oregon, our own graduate
student life starting in a tiny studio above a bar on 104th and Broadway.

Columbia might well have recovered from those shocks had it not been followed by the severe downturn in the fortunes of New York City. The 1970s were
a nadir for the city and many of the challenges manifest on the Columbia campus.
None of these major events were easily resolved or deflected. By the end of the
decade, Columbia was a shadow of its former self—academically declined, physically constrained, financially nearly bankrupt, and beset with persistent bitter-
ness and animosities. Still, within the University was a yearning to realize its
unfathomable potential. In 1980, the extremely gifted Columbia provost and
former dean of the Law School, Michael Sovern (and my law school teacher and
friend), took over as the university president. From that moment, Columbia
began its process of recovery.

But recovery from such shattering events takes time. And, when I began as
president in 2002, there was still much to do. Space had to be made available for
academic growth and dreams (hence the dramatic idea of a new campus in West
Harlem in an old industrial area known as Manhattanville); relations with students, alumni and parents, friends and surrounding communities (especially Harlem) had to be re-established and improved; highly ambitious capital campaigns
had to be designed and executed; and, above all, of course, the overall academic
quality had to be a day-in-day-out focus. More specifically, areas of academic work
intrinsic to Columbia's character and history needed to be supported—the humanities and social sciences, the arts, and the sciences—with a goal of establishing the
preeminence of intellectual creativity in vital fields of public importance (thus,
the pioneering Mind, Brain, Behavior Institute built around Columbia's Nobel-
Prize-winning neuroscience). The new campus in Manhattanville became a literal
laboratory for important experiments in these ventures and engagement with the

local communities. Over time we brought many new initiatives into the mix—especially with the international and global reach of the University: the emphasis on diversity of all kinds; the idea of making academic work more connected to the challenges facing the world outside (which I labeled the Fourth Purpose of the university); and taking on new areas of public concern in need of more academic attention (most significantly with the creation of a new Columbia Climate School). Selected pieces in this collection chronicle these developments.

Throughout this period, the evergreen issues of free speech and free press continued to define my life and work. Being a university president is a very good way to confront and practice the principle of free speech, and at Columbia, in particular, I have had plenty of opportunities to do so. Several are noted here, reflecting the evolution of my thinking about these seminal American constitutional principles, which have been with me, or so it seems, since I was a child. Both my father and his mother (my grandmother) started working at the local newspaper, the Santa Rosa Press Democrat, out of necessity when his father passed away—he as a delivery boy and she in the newspaper library. After my mother and he were married, he joined the Marines in World War II, and after the war he returned to the newspaper as circulation manager. From there he bought into a small daily newspaper in Baker, Oregon, where our family moved, and he was the editor and publisher. I did chores around the newsroom—developing films, being the janitor, melting the lead for the pigs for the linotypes, and so on. Once I started as a law professor years later, the subject I was drawn to write about, unsurprisingly, was freedom of the press—specifically, the then-differential treatment of the print media and the broadcast media under our Constitution and federal laws and regulations.

From that subject I became engrossed in the central problem of the First Amendment, namely, how far into dangerous and offensive speech should the principle extend and for what purpose? This was at the time of the highly controversial march of a small group of neo-Nazis in the Chicago suburb of Skokie, Illinois, home to many Jews and several thousand survivors of the WWII concentration camps. This led me into the fundamental underpinnings of the First Amendment, which resulted in my first book, *The Tolerant Society*. The First Amendment has remained my central intellectual focus ever since.[3] So, there has been an ongoing correspondence, and mutual illumination, between my professional and personal devotion to the issues of free speech and press and my life within a university. Perhaps like many people, I was able to use my intellectual subject to think about large issues of life, which returned to expand my thinking about the principles narrowly conceived. I certainly feel I have been fortunate to live a life where every part or sector of my being has related to all of the others.

My other area of focus emerged unexpectedly. Within a few months of becoming president of the University of Michigan, I received warning that we would be sued by a group opposed to affirmative action in higher education. This suit flowed from a huge, highly organized effort all across the country to dismantle several decades of progress by colleges and universities toward increasing the presence of African American, Hispanic and Native American students in every institution. Emboldened by successes in litigation (against the University of Texas) and ballot initiatives to change state constitutions to ban affirmative action (Proposition 209 in California being the most notorious), the anti-affirmative action groups turned their focus on one of the most prominent public universities in the nation—namely, the University of Michigan.

Two lawsuits were filed, both claiming violations of the 14th amendment of the U.S. Constitution. One was against the admissions policy for undergraduates (*Gratz v. Bollinger*) and the other against the admissions policy in the Law School (*Grutter v. Bollinger*). I had not been involved with the first policy, but I was intimately involved in shaping the latter when I was Dean of the Law School in the late 1980s. I knew this was likely to be the biggest test of the constitutionality of affirmative action ever. Prior to these lawsuits, the Supreme Court had only considered the issue once, in a well-known case called *Regents of the University of California v. Bakke* in 1978. A majority of the Court declared that "quotas" were unconstitutional, which resolved the case unfavorably to the University of California, Davis. But the justices divided sharply on whether race and ethnicity could ever be considered as factors in admissions. Justice Powell wrote the momentous plurality opinion unfortunately changing public debate on this issue ever after, saying colleges could do so for purposes of enhancing their educational goals through "diversity," but they could not for purposes of overcoming centuries of societal discrimination. This was a watershed moment and stripped the actions of colleges and universities of their most powerful reasoning—that to include Blacks, Hispanics and Native Americans in their student bodies was essential to helping society correct the vestiges of severe disadvantages endured by these groups, as found by the unanimous Court ruling in *Brown v. Board of Education* in 1954. Because of the plurality opinion in *Bakke*, no Court majority had held affirmative action to be protected under the Constitution as binding legal precedent, but it had become standard practice across higher education and now, in *Grutter* and *Gratz*, that issue would have to be resolved.

I did not intend to make defending affirmative action part of my life's mission. I believed in it and my life had been forged in the era of the civil rights movement. But now, with my presidential role and as a named personal defendant, I gladly embraced the challenge and became its advocate. First there was the complete victory with the Supreme Court's ruling in *Grutter* in June of 2003, shortly after I began at Columbia. As a result, America's colleges and universities dramatically increased the diversity of their student bodies over the next two decades, opening the minds of students and future leaders to perspectives different from their own while providing new educational opportunities to generations of college and graduate students. And then came the near-complete loss and reversal of *Grutter*—ironically for me, at least, in the last week of my Columbia presidency—as the composition of the Court shifted during the Trump presidency, in *Students for Fair Admissions v. President and Fellows of Harvard College*. Many of my speeches and writings here are devoted to this critically important issue.[4] This is a story of America, but it is also a personal story of mine.

And then there are the thoughts about how to live a good life and be good person—this, too, requires an open mind, reflected in the ability to listen carefully to another, consider their experience, recognize when you are wrong, and strive to be better. A university provides an ideal context for this search, combining young and old, all together seeking a better understanding of human beings, of society and of the physical world, to talk about matters of the utmost importance and urgency. Threading their way through these selections are my modest efforts.

In the end, much of what follows is about universities themselves—their purposes and roles in society, their organization, the leadership of them, and the very special qualities that they bring to the world, beginning with each class of entering students. Universities are structured in bizarre ways. I often say that no sane person would create a modern university as it is. And yet they work and they work so well that they are among America's finest and most successful institutions. Young people all over the world strive to attend as students. I do not mean, of course, to say that they are without flaws. There are, to be sure, many limits and defects—which are also the subject of these speeches and writings. But it is always the case that, whatever system or organizational structure you choose, there will inevitably be shortcomings that come with the choice. No system is perfect. So much academic authority is vested in the individual faculty member, and so much of the success of the university depends upon how each performs their responsibilities. They do not know the concept of a boss in the way that employees do in other settings. To many this is a strange way to run an organization. And, yet, many of the brightest people of each generation join our ranks, and every day you can see these faculty devoted to teaching their students and writing original works and conducting seminal experiments in the laboratory or out in the world. The rising criticisms of universities are overstated. All you need to do is step away from the headlines and walk on any campus on any day of the year—instantly, you will feel the exhilaration of being in a place uniquely devoted to knowledge and to the education of our youth. I am proud to have spent my life in its midst.

Many of the works herein are from convocation ceremonies when we welcome the new members of the academic community, and from commencement, when all Columbia students graduating from every school, college and affiliated institutions assemble in the superb center of the Morningside Heights campus to celebrate their accomplishments. Some 30,000 to 40,000 people gather, and the feeling is transcendent. By long tradition, the Columbia President is the commencement speaker—a very high honor and an enormous annual source of pressure and anxiety. The commencement speech is its own art form and exceptionally difficult to deliver well. Banalities flow and attention easily flags. I took every one of these occasions with the utmost seriousness, believing it a monumental privilege to be able to honor and speak meaningfully to the graduates, their families and friends. I hope that feeling is evident here to every reader.

Being a university president is how I have spent a quarter-century of my life. How to lead, how to nurture, and how to help everyone connected to these institutions is a matter of keen interest, therefore. It is not an easy job; many would say it's an impossible job. But to me it has been the best (impossible) job imaginable. There especially is the pleasure of learning about every field of study that makes up an institution dedicated to preserving and advancing knowledge and human understanding. As the president, you also connect this extraordinary little world to all the vibrant sectors of society beyond the academic gates, and then return with thoughts and ideas from abroad, as it were. For someone always trying to learn as much as possible, there could be no better position in life.

Right now, as I write this preface, it is once again a very hard time for universities and for their presidents and other leaders. Events abroad—in this case, the October 7th savage terrorist attack on Israelis in Southern Israel and the ensuing Israeli war against Hamas—have led to protests and actions on campuses and re-ignited the broader divisions around the historical Israeli-Palestinian conflict. Actual incidents and further allegations of antisemitism and Islamophobia have angered everyone and demanded corrective action. Questions for academic leaders about whether to speak and about what to say if you decide to speak have been vividly argued. As is always true in America, eventually many of the issues have evolved into free speech questions, so now once again society is asking to what extent do we or should we protect "bad" speech and under what circumstances? Inevitably, these specific issues tap into larger concerns about the modern university—Are contemporary students too intolerant, too unwilling to see the complexity of things, too encouraged and indulged to feel the self-righteousness of victimhood, too closed-minded?

Every one of these issues is discussed and considered in the speeches and writings that comprise this collection, and that is because the issues are perennial. They are hard, but they are vitally important and are never going to be resolved once and for all. That's in large part because of human nature and going through them repeatedly is how we make ourselves better people, better institutions, and a better society. Again, this points to the completely preoccupying and recurring theme of this volume: that all areas of life (whether it is with ideas or with experiences of all kinds) call for us to have an open mind, to varying degrees, which is a highly complex state of being, and, further, that given our natures it is an inherently unstable state and never one we achieve fully or permanently.

Since stepping down from the presidency on June 30, 2023, I have been on sabbatical. I have always felt that the best part of a sabbatical year is the six months BEFORE the sabbatical begins. That is when one dreams of all that you are going to do in this sacred time in which to think and write, when you are relieved of the burdens of ordinary life and do not have to face the reality of your own incapacities in the form of the blank page. So, too, one of the best periods of life is in the six months *after* you have served in the role in life that fate has afforded you. Then you are freed of the responsibility to do more; you cannot change what you have done or alter where you are headed. You can look back and take stock, and potentially even see things that were obscured in the immediate flux and pressures of the moment. You do have to face your regrets, but you can do that in the context of enjoying what has been done and accomplished. And, so, all the pieces here are untouched, unedited and unimproved. They are in the order in which they occurred. I hope they are helpful.

IN SEARCH OF
AN OPEN MIND

CHAPTER 1

INAUGURAL ADDRESS

Columbia University, Low Plaza, October 3, 2002

On October 3, 2001, less than a month after the September 11th attacks on the World Trade Center in Lower Manhattan, the Trustees of Columbia University named Lee C. Bollinger as the University's nineteenth president. Having served as the president of the University of Michigan since 1997, where he led that academic institution's high-profile defense of its affirmative action admission policies, Bollinger officially began his Columbia term on July 1, 2002, followed by inaugural ceremonies once the university reconvened for the new academic year.

Thank you, David Stern. Columbia is privileged to have your extraordinary talents so devoted to serving its welfare. And I am grateful to the Trustees, as well as to the University Community, for their trust and support.

I want to express my deepest appreciation to [United Nations] Secretary-General Kofi Annan, whose presence here reminds us of our international responsibilities and of how personal dignity is such a powerful source of authority; to Mayor Bloomberg, who personally reflects the energy and restless spirit of the City and who asserts eloquently that there are few problems for which education is not the primary answer; to Congressman Rangel, who carries forward New York's historic tradition in Washington as an architect of national programs of equal opportunity and justice; and to David Dinkins, who has served the public with such distinction as Mayor and as our Columbia Professor.

I am thankful for the greetings from Provost Jonathan Cole, Florence Grant, Karen Dacey, and my colleague and friend Ted Shaw.

It is a source of personal and University pride to have representatives from so many institutions of higher education here today. I thank you for coming. I have special thanks for our sister colleges and universities—our academic partners: to Barnard College, Union Theological Seminary, and Jewish Theological Seminary; to all institutions from the Ivy League (and especially to my good friend John Rosenwald, representing Dartmouth); to my wonderful colleagues from the University of Michigan; and to my great friend, who was himself inaugurated as the new President of New York University just one week ago, John Sexton (with whom we will find many more ways to collaborate in the years ahead).

I want to recognize my and Jean's families. First, hers. Her father, who is approaching 90, could not be here, but her brother Marco and her sister Patti are, and her cousin Paul. My brothers and sister—Brad, Tami, Jayme and Jeff—are here, too. And my parents, Lee and Pat, who as parents have sacrificed almost without limit for their children, respected the education that was unavailable to them personally, and never wavered on the importance of personal integrity.

Jean and I have a son and daughter, Lee and Carey, who are not just children we love beyond words but also people we admire for their character, their perspective on life, and the extraordinary sensitivities they bring to all they encounter.

Now my wife Jean: I could talk about her unique talents, which are so many, about her enormous capacity for empathy, about her infectious good will, or about her strength to be the person she wants to be. I could talk at length about all these qualities. But the most important thing I want to say is that after 34 years of marriage, which began with our coming to Columbia, there is a melding of purpose and sympathy between us that is nearly perfect, or as Montaigne said, "our souls mingle and blend with each other so completely that they efface the seam that joined them, and cannot find it again."

I would like to begin with an acknowledgement: I fully recognize that inaugural addresses are, as a general rule, distinctly unmemorable events. Mike Sovern, one of two living Presidents Emeriti of Columbia, used to recall how on his first day at Columbia as a freshman in 1949, Dwight Eisenhower, then President of our University, delivered a long speech of welcome. Mike said that try as he could, he could not remember one word of what the great man said. Forgetting is, of course, one of the more valuable capacities of the human mind, valuable and mysterious. It is, I am pleased to say, a little less mysterious because of the path-breaking scientific work of our master of ceremonies, Professor Eric Kandel, work for which he was honored with the Nobel Prize. Surely, not remembering is part of our genetically based instinct for self-preservation and defense. Indeed, I would not be surprised if sometime in the near future scientists uncover a particular gene whose function it is to exclude from memory inaugural speeches. With that prospect in mind, let me therefore begin by declaring that what I am about to say is not an inaugural address but really a set of personal and early reflections on Columbia and our collective future together.

Now, you may be thinking that I am employing the time-honored oratorical technique of lowering audience expectations by bringing to the surface your secret thoughts (i.e., that you are not expecting to hear memorable words). The most famous illustration of this technique is Pericles, who in his funeral oration began by observing that nothing he would say would fully satisfy either those who knew the dead soldiers or those who didn't, since any praise he might offer would be too little for family and friends and too much for strangers, arousing in them feelings of inferiority, envy, and incredulity. I confess to this motive, but I also have another higher purpose in mind: namely, to take a more or less true observation about speeches at occasions such as this and ask us to think about how what we do remember about Columbia, and what we seek to add to the store of memories about Columbia, will make all the difference in the years ahead.

II

We are gathered here this morning on one of the most stunning academic settings in the world. Personally, I never enter the space without feeling the invitation to be part of the noble and distinctive human activities of thought and discussion.

Just behind me stands Low Library, the magnificent temple to knowledge (its dome suggestive of the human mind). It is in the center of the architect Charles McKim's Athenian campus. It was the first building constructed on this campus, as a library. But for that purpose it has long been replaced by South Hall—now Butler Library, the majestic Italian Renaissance structure directly behind you. At the time that Butler Library opened in 1934, it was among the seven largest library wonders of the world, joining Oxford, Yale, Harvard, the Library of Congress, the Bibliothèque Nationale, and the world's largest library—the Soviet State Library in Leningrad. Today it remains one of the premier libraries of the world.

Directly behind me is *Alma Mater*, her robe half-concealing the owl which generations of students have patted on the head for good luck on the way to final exams. *Alma Mater* was sculpted by Daniel French, who created the revered statue of Abraham Lincoln in the Lincoln Memorial in Washington.

But, frankly, to me the most beautiful structure of all in this academic quadrangle is the steps, the steps in sunny weather with students on them, talking, reading, or relaxing.

All the buildings within your immediate sight have stories to tell: (going clockwise) St. Paul's, described by critic Paul Goldberger as a "neat combination of modesty and self-confidence (a model, in other words, for us all); Buell Hall, home of the Buell Center for the Study of American Architecture and of the oldest university foreign language cultural center in the nation; Philosophy Hall, where a brilliant professor of engineering, Edwin Armstrong, invented FM radio, which led to the founding in 1941 of the first FM radio station, which is still here, Columbia's WKCR–FM; then Kent Hall, now home to the distinguished East Asian Institute (and earlier to the Law School, now located across Amsterdam, whose alums include five Supreme Court Justices (Hughes, Cardozo, Stone, Douglas, and Ruth Bader Ginsburg), as well as two others named Roosevelt—Theodore and Franklin).

Hamilton Hall, where illustrious faculty taught and wrote: Lionel Trilling, Meyer Schapiro, Franz Boas (a founder of the field of anthropology); Margaret Mead, Ruth Benedict, Allan Nevins, Mark and Carl Van Doren, John Dewey, and Richard Hofstadter. John Jay Hall, home for a while of the great poet Federico García Lorca, and in front of which, in South Field, Lou Gehrig hit homeruns across 116th Street, now College Walk. Alfred Lerner Hall is to the West of Butler Library and gives all of us a visual sense of the importance of students to Columbia. The Journalism Building, where for the past 90 years judges have met to select the winners of the Pulitzer Prize. It was, of course, Joseph Pulitzer who founded and endowed our Journalism School (in part, he said, because "it is located in New York City"), asking of us that we serve the public good by educating a noble profession (journalism) not simply about the practical side of being journalists but also in the knowledge a great university can offer: "Why not teach," he asked rhetorically, "politics, literature, government, constitutional principles and traditions (especially American), history, political economy; also the history and the power of public opinion and public service, illustrated by concrete examples, showing the mission, duty and opportunity of the Press as a moral teacher?" He was criticized for this "visionary" scheme—by many in the press, no less.

Dodge Hall, home of the School of the Arts and site of the world's first concert of electronic music. And then Lewisohn, the focal point of our important School of General Studies.

This is just the inner circle. It spirals outward: Pupin Hall, where atomic research began in 1925, and named after Michael Idvorsky Pupin, a penniless immigrant from Serbia, who took the first X-Ray photograph in America and made possible the first long-distance telephone call. It was also home to some of the greatest scientists in modern times, among them T.D. Lee (faculty member 1953-present), Enrico Fermi, I.I. Rabi, Polykarp Kusch, and Harold Urey.

And Fayerweather, the home of our outstanding history and sociology departments, the sociology department where Robert Merton, a national medal of science recipient, developed critical breakthroughs that we now accept as settled questions.

Beyond our view, premier schools rise in succession, our outstanding Business School, School of Engineering, Architecture, Social Work, International and Public Affairs, and Law.

Then just a few miles north, in Washington Heights, is one of the major centers in the world for medical education and care, as well as basic research in health and life sciences. And, just another twenty miles up the Hudson, is the renowned Lamont-Doherty Earth Observatory, where research led to the discovery of plate tectonics. There Professor Maurice Ewing conducted major research in acoustical transmission, and today the ship bearing his name and operated by Columbia plows the oceans sending sound waves to the ocean floor to better understand this colossus of the planet.

III

Yet, the history of Columbia University—the fifth oldest university in the nation—dates back well before these buildings. We are 248 years old, and next year we begin the celebration of Columbia's 250th anniversary. Remembering our past, knowing where we came from, is critical to having an identity, whether as individuals or as institutions.

Columbia began near the site of the World Trade Center. In 1754, eight students reported to class in the vestry of Trinity Church with a faculty of one—also the first President. President Samuel Johnson taught languages, logic, composition, speech, mathematics, geography, history, business, government, astronomy, earth sciences, biology, and religion. Tuition was 100 shillings a year, not in fact a small sum ($772 in current dollars). There was, of course, no United States, no Constitution, no Declaration of Independence. The American Revolution was 21 years away. The Constitutional Convention, in which Columbia alumni would play major roles, was 34 years in the future. The population of the world at that time was under 500 million souls. Today it is well over six billion and growing at the rate of 80 million a year (with most of the growth occurring in the world's most impoverished countries). As classes opened at King's College, as we were then called, the population of New York City was 10,881.

With the American Revolution, the College's president at the time, Myles Cooper, began a long tradition of university administrations being out of touch with their times, and especially with students. He was an avowed Loyalist, and in 1775 a mob gathered outside his house. Like many an academic administrator since, he escaped ignominiously by fleeing through the back window to join a British frigate heading home. Cooper died some years later while consuming a lavish lunch in Edinburgh, yet another lesson he left for us all.

The College closed for the duration of the Revolution and then, in 1784, reopened and was patriotically renamed Columbia College. Dewitt Clinton graduated two years later. He became the first of 15 Columbians to serve as mayor of New York City. He set in motion the plotting of the basic grid of streets and avenues in the City that are still with us today.

The College quickly established itself as an educator of the greatest statesmen of the time: John Jay, America's first Chief Justice and first Secretary of State (later to be succeeded by our graduate Madeleine Albright); Robert Livingston, who helped draft the Declaration of Independence and also served as Secretary of State; Gouverneur Morris, who worked on the final draft of the U.S. Constitution; and Alexander Hamilton, who among his many accomplishments signed the Constitution on behalf of the people of New York State. These were the forebears of a long line of Columbia nation builders extending into the modern era, such as Wellington Koo, Bhimrao Ambedkar, chief author of the constitution of India, and Pixley Seme, founder of the African National Congress.

As much as I'd like to, I realize I cannot now tell the story of the next two hundred years. It must suffice to say only that it's an amazing story of distinction and movement to our present location, and that the 250th celebration will highlight that heritage.

Let me take this opportunity to recognize my two most recent predecessors. The 1960s and 70s were a vexed and difficult time (for many reasons) for universities across the country, but they brought particularly harsh consequences for Columbia and New York City.

The foundation for Columbia's fiscal strength, without which all else would collapse, was laid by Mike Sovern in the 1980s, at a time when the University also experienced both a restoration of its physical plant and an intellectual renaissance. For 13 years, Mike Sovern was the catalyst and the symbol of that restoration. Columbia became a place of greater attraction to students, and students came to know Columbia during the Sovern administration as a University that valued diversity and that protected freedom of speech. In 1987, the first fully coeducational class graduated from Columbia College. Ladies and gentlemen, please welcome my esteemed law professor and predecessor, President Emeritus Michael I. Sovern.

Over two decades ago, I was a first-year law student in a labor law class taught by a gifted young professor named Michael Sovern. I am pleased to say that I remember every word he said.

My immediate predecessor, George Rupp, is in Afghanistan, where he is leading humanitarian efforts of the International Rescue Committee, of which he is president. In the nine years of his presidency at Columbia, George Rupp advanced our University by revitalizing our core academic programs, particularly in the social sciences. Great improvements occurred in selectivity in the College and professional schools' admissions. He built new bridges of collaborative teaching and research between Columbia's schools and colleges and between the Morningside campus and the Health Sciences campus. The Rupp administration, which further enhanced Columbia's financial strength, was also marked by continued improvement in the crucial partnership between the University and our neighboring communities.

IV

As we inherit this absolutely extraordinary institution at the beginning of this new century, I want to set out some themes that I hope will be discussed and pursued as we chart our future together. It is, and has been for some years now, a glorious time for higher education in this country, and with any luck it will be for the foreseeable future. What role will Columbia play in this era, and what do we need to do to enable that to happen? To answer that we need to know who we are.

And my general answer is this: Columbia is the Quintessential Great Urban University. Looked at from any perspective, it seems to me, this is the primary source of attributes, the defining personality, of this institution. We must embrace it. We must also understand it. Here are some of the things it means to me.

First: It is less possible and less desirable to remain apart, to be removed from the world around us. Accordingly, the task for us is how to engage with that world in a useful and productive way. We must serve society and the world while enhancing the academic character of the university and preserving its distinctive intellectual outlook. The range of visitors to this campus—to teach, to speak, to visit, to seek counsel and to offer advice—is simply unparalleled. The degree to which our students are beneficiaries of this access to the world beyond these buildings is self-evident. So is the degree to which our scholarship is positively affected by this augmented contact with real problems. And on the other side, Columbians are naturally called upon more frequently to serve and they are ready to do so.

Exactly 100 years ago Nicholas Murray Butler said precisely this, in his long-forgotten inaugural address, at the start of his astonishing 43-year tenure (a record I hope to exceed, if I can simply live to be 100). It is interesting to see Butler, one of the great figures of higher education in the twentieth century (and a Nobel Prize winner), talk so comfortably and forthrightly about the importance of the university accepting the call for service to the world. My guess is that only a president of "Columbia University in the City of New York" (our official title) could say such things.

Here's what he said about scholarship and service. President Butler first distinguished the scholar from the expert. Butler agreed with Aristotle that the "true scholar" is "free," meaning in an intellectual sense. To be free, he said, is to have "a largeness of view . . . which permits [one] to see the other side; a knowledge of the course of man's intellectual history and its meaning; a grasp of principles and a standard for judging them; the power and habit of reflection firmly established; a fine feeling for moral and intellectual distinctions; and the kindliness of spirit and nobility of purpose which are the support of genuine character."

"In these modern days," Butler said in 1902, "the university is not apart from the activities of the world, but in them and of them. It deals with real problems and it relates itself to life as it is." In the combination [of scholarship and service],

Butler found the "ethical quality which makes the university a real person, bound by its very nature to the service of others." And so: "Every legitimate demand for guidance, for leadership, for expert knowledge, for trained skill, for personal service, it is the . . . duty of the university to meet." Butler made it clear that he disapproved of "academic aloofness." He urged Columbia to recruit faculty and students "competent to be the intellectual and spiritual leaders of the nation and competent to train others for leadership. Great personalities," he proclaimed, "make great universities."

This 100-year-old vision can serve as a guide for us in this new century as well. Given this enhanced involvement with the outside world, which is part of the essence of Columbia's role as the great urban university, it is crucial that we engage while retaining our distinctive academic character. In the real world, conflict and choices are always present, and that tends inevitably to affect how we think and discuss. It is harder to be intellectually "free," to have that "largeness of view . . . which permits [one] to see the other side." University engagement with the political sphere, therefore, must always be limited by the need to maintain that special intellectual angle of vision that, in the end, is what makes us of value to the society in the first place. And, for its part, when society invites our participation, it must be careful to resist the impulse it feels at times to crush that fragile intellectual spirit, for in any unrestrained battle, as Machiavelli said years ago, the state will win.

Second: Columbia, as the quintessential great urban university, is more international. I mean by this not only the presence in our university of individuals from outside the boundaries of the United States, which is significant. Columbia stands in the very top group of American Universities in terms of the number of international students. (This is a longstanding Columbia policy: it was the first university in the United States to have more than a thousand foreign students, in 1953). Today our students come from 145 nations, and a quarter of our faculty are foreign born. Rather by saying Columbia is more international, I mean something more than this; I mean international in perspective, in consciousness, in our interests and our engagements as students, teachers, and scholars. In New York City, you cannot help but feel the presence of every part of the globe, and so it is at Columbia. I, therefore, believe that in every field represented at this University there is more focus on world issues. And, so, deep down Columbia possesses naturally the sense of itself as a citizen of the world—we engage with the world, not just out of a calculation of self-interest but out of a sense of responsibility.

Third: Columbia is profoundly committed to the educational principle of diversity. Again, just as this City is the most diverse in the world, so is Columbia a highly diverse university. Among just a handful of American universities, Columbia has fiercely maintained over the years a commitment to devote its resources to a policy of need blind admissions for undergraduates. Diversity as well as educational opportunity underlie this commitment. We all have much to learn about different cultures, about different ways of organizing societies, about how life experiences shape how one sees the world, about our perceptions (often inaccurate and oversimplified) of people of different cultures, societies, race, and ethnicities. This is the true marketplace of ideas.

At home in this country, the work of integration begun by one of the greatest Supreme Court decisions of the twentieth century—*Brown v. Board of Education*—is far from over, although much progress has been made. (Many Columbians were involved with *Brown*: Robert Carter, Kenneth and Mamie Clark, Jack Greenberg, Otto Kleinberg, Constance Baker Motley, and Jack Weinstein.) Over the past four decades, our American universities have done their part to fulfill the promise of *Brown*, by seeking the educational, intellectual, and emotional benefits of diverse student populations. It would be an American tragedy if this progress were stalled by a reversal of Constitutional doctrine now nearly a half-century old, as determined opponents of affirmative action are at this moment trying to do. Very likely the issue of the constitutionality of considering race and ethnicity as factors in admissions—the most important civil rights issue since *Brown*—will come before the Supreme Court this year. The outcome will have direct relevance to Columbia, as it will for all higher education.

Fourth: Columbia, as the quintessential great urban university, is—perhaps ironically—deeply committed to tradition. Here I think of the great Core Curriculum, the longest running, most extensive core curriculum in the country. In the face of the swirling life surrounding us in this flourishing world city, it is not surprising that Columbia, as a university, would feel a greater need to hold onto what is precious from our history. And, yet, the greatness of this conservative impulse is not the wish to study Aristotle in isolation, but rather to immerse oneself in these great works while considering the great issues of our time—hence the title of the oldest Core course, "Contemporary Civilization." (Lionel Trilling said of reading King Lear that to read this "dire report of life" is "invigorating" because it "does us the honor of supposing that we will make every possible effort of mind to withstand the force of its despair and to understand the complexity of what it tells us about the nature of human existence; it draws us into more activity than we'd thought ourselves capable of.")

Fifth: Columbia, as the quintessential great urban university, is—unexpectedly—the ultimate college town. One of the most surprising things about this university is the number of students, faculty, and staff living within just a few blocks of where we are now gathered. Life here is exactly the opposite of what people commonly assume about a great university in a colossal city such as New York. It is like classical Athens, where citizens could throw on their tunics and walk to the forum and consider the world. The atmosphere is pervaded by thought and discussion; it is a community not just a campus.

Sixth: Columbia is integrated into the fabric of the neighborhoods and the City. We share life with our neighbors and we have great responsibility to them. For New York City, Columbia University is immensely important. The University brings in well over a billion dollars a year to the City economy, generating last year more than 10,000 jobs. Columbia is New York City's largest academic research center, spending $418 million on research last year (27% of all academic research spending in New York City).

This carries over more immediately to Morningside Heights, Harlem, and Washington Heights. We spend $42 million annually for goods and services from Upper Manhattan and South Bronx businesses, and we must continue to actively seek new ways to help the local economies.

But above all else the University benefits enormously by living amidst such creative and resilient communities.

Seventh and last: Columbia as the quintessential great urban university is the most constrained for space. This is not even a close question. Indeed, if college and university rankings were based on creativity per square foot, Columbia would far surpass everyone. This state of affairs, however, cannot last. To fulfill our responsibilities and aspirations Columbia must expand significantly over the next decade. Whether we expand on the property we already own on Morningside Heights, Manhattanville, or Washington Heights, or whether we pursue a design of multiple campuses in the City, or beyond, is one of the most important questions we will face in the years ahead. As we enter these discussions, we will need to continue working collaboratively with the Governor, the Mayor, and our neighboring communities and their leaders. We must be guided by a comprehensive vision for the university's real needs.

Will Rogers said of Nicholas Murray Butler that he would never be satisfied with Columbia's expansion until he had achieved the annexation of Grant's Tomb. I hereby disclaim any such thought.

So, for those inclined, genetically or otherwise, to forget inaugural speeches remember these traits of the quintessential great urban university: it is engaged, international, diverse, steeped in tradition, a college town, part of the City and neighborhood, and desperately in need of space.

V

There is so much to do, so much to build on. It is possible for us to do things at Columbia that are not possible anywhere else. We inherit a university with an astonishing history of accomplishment, one that has shown an incredible capacity to adapt to each new turn of time. Just as New York City since 1754 has grown from 11,000 inhabitants to 8 million and become the place where people from all over the planet come to become what they want to be, so Columbia has evolved from a schoolhouse of eight students and one teacher to one of the greatest universities in the world, also where people come from all over the world to become whom they want to be. The great heritage that Columbia offers can be daunting—it's not easy, I've always supposed, being an artist today in Florence. But, above all, it is exhilarating.

The principal task before us is simple to state and hard to do well. We must continue, from the level of the individual to that of the university, to know what the important and interesting questions of our time are and how best to pursue them. Some areas of especially promising knowledge must compel our attention:

The discoveries in the combined areas of medicine and health care, biology, engineering, chemistry, physics, computers, and technology—known today as the life sciences—are revolutionary in scale. No great university can minimize the potential here for transforming our understanding of life and our capacity to preserve health. And a great university will figure out how to deal with one of the most important questions of higher education, namely, how to bridge the intellectual strengths of the health sciences and professions and the fundamental science disciplines in Arts and Sciences—represented physically for us by the two campuses of Washington Heights and Morningside Heights.

Another critical area is the phenomenon of globalization. The growing reach of and the interrelationships between modern communications, economic development, disease and public health policies, education, agricultural methods, poverty, terrorism, international law, religious and regional conflict, and environmental degradation are of immense complexity and importance. The role of the United States in this new world is only beginning to be sorted out in our minds. But it is clear that we have entered a new era. And a shift in our consciousness must follow. And just as the great figures in Columbia's history worked to enhance our understanding of the momentous forces at work in their time—I'm thinking of Meyer Schapiro and the understandings of the origins of the modern art movement, or Richard Hofstadter and anti-intellectualism in American life—so will Columbia again provide intellectual leadership in the issues of our time. In this enterprise, Columbia has extraordinary opportunities to forge close partnerships with the leading institutions of the City, such as those already taking shape or expanding with the United Nations, the Council on Foreign Relations, the American Museum of Natural History, and the New York Botanical Gardens.

And a third critical area for development is the arts. It's unthinkable to be in New York City and not take advantage of the location to create a premier School of the Arts. Our young and quite extraordinary School of the Arts can become truly unique, in part by building alliances and connections the City makes possible. What I am calling for is about more than support for the arts. It is about building relationships between the various kinds of creativity a university and the contemporary art world have to offer, and creating something new in the process. That is why I am so pleased to be working on a partnership with the Royal Shakespeare Company and the Apollo Theatre of Harlem.

But, above all, we should want the most vital expression in the arts because of what it can say to us about ourselves.

VI

I want to close with two thoughts. The first is to recognize that we do all that we do in large measure to help us nurture the next generation of men and women, who will act on what we now preserve and discover. A measure of the general health of a university, just as it is of a parent, is the degree to which we actively seek to help develop the youngest among us. Columbia has much to be proud of on that measure. But, of course, there's still more to do; and we will continue, for example, to strengthen our academic advising.

The second closing thought is more of a message to our alumni here today and around the world. All of you are important members of Columbia's extended family, and I know that we will succeed in achieving our dreams for Columbia only with the support and help of our alumni. And that is not a simple plea for money, although it is always welcome. We need you as our ambassadors to potential students, as spokespeople to our external constituencies, as planners and advisors, yes, as donors, and finally as the pride of Columbia showing the rest of the world through your work and service every day the extraordinary value of a Columbia education. During my presidency, I want Columbia to be accessible to you and for your connections here to be meaningful and important.

Finally, this, returning to where I began: When President Seth Low brought Columbia to this spectacular locale, he forged a strong and whole university from what were reputedly disparate and often contentious parts, giving to the faculties for the first time decision-making powers while building a central administration that stressed cooperation and shared resources. In the words of the Trustees of that day, Seth Low "created a new Columbia." Assuming this position as President of Columbia means more to me personally than I can possibly say. But I can say that I will do everything in my power, and I will exert all of my being to continuing to build this New Columbia—most of all to make Columbia a university that the future will take pride in and draw inspiration from just as we do today.

CHAPTER 2

SEVEN MYTHS ABOUT AFFIRMATIVE ACTION IN UNIVERSITIES

Education and Law Symposium Lecture,
Willamette University College of Law, 2002

In May 2002, the U.S. Court of Appeals for the Sixth Circuit, by a 5–4 en banc vote, reversed a federal district court ruling that the University of Michigan's affirmative action policies were a constitutionally impermissible racial quota system. The appeals court cited the 1987 Bakke *decision in allowing the use of race to further the compelling interest of educational diversity, setting up two Michigan cases—*Grutter v. Bollinger *and* Gratz v. Bollinger—*for likely joint review by the U.S. Supreme Court.*

T hank you for inviting me to be part of your symposium on "Education and the Law." It is a special pleasure for me to be back in Oregon, where I spent my teenage years and absorbed the special qualities and values of this State.

I

My subject today is higher education and the legal issues related to what we usually, and I think unfortunately (for reasons I will explain later), call diversity. As many of you know, the University of Michigan, where I served as President from 1997 until just a few months ago, is the defendant in two lawsuits that challenge the constitutionality of the admissions policies in both the undergraduate and law schools insofar as they take race and ethnicity into account in order to achieve a diverse student body. (And I would add simply by way of full disclosure that I am also named personally as a defendant in the two lawsuits.) The plaintiffs in these lawsuits (white applicants who were denied admission to these schools) are represented by an organization known as the Center for Individual Rights, or CIR. For the past decade, CIR has been leading a national campaign to eliminate affirmative action. Their first success came in the *Hopwood* case, in which they brought suit against the affirmative action admissions policy of the University of Texas Law School. The Fifth Circuit Court of Appeals sent a shock wave through all of higher education when it held, in the mid-1990s, that Justice Powell's famous opinion in *Regents of the University of California v. Bakke*, which created a majority of the Supreme Court long understood as upholding affirmative action, was no longer good law.

Since *Bakke* was decided in 1978, it has been understood that the Constitution does not require public law schools to use a "colorblind" admissions process. Indeed, *Bakke* reversed a decision of the California Supreme Court that had insisted on colorblindness in admissions. An admissions process may lawfully consider race and ethnic origin, but it may not rely on racial quotas, may not use a two-track system with separate processes for majority and minority applicants, and may not place so much emphasis on race that minority applicants are admitted even though they are not deemed capable of doing good work in their courses. The University of Michigan employs admissions policies that are entirely consistent with the *Bakke* requirements. But now *Bakke* itself is being challenged.

Litigation has not been the only method of challenging affirmative action. *Hopwood* was followed by Proposition 209 in California, a proposal to amend the state constitution to forbid any consideration of race or ethnicity in public decision-making, including admissions to state universities. The California electorate adopted that proposal, and it remains in effect today, with very significant consequences for racial and ethnic diversity at Berkeley, UCLA, and San Diego, the most selective institutions in the California university system.

That's where things stood when I became President of the University of Michigan in early 1997. It was clear to everyone who was watching the unfolding of this campaign against affirmative action that it was building into a tidal wave ready to roll across the country, either in the form of litigation or by referenda like Proposition 209. Within a matter of months, CIR had filed its two lawsuits against the University of Michigan, as well as a suit against the law school at the University of Washington. Later, in Washington, a ballot proposal modeled after Proposition 209 passed, which then mooted most—but not all—of the lawsuit against the University of Washington Law School. That left the Michigan lawsuits as the primary cases in the federal courts.

I, along with others at the University of Michigan, made two decisions at this point. The first was that we would mount a full and comprehensive case supporting Justice Powell's constitutional thesis in *Bakke*—namely, that racial and ethnic diversity are critically important to a modern education for all students— and that we would show that our undergraduate and law school admissions practices were entirely consistent with that constitutional norm. And, second, we decided that we would try in every way possible to explain to the broader public the fundamental importance of the issues at stake in the litigation and why it is, therefore, so critical that the course of constitutional law since *Bakke*, really since *Brown v. Board of Education* was decided nearly a half-century ago, not be abandoned.

The University is supported in its argument by individuals such as President Gerald R. Ford and Secretary of State Colin Powell, and by virtually every major institution in our society, including all of higher education—the Association of American Universities (AAU), the American Council on Education (ACE), the Department of Justice, churches, labor unions, and elementary and secondary school educators, General Motors, and twenty other Fortune 500 corporations. The corporations argue in their brief that racial and ethnic diversity in higher education is vital to their efforts to hire and maintain an effective workforce prepared for the opportunities presented by a global economy. They state that managers and employees who graduated from institutions with diverse student bodies demonstrate creative problem-solving by integrating differing perspectives; exhibit the skills required for good teamwork; are better prepared to understand, learn from, and collaborate with persons from other racial, ethnic, and cultural backgrounds; and are more responsive to the needs of all customers.

Last fall the two cases were decided, each by a different federal district judge (the cases were not consolidated but were tried independently). In the undergraduate admissions case, the judge held that *Bakke* is still good law and that Michigan's policy of considering race and ethnicity as factors and for educational purposes was consistent with that constitutional decision. In the law school case, however, the federal judge held just the opposite, that race and ethnicity cannot be considered as factors in admissions, even for educational purposes. These two decisions are currently on appeal to the Sixth Circuit, and we are awaiting that outcome. I must say that I am very optimistic that the Sixth Circuit will rule in Michigan's favor.

Let me just complete the picture of the current legal landscape on affirmative action. Besides *Hopwood*, the ballot propositions in California and Washington, and our cases in Michigan, there are now two other federal court of appeals decisions on affirmative action. The Ninth Circuit Court of Appeals held in what remained of the University of Washington case that *Bakke* is still valid under the Fourteenth Amendment. But the Fourth Circuit Court of Appeals has held, in a case involving the admissions system at the University of Georgia, that affirmative action in university admissions is now unconstitutional. That case, however, was oddly presented to the trial court, and hence to the appellate court as well. No evidence of the benefits and purposes of affirmative action was presented because the case was handled not by the University of Georgia, but by the Attorney General of the State, who opposed the University's policy.

The upshot is that we now have a sharp split in the circuit courts on the issue of the constitutionality of affirmative action. The Fifth and Fourth Circuits have held against, while the Ninth has held in favor, and (I predict) the Sixth will as well. This, of course, makes a perfect context, or opportunity, for the Supreme Court to take the Michigan cases, as I expect it will following the decision of the Sixth Circuit. Moreover, of all the litigation thus far on affirmative action in education, the Michigan cases have by far the most extensive records.

II

What I would like to do this afternoon is to review what I believe are the major misconceptions about affirmative action in admissions, what I call the myths about racial and ethnic diversity in higher education. It has been my firm belief, as a participant and observer of this great issue of our time, that many people have seriously mistaken views about what is involved in university admissions and what is really at stake in the constitutional and policy debates now underway. These misconceptions or myths impede our ability to think clearly about what surely is one of the most important constitutional issues since *Brown v. Board of Education*. Here, then, are seven significant myths about affirmative action in universities and why it is important that they be dispelled.

The first myth is that race is no longer a significant factor in American life, that somehow we have gone through the era of *Brown v. Board of Education* and all of the decades of cases since then, and we are now in a position in which race no longer matters in American life. In large part, that is a myth. That should be even clearer now, after the last six months, than it was before. In the lawsuits, the University of Michigan makes the case that it is a myth through statistical analysis, demographics, and other expert testimony. Wishing that race is no longer a factor in American life doesn't make it so.

Americans of different races lead surprisingly separate lives today. Metropolitan Detroit is now the most segregated metropolitan area in the entire country; and Livonia, Michigan, a suburb of Detroit, is the whitest city in the United States of over 100,000 people. These two extremes reside right next to each other. Indeed, America as a whole is more segregated today than it was at the time of *Brown v. Board of Education*. Ninety-two percent of the University of Michigan's white students and 52 percent of its African American students grow up in racially separate communities. The result of this separation is that Michigan's incoming students have rarely had the opportunity to get to know and learn from peers of different races before coming to campus. And the same circumstance exists across the country. Some estimate that by the year 2030 (by the 25th college reunion of the students who are applying for college this fall) forty percent of Americans will be members of a racial minority group. Where will these different parts of society come into contact so that they can learn from one another—about their differences but also about their commonalties—if not in our system of public and private higher education? Race still matters.

But what is so key about race in higher education? If differences of opinion are what is important, why not accomplish that with an all-white student body? The answer is that race and ethnicity continue to be uniquely important factors in American life. Race remains, alas, the "American dilemma." When individuals meet on the street, when they decide where to live, when they decide whom to befriend, when they decide with whom to work, race matters. A well-educated undergraduate, a well-trained lawyer, should have experience interacting with persons different from themselves. They should understand how the experience of race can influence people's perceptions of our nation's social, legal, political, and economic systems. A first-class education is one that creates the opportunity for students, expecting differences, to learn instead of similarities. Likewise, encountering differences, rather than one's mirror image, is an essential part of a good education.

Faculty members relate experiences where the learning taking place in their classrooms has been powerfully affected either by the presence of students from different races, or the lack thereof. Students' racial identities may affect their perception of important works of literature, their views on the political process and the role of government. A diverse classroom also allows students to dispel stereotypes they may harbor about race and viewpoint.

The second myth has it that diversity—and we use that word so often that it can come across almost as a cliché—is good, but that it is optional, an augmenting part of our educational program—"enriching," one might say, but hardly essential. So, the first myth is that race doesn't matter. Then, even if one agrees that diversity in higher education is a good thing, there is still, maybe, a sense that it's not that important, that we can do without it if it is difficult to achieve. My point is that that is a myth: ethnic and racial diversity within a university setting is absolutely essential to the accomplishment of a university's missions, and is at the very core of what a university does.

Interacting with people of different backgrounds creates the environment in which learning and empathy are fostered—it is the very essence of what we mean by a "liberal" or "humanistic" education. The analogy I use is Shakespeare: Why is it that Shakespeare is thought to be one of the greatest if not the greatest writers of all time? One of the explanations, espoused long ago by the critic William Hazlitt, is Shakespeare's uncanny genius for being able to cross into different characters' minds. Within a few lines, within a few minutes of a play, one has the distinct impression of a particular human being, one who thinks and feels and reacts in unique ways. That, in large part, is what exposure in an educational context to cultural diversity involves—the opportunity to come to a greater understanding of others' points of view, and how their life experiences might have caused them to be who they are and form the opinions that they hold. Grappling with race in America is, therefore, a powerful instance of, a powerful metaphor for, crossing sensibilities of all kinds, and crossing sensibilities is part of the core of Shakespeare's genius and of great education.

Some will be quick to note that not all people of the same race hold the same opinions. And that is certainly true. There are too many people, of all backgrounds and all political stripes, who think that is the case. And clearly the best way to undercut that assumption is to have members of the majority come into contact with greater numbers of persons of color, and vice versa. Moreover, while not all African Americans, for example, hold the same views, the experience of being an African American in this country is typically different from that of being a Caucasian, and the classroom—and the campus generally—are enhanced by having an admixture of people with different human experiences. One more point here: we all recognize that people's behavior in a meeting, say, is affected by the gender and racial make-up of the group: that is, the mere presence of a diverse group—women, minority, men, majority—affects for the better how we act and what we say, even without our knowing the personal viewpoints or opinions of the other people present.

Having a racially diverse class enables a law school to do a better job of preparing students to be effective lawyers, and the same rationale applies to medical schools and doctors. Students are exposed to classmates who have had different life experiences, and their prior assumptions are challenged. When an applicant's file reveals that he or she might add to the diversity of perspectives that are voiced in class, that helps the applicant's chances of admission.

The word diversity is a much-used term now, and because it causes us to focus on the differences among people, its use can lead us away from our similarities. Across race, across ethnicity and religion, we often have more in common than we might have imagined. It is in part for that reason, and in part because of the profundity of what is at stake, that I would prefer to speak in terms of integration, and of education's role in helping us achieve an integrated society. What we learn from integration is as much or more about similarity as it is about difference. It is only through interacting with others that you discover what you have in common as well as where you differ. A great soul, one person has observed, can be deeply moved by abstract statistics, but for most of us it usually takes a human face—a specific personal experience—to move us to understanding and learning of the most profound kind. I would hope, therefore, that we not be beguiled by our current language about diversity into thinking that we are concerned with learning from diversity only about differences, important as that is. Nor should the use of the word diversity cause us to assume that diversity is in this context something of a discretionary add-on or enrichment, rather than something at the very core of the educational process.

The Center for Individual Right's challenge to "affirmative action" in higher education admissions is not merely a challenge to the mechanical or procedural particulars; the fact that race is considered at all is what makes the process unacceptable to them. Theirs is a challenge to our philosophy of education and to the historical purposes of our great universities. That is a challenge I have welcomed—because I am confident that a diverse learning community is a better learning environment. And I am convinced that a diverse educational community furthers a historical mission of universities—the education of all students in order for them to be good and productive citizens.

The third myth is that there is so much self-segregation on campuses that all the effort to integrate a campus and create diversity doesn't really accomplish very much. Again, that is a myth. It goes back to my earlier observation that most of the students come from all-white or all-black high schools and lives. Interaction takes practice, it takes experience, it takes time and patience. If this is as difficult as I suggest in part that it is, given where our students are coming from, the fact that there is some self-segregation is more proof of the importance of the task than it is a sign that somehow we are failing. What do you expect? This is very, very hard for people to do. And it is very, very important for our nation. That is why it is so necessary in higher education. If not there, then where?

The other reason that it is a myth is there is far less self-segregation than people assume. I would invite people to go to the University of Michigan campus or the Columbia University campus, walk around, and see for themselves.

The fourth myth is that the process of admissions is essentially a process of rank-ordering the candidates by credentials—by SAT scores, grades, and so forth, and then we draw a cut-off line: above the line, you get in; below the line, you get on a waiting list or are denied admission. And then we take into account race, and we make sure that we have a critical mass of minorities—and that race is the one exception to the decision-making process. That is a myth, a fundamental misconception about the way the admissions process works.

Most public and private universities across the country, including Michigan and Columbia, use a variety of factors to determine a student's admissibility. These include, among others:

> High school grade point average;
> The rigor of the high school courses taken;
> Alumni relationships (parent, sibling, or grandparent);
> Quality of the essay;
> Personal achievement;
> Leadership and service;
> Socio-economically disadvantaged student or education;

Athletic ability;

Underrepresented racial or ethnic minority identity or education; and

Residency in an under-represented region.

Any or all of these factors can influence a student's admissibility because they are all characteristics that contribute to the quality of the University and the diversity of the student body. No one factor is determinative. Obviously, each year, the limited size of the entering class means that thousands of talented applicants cannot be admitted. The task of the admissions office is, using good judgment and a fair and legal process, to assemble a student body it believes collectively will provide the best possible learning environment.

Admissions officers are alert to the potential of those who may not have had full opportunity to manifest their talent (immigrants, for example), those who have served the country (including veterans), or who have unconventional talents (oboe players and talented sculptors and athletes). They must be responsible to the communities from which they derive (e.g., state residents) as well as to the nation itself (through geographic diversity). By employing admissions policies aimed at a comprehensive diversity—of which racial and ethnic diversity is an important part—the University is able to achieve its mission of educating students to participate fully in our heterogeneous democracy and the global economy.

It is important to understand that admissions offices are not making thousands of individual, unrelated decisions; they are trying to make the best judgment about individual applicants in order to form the strongest class that will study and live and interact together over an extended period of time—three or four years. The question for each applicant is what can he or she contribute to the whole, not where they stand in splendid, isolated comparison with everyone else. Applicants have a right to be treated fairly within the admissions process, but there is no right to be admitted to a university without regard to how the overall makeup of the student body will affect the educational process or without regard to the needs of society after they graduate.

Are we, for example, really prepared to say that medical schools cannot consider race in determining who will be available to provide the medical care for our nation? We know that minority physicians are more likely to practice in areas where there are high concentrations of minorities; therefore, diversity among practicing physicians and medical administrators increases the availability of health care within underrepresented minority communities. And while the minority population in our country is growing, in absolute and percentage terms, the number of African Americans and Latinos admitted to medical schools has declined markedly in recent years. It is clear that the changes in admissions policies in California and Texas have contributed significantly to this decline. And so the stakes are high not only for medical and health education—but also for health care in this country—if an adverse decision in these cases in the end imposes a federal constitutional bar to the consideration of race in admissions.

The fifth myth is that the gap is too big. One can understand how important diversity is, and how central it is to the educational process, but there is a sense on the part of some that the "plus factor" in the admissions process given to underrepresented minorities is too large. Well, I would say, the gap is too big or too small or just right depending upon your educational premises and depending upon our judgment as to who can do the work at the university. If your educational purposes are such, as I have argued, that a sense of empathy and a presence of different points of view and experiences are central to the educational process for all students, and if all the students whom you admit can do the work, then the leg up is not too big. Nothing is too big or too small except in relation to purposes and values.

The sixth myth is that we can achieve diversity using other means. Could the Michigan Law School, the undergraduate program, or the Medical School obtain a racially diverse class with a "colorblind" process, by placing greater emphasis on socioeconomic factors? The answer is no; racial diversity and socioeconomic diversity are not the same thing (because, in short, most of our poor people in this country are white). When a colorblind process emphasizing socioeconomic diversity was adopted at the law school at the University of California at Berkeley, African American enrollment in the entering class fell by approximately 60 percent.

In his opinion in *Bakke*, Justice Blackmun wrote (and he was joined in this by Justices Brennan, White, and Marshall), "I suspect that it would be impossible to arrange an affirmative-action program in a racially neutral way and have it successful. To ask that this be so is to demand the impossible. In order to get beyond racism, we must first take account of race. There is no other way. And in order to treat some persons equally, we must treat them differently. We cannot—we dare not—let the Equal Protection Clause—perpetuate racial supremacy." That was right in 1978, and it is still right today.

Some schools in other states have tried a "colorblind" admissions process in which they accept the students in the top four percent or perhaps ten or twenty percent of each high school in the state. There are several problems with this approach: first, this approach is completely ineffective for graduate schools and professional schools. Second, it would result in admitting some top students from weak high schools who may not be academically prepared to do the work, and reject very able students who are below the cut-off at a very strong school. Third, all opportunity for individual evaluation and assessment of the candidate is lost. And so the process is colorblind, but blind to the applicants themselves as well! And fourth, for such an approach to work, de facto segregation would have to continue in high schools, which, given the purposes of such an approach, would be ironic in the extreme. The conclusion is clear: the best way to admit a racially diverse class is, not surprisingly, to use an admission process that uses race as a factor—the approach followed by virtually every selective college and university admissions for the past thirty years.

If, in the future, colleges and universities are not permitted to consider race as a factor in their admissions processes, it will have a devastating effect on their ability to assemble a diverse student body. It is likely that the number of minority students enrolled at universities would decline significantly. The experience at California's flagship public universities, Berkeley and the University of California at Los Angeles (UCLA), bears out this prediction. Admission levels of underrepresented minorities—Blacks, Hispanics, and Native Americans—remain well below where they were prior to Proposition 209. At Berkeley, they are down 44 percent and at UCLA they are down 36 percent from pre-Proposition 209 levels. And the decision will not affect Michigan alone: all public institutions across the country would be affected, and all private higher education institutions as well, given that, under Title VI, those schools are prohibited from discriminating on the basis of race—and other things—in the admissions process, and an adverse decision in the Michigan cases would in effect change the statutory definition of race discrimination in admissions.

The last myth is that this policy, well-intentioned and even important as it is, materially diminishes the likelihood of a white student being admitted, and is therefore unfair. This notion that enormous numbers of whites are being denied admission because of the preferential treatment of under-represented minorities is simply false. In fact, admissions policies such as Michigan's do not meaningfully affect a white student's chances of admission. The numbers of minority applicants are extremely small compared to the numbers of white students who apply to universities across the country. It is not mathematically possible that the small numbers of minority students who apply and are admitted are displacing a significant number of white students. In their book *The Shape of the River*,

William Bowen, former president of Princeton, and Derek Bok, former president of Harvard, looked at the nationwide statistics concerning admissions to selective universities. They determined that even if all selective universities implemented a race-blind admissions system, the probability of being admitted for a white student would only go from 25 percent to 26.2 percent.

The source of this whole problem of admissions affirmative action is, in large part, the need for remediation of K-12 public education in under-resourced school systems. Addressing that issue, however, and seeing the educational benefits will take many years, during which we will lose several generations of students; in the meantime, colleges and universities have had decisions to make—classes of students to admit.

The effects of unequal—and inadequate—funding of public school on the quality of education for racial and ethnic minority students are hard to overstate. And those effects are, in large part, the source of the problem that the admissions affirmative action leg up seeks to address—making sure, as we do so, that we don't take students who can't do the work. Renowned researcher Linda Darling-Hammond notes that the wealthiest ten percent of school districts spend almost ten times more than the poorest ten percent. And poor and minority students are disproportionately concentrated in the least well-funded schools. Predominantly minority schools have difficulty hiring the most qualified teachers, which, she has concluded, is a major contributor to the students' achievement gap. One study of 900 Texas school districts found that, "holding socioeconomic status (SES) constant, the wide variability in teachers' qualifications accounted for almost all of the variation in black and white students' test scores." In general, Darling-Hammond notes, "urban schools suffer from lower expenditures of state and local dollars per pupil, higher student-teacher ratios and student-staff ratios, larger class sizes, lower teacher experience, and poorer teacher qualifications." Those factors are, I think, important to keep in mind as we consider the disappointed majority applicant.

III

The outcome of the Michigan cases will profoundly affect the quality of higher education, professional education, and graduate education that all students—majority and minority—receive in this country. It will help determine the demographics of those classes. It will determine whether the graduates, majority and minority, will be leaders who have the education and experience that will enable them to thrive in social and business contexts that are increasingly diverse and international. And it will affect the historic commitment of this nation to build an integrated society after over two hundred years of slavery and exclusion for African Americans and others. This was—and is—the challenge of the greatest decision of the last century, *Brown v. Board of Education*.

In an eloquent *New York Times* op-ed piece supporting the University of Michigan's admissions policies, President Gerald R. Ford wrote, "Tolerance, breadth of mind and appreciation for the world beyond our neighborhoods: these can be learned on the football field and in the science lab as well as in the lecture hall. But only if students are exposed to America in all her variety," and then he goes on to say, "I have often wondered how different the world might have been in the 1940's, 50's and 60's—how much more humane and just—if my generation had experienced a more representative sampling of the American family."

And, so, far from being some sort of nice but non-essential add-on, racial, ethnic and other kinds of diversity in a university setting is at the core of what the university does, it is absolutely central to the quality of students' educational experience, and the diversity of its graduates is, as America's business leaders have forcefully argued, one of the most valuable contributions higher education makes to the nation's common weal. The greatest question is this: Do the ideals of *Brown v. Board of Education*, reflecting our profound commitment to integration and to the fundamental role of education in realizing that national goal, still have vitality and meaning at the beginning of this new century, or will they slip into obscurity, a noble but largely failed effort of the romantic and idealistic twentieth century?

Thank you.

CHAPTER 3

STATEMENT ON THE FUTURE OF JOURNALISM EDUCATION

Columbia University, April 15, 2003

At the time Lee C. Bollinger began his tenure as Columbia University president in the summer of 2002, an ongoing search for a new dean of the University's well-known Journalism School was nearly complete. But, given the ascending importance of journalism in a world of rapid globalization and technological change, he suspended the search. He announced the appointment of a new task force comprised of faculty from across the University, as well as outside experts and practitioners, to reconsider the nature of a model journalism education within the setting of a great university.

At the beginning of the last century, Joseph Pulitzer bequeathed two major gifts to Columbia University: one to establish the premier school of journalism in the nation and the other to create a prize, sponsored by a great university and judged by great journalists, to honor the highest levels of journalistic achievement. These gifts came at a time of tremendous, destabilizing social change in America, a time in which the role of journalism was also changing rapidly. And they were motivated in part by Pulitzer's belief that journalism needed institutions that would help it adjust to a new role in a new era. There can be little doubt that together these have been significant contributions to the development of journalism over the last century.

As we enter another new century, at a time of similarly profound and destabilizing changes, the role of the media in America is even more critically important to society than it was a century ago and is again in the process of rapid change. And so it seems timely to review where we are and consider afresh how journalism education in a great university can contribute to the process by which the media adapt to a new world. To that end, I convened a group of people of extraordinary accomplishment in and about journalism and higher education to consider the question of what a model school of journalism for the twenty-first century should look like.

The Task Force was composed of members of the School of Journalism faculty, faculty from other departments and schools at Columbia, and practicing journalists from nearly every branch of the media. We met six times from October 2002 to March 2003. Attendance and participation were remarkable, attesting to the commitment of the members and the importance of the subject. I served as chair. The conditions for discussion were the following: This was not to be a review of the Columbia School of Journalism, or of journalism schools in general. There would be no effort to conduct new research or an extensive review of the literature about journalism education. The reason for this was not to think about the issues behind a veil of ignorance, but rather to avoid the typical problem in such discussions of spending too little time in sustained discussion, reflection, and judgment. For our purposes, the expertise represented around the table was sufficient in itself. Lastly, I said from the outset that I did not expect the Task Force to issue a report, with members expected to sign on to or dissent from a final document. Consequently, the views below are my own—judgments informed by a remarkable group of people to whom I am deeply indebted both individually and collectively.

I start from the premise that journalism and a free press are among the most important human institutions of the modern world. Democracy, civil society, and free markets cannot exist over time without them. The quality of life within these systems is closely tied to the quality of thought and discussion in our journalism. This is truer today than it was a century ago, and it is likely to be truer still a century from now. And nothing demarcates the inexorable processes of globalization more than the growing reach of media into every city, hamlet, and home on the face of the earth. Journalism has an ascending importance in the modern world, and more than at any time in human history the character of the press is a key determinant shaping and defining national and global society.

Yet, there are concerns about the press, including a growing fear about how concentration of ownership narrows the scope of public debate and how commercial and technological forces increasingly drive the structure and behavior of the press. There is understandable anxiety that monetary pressures are threatening the quality and standards of journalism.

One of the best ways (and perhaps a necessary one) of dealing with these realities—the growing importance of journalism and the concern about commercial and other interests becoming too dominant—is for journalism to embrace a stronger sense of being a profession, with stronger standards and values that will provide its members with some innate resistance to other competing values that have the potential of undermining the public responsibilities of the press. There is nothing inherently inconsistent about good journalism operating in a market. Capitalism is a well-proven method of serving public needs and preferences, both for goods and services and for information. But like any system, its advantages turn into harms unless moderated by an internalized value system. Throughout much of the twentieth century, the electronic media were subject to congressionally and administratively mandated responsibilities to operate in the "public interest." In the current deregulatory climate, however, as the government has relaxed its "public interest" standards, this system does not provide the counterweight it once did. That puts more pressure than ever on what remains as the primary check on commercial excesses, namely the professional identity that insists that some things simply will not be done for money.

The real question is who will set the standard against which everything else can be compared and whether those who set the standard will have the imagination to set it as high as it might be. Our great universities have a crucial role to play in this process, similar to the role they have played in the professions of medicine, law, and engineering, for example. We must take up that responsibility more than we have, by devoting our energies to developing an appropriate curriculum, by increasing our research capacities, and by fulfilling our role of serving the public good in the ways that universities can beyond teaching and research. This will, of course, require greater investments in journalism education, and we ought to be ready to make those investments. A professional school should prepare students for performance within the profession at the highest levels.

A great journalism school within a great university should always stand at a certain distance from the profession itself. Its faculty should be made up of leading practitioners of the profession who, in the manner of other university faculty, both teach and actively explore, in their ongoing work, the greatest possibilities of journalism. The faculty should also reflect on the profession—drawing our attention to important issues, engaging in research to assist in their resolution, and communicating these findings to students, the profession, and the interested public. Like journalism itself with respect to the general society, journalism schools must maintain an independent perspective on the profession and the world. Among other things, they are the profession's loyal critics. The habits of mind developed in the academic atmosphere of engaged reflection will inevitably suffuse the educational process, leading to an emphasis on some aspects of professional life and the neglect of others. A great university will also be able to offer knowledge and intellectual exchange with people in other fields related to the professional school, just as a professional school will contribute its knowledge and expertise to other parts of the university. Ideally, a professional school should make the university as a whole integral to its teaching and research missions.

More specifically, a professional school must instill certain basic capacities in its students. (1) Students must receive an introduction to the skills and craft of writing and reporting which are the foundation of the profession. This would include the skills of analyzing and organizing information for news stories of all lengths as well as for investigative reports. (2) Students must acquire an intellectual ability to deal with new situations, as knowledge and working conditions shift over time or as their own knowledge proves inadequate (in other words, students must learn how to "think like a journalist"). (3) Students ought to become familiar with how their profession developed. Who were the great figures and what were their contributions? How did the field evolve into what it is today, and what are the trends at work now and where are they leading the profession? (4) Students must acquire a sense of an identity as a professional, which includes the moral and ethical standards that should guide professional behavior.

My sense is that for a modern journalism school some new courses and programs to meet these objectives will need to be created. As these are conceived, it is important to remember that it often takes many years for materials and texts to be assembled. It may be possible, as one of many examples, to develop courses where students become immersed in reading and comparing significant journalistic pieces along with other materials about the same subject and then discuss what the authors tried to do, what alternative stories might have been written, and what this analysis reveals about the practice of journalism and about society. Students would be expected to articulate and defend their views in class, and then to write and produce a different story. These discussions would, of course, naturally invite considerations of journalistic ethics and norms. And, given the multiplicity of media forms through which journalists are expected to communicate, this kind of course would provide the opportunity to learn the techniques of various media and to see how structure and content change across them. While this kind of educational experience takes place now in journalism education, my sense is that it does not hold nearly the centrality nor the level of engagement that it might.

One of the most significant needs for journalists today is to have a high level of knowledge about the subject they are reporting and communicating. This raises a matter of enormous complexity and significance for a school of journalism. Of all the criticisms of the press, one of the most serious—and, happily, the most remediable—is the lack of context for stories. Journalism functions by reference to current events (just as law operates by cases and statutes and medicine by diseases). At its best, journalism mediates between the worlds of expertise and general knowledge. To do that well—to write for the present and to weave in broader meaning—is remarkably difficult. A necessary element is substantive knowledge, the kind of knowledge you cannot just pick up in the course of doing a story. Having a foundation of general knowledge enhances one's capacity to deal with new areas and specific issues. Moreover, the deep sense of personal satisfaction in journalism, as in other parts of life, comes from probing into the heart of a matter. It is the superficial skipping from event to event that produces both sophomoric journalism and unfulfilled journalists.

Journalism may be moving increasingly to a system in which reporters have an underlying expertise, and to the extent that is true, universities ought to provide opportunities for students to develop that expertise. Specialization has its risks, and we should be alert to them. Some argue that expertise impairs a journalist's ability to write for a non-expert audience, but that seems to me implausible. Not all experts are capable of writing for a general audience (it is, indeed, a special skill), but those who can are usually better explainers than are the best of those who do not have that expertise.

On the other hand, my guess is that it is far too early to declare the end of the generalist editor and reporter, who moves from the education beat to the Hong Kong desk and then on to national politics. For them, and for future general managers of news-gathering operations, we need to provide a knowledge base and intellectual approach that will serve journalists well over their whole careers. That achieving complete knowledge of every subject is impossible should not lead us to give up on developing any kind of deeper knowledge in a journalism school education. That a journalism school is located within a great university, which houses an extraordinary amount of expertise on virtually any subject, means that it would be an intellectual tragedy not to ensure that students partake of the feast. One way of doing so is simply to reserve space in the broader university curriculum for students to explore other fields. This requires a willingness on the part of faculty and departments outside the journalism school, which I have every reason to believe exists.

But my sense is that we can do better than that. The educational goal ought to be to develop a base of knowledge across relevant fields that is crafted specifically for what leading journalists need to know: for example, a functional knowledge of statistics, the basic concepts of economics, and an appreciation for the importance of history and for the fundamental debates in modern political theory and philosophy. To address this assignment would require joint efforts of experts from around the university working closely with faculty in the journalism school. In addition to core knowledge, the faculty might decide upon a few of the most important subject areas of our time (e.g., religion, politics, life sciences, and the forces of globalization) and develop specific materials and course work in these as well.

All professional schools devote a significant part of their educational programs to having students do what they will do as professionals. Medical students diagnose diseases, arts students draw and act, and law students analyze cases. The integration of action and thought is one of the most powerful learning devices and, when done well, one of the most exhilarating. It is to be expected, therefore, that a journalism school curriculum will teach students how to be journalists by having them do some aspects of journalism. To pit the teaching of craft against the teaching of intellectual capacity is to pose a false choice. The questions are what part of doing journalism should be used for educational purposes and how should the integration with other forms of learning occur?

There are several things to keep in mind as one answers this. First, we must always be aware that we have precious little time with a student. No moment should be wasted, and everything we do should be evaluated against possible alternatives that might better prepare a student for his or her future. Second, we ought to think about what will best serve a student over the full course of his or her career. We will better serve the student, as well as the society, by laying the foundation for a professional lifetime. Third, we must beware of placing too much emphasis on the beguiling qualities of basic skills training. Students naturally seek out this training, often because they are eager to become professionals and it is enticing to perform that role right away, and sometimes also because getting a job is foremost in their minds and they think basic skills will enhance their immediate employment prospects. Although students should finish journalism school in possession of the skills required to work right away as daily print or broadcast reporters, they must acquire not only these foundational skills, but also a mastery of journalistic inquiry and expression at their highest, most sophisticated, level. This implies an educational environment where clear expression interacts with complex understanding. Fourth, there is an important relationship (one that people within a university are especially sensitive to) between the type of education offered and the kind of people we can attract as faculty members. If journalistic education is to place a greater emphasis on imparting a degree of expertise in subject matter, it will be essential to attract faculty who have demonstrably acquired such expertise themselves, in addition to their expertise in the craft of journalism.

In considering how to impart this combination of skills and capacities to students, we ought to explore ways outside of the classroom too. A major publication within the school could be edited and managed by students. It should also be possible to develop a system of one- or two-year clerkships with outstanding practitioners immediately following graduation.

This raises the question of the appropriate time-to-degree in a modern journalism school. The answer, to my mind, is that the minimum is the time it will take for students to absorb the distinctive qualities of mind that a university education can offer. It is very difficult, although not impossible, for this to occur in a year's duration or less. Over time our aim should be to extend the curriculum into a second year, as virtually every other master's degree program in the university has done. (Of course, the program—its length and content—may vary depending upon the educational needs of particular groups of students, such as mid-career journalists returning to school). The question of duration is ultimately related both to the amount of material that a student should be expected to master and the emotional or psychological commitment he or she must have to the educational experience in order for the professional attitudes we want to instill to take hold.

The curriculum should not be constrained by the salary structure in the profession. If a two-year course of study is deemed necessary, and if the prospects of professional compensation are so low (relative to tuition and other educational expenses) that there is a significant disincentive for the most talented young journalists to undertake a professional education, then universities ought to build a financial aid program that will change this socially dysfunctional incentive structure. That is what we have done in other fields, such as graduate studies in the arts, humanities, social sciences, and other sciences. (It is interesting to note that we have done precisely this in reverse, so to speak, in fields like law, where salaries in private practice are high relative to the costs of a legal education but also high relative to salaries paid in the public service sector. To encourage graduates to pursue careers in public service, leading law schools have created student loan forgiveness programs for graduates who promise to take public service jobs for a specified number of years.)

Finally, one might ask what would be a good measure of the success of a journalism education. One vital measure should be whether the most promising and talented people entering the profession choose to attend journalism school. As I indicated before, we will never have an official system of licensing of journalists, given our First Amendment, so that the possibility of becoming a journalist without having a degree in journalism will continue. Our aim should be to create educational programs that are so compelling that the most promising future leaders in journalism decide that a professional education is critical to a successful career and life.

I would like to thank the members of the Task Force. They have my deepest appreciation for the time, energy, and advice they provided as we explored the future of journalism education. It is an understatement to say that their expertise and insights helped my thinking evolve on this critically important issue. I am eager to work with the new Dean and the faculty to see how we might shape the education of journalists in the years ahead.

CHAPTER 4

A RESOUNDING VICTORY FOR DIVERSITY ON CAMPUS

Washington Post, June 24, 2003

On April 1, 2003, the U.S. Supreme Court heard oral argument over the use of affirmative action in the University of Michigan's undergraduate and law school admissions policies in the cases of Gratz v. Bollinger *and* Grutter v. Bollinger. *On June 23, 2003, in a majority opinion authored by Justice Sandra Day O'Connor, the Court held that, while the university's undergraduate admissions policies did not meet the* Bakke *standard, the U.S. Constitution "does not prohibit the law school's narrowly tailored use of race in admissions decisions to further a compelling interest in obtaining the educational benefits that flow from a diverse student body."*

Yesterday the Supreme Court delivered the most important decision dealing with affirmative action—perhaps the most important decision dealing with race in America—in a quarter-century. The court's decision is a great victory for American higher education, and for the nation as a whole.

Writing for the majority in the case dealing with the admissions policy of the University of Michigan Law School, Justice Sandra Day O'Connor declared that the Constitution "does not prohibit the Law School's narrowly tailored use of race in admissions decisions to further a compelling interest in obtaining the educational benefits that flow from a diverse student body."

While a 6 to 3 decision struck down an aspect of the University of Michigan's undergraduate admissions procedure, which it viewed as being "not narrowly tailored to achieve educational diversity," the court affirmed the central principle set forth in Justice Lewis Powell's seminal opinion in *Regents of the University of California v. Bakke* in 1978—that race may be considered by colleges and universities as a factor in making admissions decisions.

The court also explicitly endorsed the view that the government (here the public University of Michigan) does have a compelling interest in obtaining the educational benefits that derive from having a diverse law school student body. It recognized that those educational benefits are "substantial," "important and laudable." It stated that the university's law school admissions policy "promotes 'cross-racial understanding,' helps to break down racial stereotypes, and 'enables [students] to better understand persons of different races.'" Referring to friend-of-the-court briefs from major American businesses and "high-ranking retired officers and civilian leaders of the United States military," the court noted that the "benefits are not theoretical but real."

Especially gratifying is the court's statement, quoting *Brown v. Board of Education*, that "'education is the very foundation of good citizenship.' For this reason, the diffusion of knowledge and opportunity through public institutions of higher education must be accessible to all individuals regardless of race or ethnicity . . . Effective participation by members of all racial and ethnic groups in the civic life of our Nation is essential if the dream of one Nation, indivisible, is to be realized."

The court's decision, then, suggests that the court knows what the nation knows: that, unfortunately, race still matters in the United States, and that as we as a nation seek to treat all Americans fairly, treat them equitably and as individuals, college and university admissions offices cannot be barred from looking at race. As Justice Harry Blackmun wrote in *Bakke*, "It would be impossible to arrange an affirmative-action program in a racially neutral way and to have it successful . . . In order to get beyond racism, we must first take account of race. There is no other way."

What, many might ask, at the end of the day does this really mean for higher education in this country? Against the alternative of eliminating consideration of race in admissions, the decision is of immense significance. There are no effective alternatives to achieving an integrated student body, at least without sustaining enormous costs to the quality and character of education. Furthermore, a negative decision would have reached throughout the nation's colleges and universities, private as well as public, because statutory law incorporates any 14th Amendment doctrine directly applicable to public institutions. The alternative, in short, would have been a change in educational course of enormous proportions.

What the positive decision in this case did was, however, even better and more significant than *Bakke*. No simple majority emerged from that earlier case; Powell's famous opinion upholding the use of race under limited circumstances stood alone and required extensive analysis to make it into precedent. Now we have a clear majority and a clear precedent. Moreover, the rationales for the educational benefits of diversity are more extensive than any that have been given before. That helps make the value of the decision as a precedent even stronger. To that must be added the critical fact that the court has not speculated about what kind of admissions policy will be sustained as constitutional; it has upheld a specific policy against which all of higher education can measure its own programs.

And, finally, it is of the highest importance to recognize that the law school policy can be applied throughout all other colleges and universities. Nothing about this policy makes it peculiarly relevant for admissions decisions regarding law schools. The Michigan undergraduate admissions policy, which the court found flawed, awarded points for race and ethnicity. The only reason for that system was to ensure consistency across many different applications reviewed by many different admissions counselors. Nothing precludes the university from now embracing a non-quantitative method that permits counselors to consider "race" as one among many factors. And that will be true of every college and university admissions program in the country. It is, therefore, misleading and inaccurate to think of what the Supreme Court has done as a "split" or "murky" decision in this area of constitutional law. It is about as clear as constitutional law gets.

By rejecting an absolutist argument—by affirming the notion that race may be considered in an appropriate manner in the admissions process—the court has helped ensure that public and private colleges and universities in the United States will remain accessible to all Americans of all backgrounds. And it has helped ensure that American higher education will continue to educate our youth for the increasingly diverse world they will inherit.

CHAPTER 5

EDUCATIONAL EQUITY AND QUALITY: *BROWN* AND *RODRIGUEZ* AND THEIR AFTERMATH

Address to the College Board Forum, New York City,
November 3, 2003

In 2003, the College Board Forum invited President Bollinger to address issues of educational access and quality. In this speech, presented around the time of the fiftieth anniversary of Brown v. Board of Education, *Bollinger explained* Brown's *reach beyond de jure segregation to the lasting equity and quality disparities inherent in the funding mechanisms for K–12 public education. In reexamining the 1973 case of* San Antonio Independent School District v. Rodriguez, *in which the Supreme Court held that the state school-finance system did not violate the Equal Protection Clause of the Constitution, Bollinger explored how the judicial battle shifted to the states, creating possible avenues for further progress.*

In May, we observe an important fiftieth anniversary. I am not referring to Roger Bannister's running the first sub-four-minute mile on May 6. I am referring, of course, to *Brown v. Board of Education*, which was handed down eleven days later. In that unanimous decision, written clearly and succinctly by Chief Justice Earl Warren so that it could be understood by all Americans, the Supreme Court dramatically affected the quality and character of public education in this country. It defined what "equal educational opportunity" means in a racial context, and clearly articulated, with inspirational power, the importance of education—to individuals and to the nation as a whole. The Court wrote:

Today, education is perhaps the most important function of state and local governments. Compulsory school attendance laws and the great expenditures for education both demonstrate our recognition of the importance of education in our democratic society. It is required in the performance of our most basic public responsibilities, even service in the armed forces. It is the very foundation of good citizenship. Today it is a principal instrument in awakening the child to cultural values, in preparing him for later professional training, and in helping him to adjust normally to his environment. In these days, it is doubtful that any child may reasonably be expected to succeed in life if he is denied the opportunity of an education. [And listen especially to this next sentence:] Such an opportunity, where the state has undertaken to provide it, is a right which must be made available to all on equal terms.

Few people, if any, would argue about the centrality of education in our country today. Indeed education is probably even more important now than it was fifty years ago. What conclusions follow from that recognition are a matter of great debate, however.

Brown is a case, I would assert, about at least four separate but related things. *Brown* is, of course, a case about segregation; the court struck down de jure racial segregation in public schools, and in so doing set the stage for ending de jure segregation generally. And yet fifty years later, de facto segregation in primary and secondary education and in society is on the rise; and too often, neither minority nor majority students garner the educational and social benefits that come from being part of a diverse student body.

Brown was about segregation, but it was also about a theory of education. It stands for the proposition that racially separate education is inherently unequal. It lays the legal and educational foundation for the recent Supreme Court decisions in *Grutter* and *Gratz v. Bollinger*, involving the admissions policies at selective colleges and universities across the country. Those cases state explicitly that diversity in an educational context contributes to the education of all, and society as a whole. And so the fact that de facto segregation is so common across our country is even more disappointing.

Brown is about not only segregation and about a theory of education; it is also about equity in education. Indeed the underlying value in *Brown* is perhaps as much equity as it is desegregation. The Court concluded that it was impossible for racially segregated education to be equal—and so public education had to be racially integrated.

Of course, equitable mediocrity in education was not what was sought by either blacks or whites. *Brown* was not about an equal lack of education opportunity for white and black students, rich and poor. Equity in educational funding and opportunity means, of course, that all students of all backgrounds have available to them at least an adequate education.

These four themes or ideals—desegregation, a theory of education that recognizes the harms that come with segregated education and the benefits of integrated education, equity of educational opportunity, and educational quality—remain the themes and ideals that the courts and our society have continued to wrestle with for the last half century. Our national commitment to these ideas and our progress toward them have differed depending on the idea, and they have ebbed and flowed over the last five decades. The real issue is what are our ideals today, and how committed are we to implementing them in practice.

In the years before *Brown*, the legal team at the NAACP deliberately chose a legal strategy that challenged educational segregation head on, rather than seeking to mitigate the inequity that existed between black and white schools. That was, of course, the right strategy, both on pragmatic and principled grounds. Our educational system, our citizenry, and our nation are all better as a result. And yet, now, fifty years after *Brown*, we still struggle with the tenacious challenge of educational equity generally. We do so in a racial context because of de facto segregation and because of the correlation between race and wealth, but we also wrestle with it in an economic context, given the fact that public education relies so heavily on property taxes. We know that many of the school districts that are the most property-poor are heavily minority districts. (Currently more than two-thirds of the black and Latino students in this country attend essentially segregated schools in which most students are also poor.)

One of the key obstacles to equal education remains, therefore, unequal funding for public education. Despite that inspiring and apparently egalitarian language in *Brown*, another Supreme Court decision handed down thirty years ago stands as a formidable impediment to achieving equity in public school financing. And so even as we anticipate celebrating the fiftieth anniversary of *Brown*, we should also reexamine the issues and reasoning of *Rodriguez v. San Antonio Independent School District*, 411 U.S. 1 (1973), and consider the legal and educational challenges that continue in its wake.

Today I want to do just that—reexamine *Rodriguez*, consider two lines of legal argument that have been pursued in the years since *Rodriguez*, and finally, suggest possible avenues for further progress toward equity and quality public education. After all, the title of today's forum, Providing a Quality Education for All Students, speaks to both equity and quality.

One might note that in these two cases—*Brown* and *Rodriguez*, one sees signs of the evolving history and demographics of our nation—one a 1954 case dealing with African American students segregated from white students, the other dealing with a Texas school district, ninety percent Hispanic American and six percent African American that was grossly under-funded compared with neighboring, largely white school districts. Of course, the civil and educational rights of African American and Hispanic Americans—indeed all Americans—are inextricably related—as you will see in the story of *Rodriguez*.

On May 16, 1968 (which I can't help but notice, was just six weeks after the assassination of Reverend Martin Luther King, Jr.), 400 students from Edgewood High School in San Antonio staged a walkout and demonstration. Among their grievances were inadequate supplies and the lack of qualified teachers. Parents formed an advocacy group, and a class action lawsuit was filed in federal court. The plaintiffs argued that their school district had among the highest tax rates in the county but raised dramatically less per student than the nearby wealthy district, the predominantly "Anglo" Alamo Heights district.

As Justice White would later note in dissent, the District Court "postponed decision for some two years in the hope that the Texas Legislature would remedy the gross disparities in treatment inherent in the Texas financing scheme. It was only after the legislature failed to act in its 1971 Regular Session that the District Court, apparently recognizing the lack of hope for self-initiated legislative reform, rendered its decision."

The District Court held that the state's school-finance system violated the United States Constitution. It found that wealth is a suspect classification and that education is a fundamental right, and therefore the law could be upheld as constitutional only upon a showing that the state had a compelling state interest for the finance system. The court concluded that not only was there no showing of a compelling state interest that necessitated this specific means of achieving the goal, but there was not even a reasonable or rational reason for funding education the way the state had.

When Texas appealed the case to the Supreme Court, the attorneys general of twenty-five states filed amicus briefs. They supported not the State of Texas and its law, but Rodriguez. Plaintiffs' spirits were also buoyed by the fact that in 1971, in *Serrano v. Priest*, the California Supreme Court had held that the California education finance system violated the Equal Protection Clause of the United States Constitution and comparable sections of the state constitution.

The Supreme Court handed down its decision in March 1973, thirty years ago this year. (I was at that time a clerk to the Chief Justice.) The vote was 5-4. The Court rejected the plaintiffs' argument that the gross disparities in funding among school districts violated the Equal Protection Clause of the Fourteenth Amendment, stating that under the federal constitution, education was not a fundamental right. Had just one of five justices voted the other way, public education funding—and public education itself—might look very different today.

Parent Demetrio Rodriguez said, "The poor people have lost again." In his dissent, Justice Thurgood Marshall called the *Rodriguez* decision "a retreat from our historic commitment to equality of educational opportunity." Hopes that the federal judiciary would further education finance reform were dashed. But the wheels of legal development sometimes roll slowly.

The Court's decision that education is not a "fundamental right" is of profound significance. If education were considered a "fundamental right explicitly or implicitly protected by the Constitution," then courts would examine state school funding schemes that produce gross disparities in funding to different districts with great care or skepticism; the laws would receive what is called "strict scrutiny"; they would not be given the deference that the judicial branch typically gives a statute passed by the legislative branch and signed by the executive. Under "strict scrutiny," a court would ask not merely whether a law is "reasonably related" to a "legitimate purpose," but rather whether the means set forth in the law are "necessary" to the achievement of a "compelling state interest." Few statutes can withstand strict scrutiny, either because there is usually another, less problematic means to achieve the same goal, or because the purpose of the law is not deemed sufficiently compelling—(i.e., so necessary that such an intrusion on our rights must be tolerated).

In *Rodriguez*, the Court quoted the same inspiring passage from *Brown* quoted above, noting that it remained equally valid, that their decision did not "in any way [detract] from our historic dedication to public education," and that they agreed with the court below that " 'the grave significance of education both to the individual and to our society' cannot be doubted.' " But, the Court added, "the importance of a service performed by the State does not determine whether it must be regarded as fundamental for purposes of examination under the

Equal Protection Clause." If it did, the Court asserted, it would be acting as a "super-legislature."

The fact that earlier Supreme Court decisions had found rights such as "travel" to be "fundamental" under the 14th Amendment did not persuade the majority in *Rodriguez* that "education" should have the same constitutional status. Clearly, the majority was concerned about a "slippery slope": if education were deemed a fundamental right, why not subsistence or housing? The majority's language expresses this deep worry: "It is not," the majority said, "the province of this Court to create substantive constitutional rights in the name of guaranteeing equal protection of the laws. Thus, the key to discovering whether education is 'fundamental' is not to be found in comparisons of the relative societal significance of education as opposed to subsistence or housing. Nor is it to be found by weighing whether education is as important as the right to travel." "Rather, the answer lies in assessing whether there is a right to education explicitly or implicitly guaranteed by the Constitution."

Of course, education might well be thought of as especially proximate to other basic rights protected by the Constitution, such as the right of free expression and the right to vote. And, indeed, the parents made this exact argument. But the court majority simply disagreed.

It was not persuaded by the argument "that the right to speak is meaningless unless the speaker is capable of articulating his thoughts intelligently and persuasively [; that] the 'marketplace of ideas' is an empty forum for those lacking basic communicative tools [; and that] the corollary right to receive information becomes little more than a hollow privilege when the recipient has not been taught to read, assimilate, and utilize available knowledge."

Nor was the Court persuaded by the argument that "Exercise of the franchise . . . cannot be divorced from the educational foundation of the voter. [that] . . . a voter cannot cast his ballot intelligently unless his reading skills and thought processes have been adequately developed." It asserted that while "the Court has long protected the rights to vote and speak, it has "never presumed to possess either the ability or the authority to guarantee to the citizenry the most effective speech or the most informed electoral choice." Worthy goals though they may be, they should not be pursued by such "judicial intrusion into otherwise legitimate state activities."

The Court was concerned, therefore, not only about a "slippery slope," but also about the values of federalism—a decision upholding the lower court

decision would potentially "abrogate systems of public financing public education presently in existence in virtually every State."

In his concurrence, Justice Potter Stewart acknowledged that the method of
financing schools in Texas and "in almost every other State, has resulted in a system of public education that can fairly be described as chaotic and unjust." Yet,
he continued, "It does not follow, however, and I cannot find, that this system
violates the Constitution of the United States." To hold otherwise, he said, with
a degree of hyperbole that revealed perhaps his own doubts about his conclusion,
would be "an extraordinary departure from principled adjudication under the
Equal Protection Clause of the Fourteenth Amendment."

I cannot help but think that *Rodriguez* was wrongly decided, that the arguments
of the four dissenting Justices (Brennan, White, Douglas, and Marshall) are persuasive, and that as a matter of educational and national policy the consequences
have been nothing short of tragic. The simple fact of life is that education is the
sine qua non of citizenship and all it entails. If you are educated but poor it's
harder to participate meaningfully in the democratic process— but you still can
do it. But to be uneducated is to be barred from participation, whether you are
rich or poor. While I do not expect, realistically, that *Rodriguez* will be overturned
in the short term, I do believe that in time our law should and will come to recognize a fundamental right to education under the federal constitution. Developments in the states since *Rodriguez* show, that there is, in fact, less to be worried about in declaring education a fundamental right than reasonably may have
been feared in 1973. Moreover, they also show that, in the end, only a national
constitutional norm will help our society rectify the structural injustices of public education. I now want to turn to those developments.

With the 1973 *Rodriguez* decision, the battle to alleviate gross disparities in public education funding shifted to the states. State courts were asked whether such
funding systems violated their own constitutions. In virtually all states, schools
were—and still are—operated by local districts with a mixture of funding from
local property taxes and state grants (and some federal grants). Lawsuits challenging
state education funding methods have been brought in at least 45 of the 50
states—19 of them successfully. It is in state courts—interpreting state
constitutions—that the legal battle and the policy debates remain.

Unlike the federal constitution, which has no explicit protection for education, at least 48—if not all—state constitutions contain clauses that explicitly
protect education. Therefore, plaintiffs challenging education funding laws have

an easier case to make than they do under the federal constitution. There is great variety in the wording of these education clauses; some use only general education language. For example, the Connecticut Constitution states, "There shall always be free public elementary and secondary schools in the state." Other clauses speak to the quality of public education—such as New Jersey's: "The Legislature shall provide for the maintenance and support of the thorough and efficient system of free public schools for the instruction of all the children in this State between the ages of five and eighteen years." Some clauses articulate a stronger requirement, and some state constitutions include a rather emphatic education clause, such as Washington's, which states, "It is the paramount duty of the state to make ample provision for the education of all children residing within its borders . . ."

The legal arguments that might be made to strike down a public education funding system depend in part on the precise language of the state constitution's education clause. The more emphatic and specific the language, the stronger—and more numerous—the potential arguments for striking down a funding system.

In the years after *Rodriguez*, the cases typically relied on arguments of inequity or "equality." For example, after the plaintiffs in *Rodriguez* failed in their federal constitutional claim, plaintiffs from the same Texas school district challenged the state's education funding law under the state constitution's education clause. This time, in *Edgewood Independent School District v. Kirby*, the plaintiffs won: the Texas Supreme Court found the system unconstitutional because the framers of the state's education clause, which calls for an "efficient system of public free schools," "never contemplated that such gross inequalities could exist with an 'efficient system.'" After multiple legislative responses and two more court challenges, a new funding approach passed state constitutional muster.

However, equity claims were not always successful, even when the language of the state constitution seems promising. In Minnesota, for example, the Supreme Court concluded that education funding differentials arising from relying on property taxes were constitutional; it rejected an argument that such a system violated the education clause, which required nothing less than "a general and uniform system of public schools."

There is also the issue of how to define equality. As one commentator points out, states might look at the "disparity in the capacity to fund education," the "disparity in the actual funding provided for schools in the different districts," the "actual caliber of the educational services available to a district's children . . .

comparisons of school facilities, class sizes, teacher qualifications, and the like . . ." or, boldest of all, "the ultimate outcomes delivered by the educational system . . . whether children in different districts are equally well educated by their schools and equally well prepared to participate in the work place, in higher education, and in the democratic process."

Sometimes plaintiffs have won on equity grounds even without the court concluding that a fundamental right in education warranted strict scrutiny. For example, in striking down the state's school funding law, Vermont's Supreme Court noted that the case does not turn on "the particular constitutional test to be employed. Labels aside, we are simply unable to fathom a legitimate governmental purpose to justify the gross inequities in educational opportunities evident from the record." While Vermont's Supreme Court recognized the importance of local control, it noted that "The state may delegate to local towns and cities the authority to finance and administer the schools within their borders; it cannot, however, abdicate the basic responsibility for education by passing it on to local governments, which are themselves creations of the state."

In the Vermont case, as in others, the state's rationale for the existing school funding system is preservation of local control. As the Vermont Court noted, however, the values of equity and local control are not necessarily in conflict. It stated that "[r]egardless of how the state finances public education, it may still leave the basic decision-making power with the local districts. Moreover, insofar as 'local control' means the ability to decide that more money should be devoted to the education of children within a district, we have seen—as another court once wrote—that for poorer districts 'such fiscal freewill is a cruel illusion.'"

But even if there were a conflict with local autonomy, I confess I find it hard to imagine a rational reason why the funding level of a school—the funding available to educate a child—should be largely a function of the aggregate property values in the school district in which the child lives. One can well imagine that education has historically been thought of as a local matter because in the eighteenth and early nineteenth centuries, education may have seemed to some the most local of local issues. The schoolmaster and the schoolhouse served to educate the local children. If they were not educated, it was they who suffered, not others; if they became educated, it was they who benefited. That makes some sense when the economy was agricultural, and people and their livelihood were tied to the land. But with industrialization and increased commerce comes not only greater mobility of individuals, but greater fluidity of labor and broader consequences of education. In the nineteenth century, the Morrill Act's creation of the Land Grant colleges during the Civil War reflected the nation's new recognition that the economic and social benefits of education flow not only to the student but also to the state and the economy at large. Moreover, as Jefferson and others keenly recognized even in the eighteenth century, broad-based public education is essential to the success of a democratic form of government. Education is the most public of all public goods.

Indeed, we see the increased role that the federal government has come to play in educational matters in recent years as it recognizes the crucial stake that the nation as a whole has in educational quality. I am thinking of initiatives from President George Bush's 1989 National Education Summit, which set out to articulate national educational goals to recent federal legislation related to educational accountability. That increased federal involvement also reflects an acknowledgement that the federal government must play a key role in education today—despite the fact that education has historically been a jealously guarded state and local matter. This sense of an increasing stake of the society as a whole in local education will, ultimately, I believe, be reflected in the Constitution too.

Equity claims predominated in the legal challenges to education funding laws in the 1970s and 1980s, and plaintiffs won about a third of those cases, beginning with California in 1971. But since then there has been a new and intriguing development in the field of education reform, which involves an increasing number of cases focusing less on equity and more on the adequacy of education afforded students. When, in 1989, cases began to shift to making adequacy claims, plaintiffs won two-thirds of the cases, including cases in Kentucky in 1989 and in Ohio and Wyoming in 1997. Perhaps this shift and success has been due in part in recent years to the widely held feeling that public education was often failing students. While the assumption in *Rodriguez* was that most students were adequately served by the public education systems, in the eighties (particularly after the publication of *A Nation at Risk* in 1983) there was a sense that the opposite was the case.

We can see the two different legal arguments or strategies for striking down state public education funding systems side by side in New England's Twin States—New Hampshire and Vermont. In 1993, the New Hampshire Supreme Court found that the State Constitution's education clause imposes a duty on the state to provide adequate funding for broad educational opportunities for all children.

The Court did not address itself to equality arguments. The case was remanded for a determination of whether the education funding system fulfilled that obligation, and the iterative legislative process began. In Vermont, on the other hand, the state Supreme Court decided that the state's educational funding system "deprives children of an equal educational opportunity."

The legislative response called for by these different judicial decisions in the two states differed accordingly. In New Hampshire, the question was, essentially, how much funding was necessary or adequate. In Vermont, the question was, essentially, how to mitigate the disparity between education funding in property-wealthy towns and property-poor towns. While it is undoubtedly too early to make a judgment about these alternative approaches, a fair if tentative evaluation would be that determining "adequacy" in New Hampshire has been difficult but doable; imposing equity in Vermont has proved both difficult and divisive.

The adequacy has several distinct advantages. Each of the educational clauses in state constitutions imposes an express duty on the state to provide for a system of public education. That duty—regardless of the precise wording of the education clauses—necessarily means (unless language is vacuous) that the state has an obligation to provide an adequate minimum level of education.

Moreover, unlike striking down a financing system on equity grounds, invalidating a state finance law on adequacy grounds gives rise to no "slippery slope" problem: it creates no precedent that might support assertions of other fundamental rights—to basic shelter or subsistence, for example.

Some believe that changes in school funding based on adequacy will be longer lasting than changes imposed as a result of changes designed to establish educational funding equity. Time will tell.

Concerns that establishing a right to an adequate education would result in courts and legislatures setting the constitutional definition of "adequate education" too low have proven to be largely unfounded. Many states have rejected archaic or basic competencies as standards and have arrived at seemingly rigorous definitions. The Supreme Court of Kentucky, for example, has listed seven specific standards, requiring sufficient

(i)   . . . oral and written communication skills to enable students to function in a complex and rapidly changing civilization;

(ii)   . . . knowledge of economic, social and political systems to enable the student to make informed choices;

(iii)   . . . understanding of governmental processes to enable the student to understand the issues that affect his or her community, state, and nation;

(iv)   . . . self-knowledge and knowledge of his or her mental and physical wellness;

(v)   . . . grounding in the arts to enable each student to appreciate his or her cultural and historical heritage;

(vi)   . . . training or preparation for advanced training in either academic or vocational fields so as to enable each child to choose and pursue life work intelligently; and

(vii)   . . . levels of academic or vocational skills to enable public school students to compete favorably with their counterparts in surrounding states, in academics or in the job market.

Indeed, while the Kentucky case was brought on behalf of poor school districts seeking equitable funding, the Court invalidated the entire state education system because they deemed it "inadequate and well below the national effort."

Perhaps it should be explicitly acknowledged that there is not necessarily a linear or even inevitable correlation between the level of funding and the quality of education. A school district does not necessarily deliver a better or worse education simply because it receives more or fewer dollars than another district. But as a friend of mine is fond of saying, the race doesn't always go to the swift, or the battle to the fittest, but that's the way to bet. Resources do, in fact, generally correlate with quality. As the Vermont Supreme Court wrote—and indeed the state did not contest, "Unequal funding yields, at a minimum, unequal curricular, technological, and human resources." Wealthier school districts are generally stronger than poor districts. As Demetrio Rodriguez commented in 1992, "If money is not necessary, why is it people have been fighting us over it for twenty-two years?" Or one might also ask, as others have, if money isn't important, why do wealthy districts choose to spend so much more on education? Or consider the answer of the New Jersey Supreme Court:

Poorer urban districts . . . are entitled to pass or fail with at least the same amount of money as their competitors. If the claim is that these students simply cannot make it, the constitutional answer is: give them a chance. The Constitution does not tell them that since more money will not help, we will give them less; that because their needs cannot be fully met, they will not be met at all.

Similarly, in striking down Arkansas's school funding scheme as both inadequate and inequitable in 2002, the Arkansas Supreme Court rejected as "farfetched" and "implausible" the State's argument that enhanced school funding does not correlate with better student performance, concluding that adequately compensated "teachers, sufficient equipment to supplement instruction, and learning in facilities that are [adequate], all combine to enhance educational performance . . . All of that takes money."

There is, of course, a spirited debate today over whether increased resources yield better test scores on standardized tests. There are many compelling anecdotes of extraordinary improvements in educational outcomes following significant new investments of resources. This is an important debate, but it is not worth the attention it tends to get. We Americans have far too great a penchant for reducing questions to numerical outcomes and rankings, and it is particularly prevalent and problematic in education. The fact is that along with resources goes the quality of life we offer our children, and their families, and the explicit respect and dignity of being full members of society. A poor school, relative to others, inevitably conveys a message of what the rest of society thinks of its students, their potential, and their worth. We have taken that lesson to heart with our commitments to students with disabilities—even though presumably all the funds spent to that end have not raised average test scores at their schools—and we should take it to heart more broadly for socio-economically disadvantaged students—indeed all students. If we want students to think they matter, we need to provide an education that suggests this is the case.

Thus, despite daunting legal, social, and educational challenges, hope endures. Teachers, administrators, and policy experts continue their work. Legal challenges to inequitable funding systems and inadequate education continue, based on state constitutions' education and equal protection clauses, and other arguments.

And there may also be hope—for another day—in the most unlikely of places—in *Rodriguez* itself. Ironically, while it was the failure of the Supreme Court in *Rodriguez* to find a fundamental right to education that led plaintiffs to state courts and state constitutions, that process caused the legal grounds for challenging educational funding laws to shift from causes of action based on inequity to causes of action based on inadequacy. And the question of inadequacy remains very much open—under not only state constitutions, but also under the federal constitution. Indeed, Justice Powell's majority opinion in *Rodriguez* expressly stated pointedly:

The State [of Texas] repeatedly asserted in its briefs . . . that it now assures "every child in every school district an adequate education." No proof was offered at trial persuasively discrediting or refuting the State's assertion.

. . . even if it were conceded that some identifiable quantum of education is a constitutionally protected prerequisite to the meaningful exercise of either [First Amendment freedoms or the right to vote], we have no indication that the present levels of educational expenditure in Texas provide an education that falls short . . . [N]o charge fairly could be made [in the present case] that the system fails to provide each child with an opportunity to acquire the basic minimal skills necessary for the enjoyment of the rights of speech and of full participation in the political process.

And despite the fact that *Rodriguez* was, to my mind, a missed historical opportunity, the decision explicitly left open the issue of adequacy as a federal constitutional right, some "basic minimum" to which every child in the country is entitled. In fact, the Court reiterated this point in a later case, stating that it had not "definitively settled the questions whether a minimally adequate education is a fundamental right and whether a statute alleged to discriminatorily infringe that right should be accorded heightened equal protection review."

Clearly, Justice Powell was troubled in *Rodriguez* by the complexity of the issues involved and the lack of clear solutions of judicially appropriate standards of evaluation. He feared that a decision for the plaintiffs would precipitate "an unparalleled upheaval in public education." But over the last thirty years, state courts have made significant progress in defining and articulating justiciable standards of equity and adequacy. The challenges to state educational funding laws have stimulated or compelled an interaction between the state judiciary and the legislative and executive branches—about equity, about what an adequate education is, about the purposes of education and about the benefits of education and who receives those benefits. Since 1973, every single state has passed some form of public education finance reform. It is fifty different stories in fifty different states, but while lengthy, frustrating, and often difficult, they have been in the main, good for education, good for democracy, and good for society.

But we all are painfully aware that this country still struggles with equity in public education as it relates to financing; and we also still struggle with the challenge of quality—of adequacy—in public education. Because of *Brown* and succeeding cases, there is at least the possibility that students of different racial and ethnic backgrounds will benefit from sitting down and learning together. But whether what students are learning is adequate—in either educational or constitutional terms—is still very much at issue. That remains the challenge for all of us—educators, advocates, lawyers, and citizens—as members of a society that would seek to ensure that, in education, no child is left behind.

CHAPTER 6

ACADEMIC FREEDOM

Benjamin N. Cardozo Lecture, Association of the Bar of the
City of New York, March 23, 2005

---

*During the 2004–2005 academic year, Columbia experienced its own version of the
growing controversy on U.S. campuses about academic freedom, freedom of expression, political debates over Israel, and claims of anti-Semitism. A documentary film
titled* Columbia Unbecoming *alleged that some faculty members in the Department of Middle East and East Asian Studies expressed pro-Palestinian, anti-Israel
views in their teaching and penalized Jewish students who disagreed with them. While
some students and faculty rejected this characterization, President Bollinger named
Professor Ira Katznelson to lead an ad hoc committee reviewing these claims. Then,
in February 2005, shortly after Professor Rashid Khalidi, director of Columbia's Middle East Institute, publicly commented on the matter, New York City public schools
chancellor Joel I. Klein terminated Khalidi's role as a lecturer for a teacher development program.*

We gather at a time of enormous stress for colleges and universities across the country. It is a time of contentious debate on campuses—among students, among faculty, and within administrations. Some of these debates concern matters of national or global importance. Many are joined—even incited—by outside forces, from political pressure groups to the mainstream media to increasingly strident voices on the Web.

For those of us who inhabit the academic world, these can be troubling times. It is a time when a notion we all hold very dear—academic freedom—is invoked by people on opposite sides of any given debate, often by people who have very different ideas of what academic freedom means. Some even question the basic premises of academic freedom.

What is called for in times like these is a renewed understanding of what our principles are in theory and what they mean in practice. As always, we must also understand what purposes they serve, so we know what's ultimately at stake.

Academic freedom goes to the heart of the university, to the rights and responsibilities of faculty and students, to the nature of teaching and scholarship. As such, it cannot be reduced to a soundbite or slogan, as some would have it, without jeopardizing our working grasp of the principle itself. In stressful times especially, we must make every effort to hold in our minds the complexity of what we say we believe. That is what I will endeavor to do this evening.

Let me begin, then, by surveying the climate in which our conversation takes place.

There is a deep sense of vulnerability in our universities. It is hard not to believe that the extraordinary action of Harvard's faculty of Arts and Sciences in taking a vote of no confidence and censuring its president, Larry Summers, will in time come to seem symbolic of larger societal issues, much larger than the immediate questions they well may have thought they were addressing. In the last national presidential election, many of our country's most distinguished scientists felt the singular need to enter the public arena and criticize the Bush administration for systematically choosing politics over science in various public policy settings where the norm had theretofore been scientific objectivity. Meanwhile, politically powerful conservative figures and groups (e.g., the National Association of Scholars) within the country regularly and publicly castigate our leading colleges and universities as bastions of outdated political liberalism, intolerant of diverse perspectives, committed to political ends under the mask of scholarship, living by a double standard of free speech for us but not for our opponents, and harboring extremists and especially anti-American extremists.

One notable manifestation of these attacks is a national group called Students for Academic Freedom (SAF), founded in 2003, by the conservative activist David Horowitz, with members on about 150 campuses. At the core of SAF's campaign is a so-called "academic bill of rights," written by Horowitz and peddled to legislators across the country. Among other things, the bill calls for "fostering a plurality of methodologies and perspectives" in the hiring process; creating "curricula and reading lists in the humanities and social sciences [that] reflect the uncertainty and unsettled character of all human knowledge in these areas by providing students with dissenting sources and viewpoints where appropriate"; and inviting speakers with different points of view to campus. Horowitz's agenda has gained traction in statehouses across the country: legislation enacting variations of the academic bill of rights is moving ahead in 19 states. A Republican congressman from Georgia introduced Horowitz's bill as a nonbinding resolution in the U.S. House of Representatives in 2003.

It is by no means a new phenomenon that an individual professor's public comments provoke a national political firestorm and, then, calls for the professor's dismissal (as we shall see). This is especially true in periods of perceived national emergency. We have that today, but seemingly augmented by the new forms of media and communications that have emerged in the last decade.

Take, for example, the controversy surrounding Ward Churchill's invitation to speak at Hamilton College in 2004. None of us could have anticipated the speed with which conservative activists around the country organized to stop him from speaking. What started with an op-ed in the Hamilton student newspaper rapidly snowballed into a national media campaign.

We experienced a version of this at Columbia in 2003, just as the United States was undertaking the invasion of Iraq. An assistant professor speaking at a public forum, called to protest the war, expressed the wish for "a million Mogadishus" in order to stop what he saw as America's colonializing hubris. This statement was seized by local and then national media, including the commentator Bill O'Reilly. In the week after the protest, I received more than 20,000 emails, and the phone lines in my office became inoperable. Nearly 140 lawmakers from the U.S. House of Representatives and from state legislatures wrote to me demanding that the faculty member be discharged. The professor had to be moved to an undisclosed new apartment because of threats. I and others expressed vehement objection to the professor's statements. But its rapid transformation into a national scandal is, I think, symptomatic of a kind of persecution that arises during wartime.

At this moment, Columbia is facing another, slightly different—but very difficult—challenge. A number of students, supported by some faculty, have asserted that certain professors in our department of Middle Eastern and Asian Languages and Cultures have taught courses on the Israeli-Palestinian controversy that are biased against Israel, Zionism, and Jews, and have intimidated students who try to express reasonable and alternative viewpoints on the subject. A few professors have also allegedly called Zionism—and the very existence of Israel as an avowedly Jewish state—"racist," and have urged the rest of the world to treat it as a "pariah state." Some groups outside the University and segments of the media have condemned the professors and the University for these actions and called for their dismissal. Some have gone so far as to depict Columbia as a "campus of hate," filled with anti-Semitism.

The University's policy with respect to two aspects of the controversy is clear and, I believe, right: We will not tolerate intimidation of students in the classroom for appropriately expressing reasonable and relevant points of view. A faculty committee, advised by Floyd Abrams, is nearing the end of its review of any claims of intimidation. And we will not punish professors (or students) for the speech or ideas they express as part of public debate about public issues. I can also say with complete confidence that it is simply preposterous to characterize Columbia as anti-Semitic or as having a hostile climate for Jewish students and faculty.[1] Columbia is deservedly proud of the strides it has taken over the years as a leading world center of Jewish studies and a place where everyone of whatever background, race, or religion can flourish.

These controversies raise important questions about the work of the modern university. In particular, what are the rights and responsibilities of professors to set and control the content of the classroom? (I am using "classroom" throughout as shorthand for the educational experience.) Is it within the prerogatives of the professor to teach a single perspective on the subject, perhaps reinforcing this choice with selective readings? Is there a line between academic inquiry and politicization of a course? If so, how is it set and who enforces it? Should we care whether an individual professor uses the classroom as a place of political advocacy, as long as elsewhere in the curriculum there are offerings by advocates for other sides of the same topic?

I do not intend my discussion of these questions, as they relate to academic freedom, to be merely one about "rights." As with any "right" or freedom, we can only understand what academic freedom means when we also understand what we are striving to accomplish. So, I want to also talk about what we value and aspire to in the university and why that serves society—and justifies academic freedom in the first place. I believe we are neglecting a critically important function of universities—a function that arises out of the particular intellectual character nurtured within the modern university and beneficial to democratic society. It is what I would call "the scholarly temperament."

Let me say, I am deeply, deeply proud of Columbia University, proud to be a member of the faculty, proud of the extraordinary students we have, and proud to serve as the president. I cannot imagine a community more committed to the life of the mind, in the best sense, and I see it in facets of the institution every single day. All that I have to say tonight about academic freedom and the ideals of the university constitute the stuff of daily life in this remarkable place. Thus, I approach the subject with a confidence that, while, at certain moments we do not reach as close to the ideal as we would like, Columbia nevertheless approaches the ideal as much or more so than any institution I know.

Let's begin by examining the principle of academic freedom itself—its origins and its less-than-wholly-successful life in the real world.

I. ACADEMIC FREEDOM

The current, American conception of academic freedom can be traced to early 19th-century Germany. The founders of the University of Berlin adopted two basic principles upon its establishment in 1810: Lehrfreiheit ("freedom to teach") and Lernfreiheit ("freedom to learn"). Professors had the right to research and teach according to their interests, and students had the right, free from administrative coercion, to choose their own course of study.[2] (It is worth highlighting that in these origins the rights of students were encompassed by the idea of academic freedom, something I believe we need to integrate more into our contemporary thinking.)

In the late 19th century, American universities overwhelmingly adopted the German model. They established individual graduate schools, each dedicated to a specific field of knowledge. They also adopted the general principles of the "freedom to teach" and the "freedom to learn"—since, it was believed, in order for graduate students and faculty to break new intellectual ground, they had to possess the freedom of inquiry.[3]

Historians trace the codification of academic freedom, meanwhile, to a series of conflicts in the late 1800s that pitted individual faculty members against university trustees and administrators.[4]

The most famous was a case involving Edward A. Ross, a Stanford economist who made a series of speeches in support of the Democrat William Jennings Bryan in 1896. Jane Lathrop Stanford—widow of Leland Stanford, ardent Republican, and sole trustee of the university—was so outraged by Ross' activism that she demanded his dismissal. The president of the university eventually acceded to her demands; Ross was forced to resign in 1900.[5]

Ross' mistreatment at the hands of Stanford administrators became the basis for the charter document of the American Association of University Presidents, entitled the "Report on Academic Freedom and Tenure." Co-written in 1915 by Arthur Lovejoy, a Stanford philosopher who resigned over Ross' firing, and Edwin R.A. Seligman, a Columbia economist, the report sought to remove university trustees as arbiters of research and teaching, and to assert instead the authority of self-governing faculty members. The report stated:

The distinctive and important function [of professors] . . . is to deal at first hand, after prolonged and specialized technical training, with the sources of knowledge; and to impart the results of their own and of their fellow-specialists' investigations and reflection, both to students and the general public, without fear or favor . . . The proper fulfillment of the work of the professoriate requires that our universities shall be so free that no fair-minded person shall find any excuse for even a suspicion that the utterances of university teachers are shaped or restricted by the judgment, not of professional scholars, but of inexpert and possibly not wholly disinterested persons outside their ranks.[6]

This notion—that faculty members, not external actors, should determine professional standards for the academy—remains, today, a powerful and widely accepted idea. It is the foundational principle of academic freedom.

It has not, however, gone untested. Indeed, the 20th century presented a flurry of challenges to academic freedom, especially in times of great national stress.

When the United States entered World War I in 1917, the nation's political leaders sought to enforce public support for the war effort. That year, Congress passed the Espionage Act, which prescribed a $10,000 fine and 20 years' imprisonment for obstructing the draft or disclosing information about the nation's defenses. A year later, Congress passed the Sedition Act, which made it a federal offense to use "disloyal, profane, scurrilous, or abusive language" about the Constitution, the government, the flag, or the uniforms of the Army and Navy.

Such legislation, along with a widespread fear that new immigrants still harbored loyalty to their European homelands—particularly to Germany—gave rise to a brand of fanatical American nationalism. Citizens felt great pressure to publicly proclaim their allegiance to the United States. Submitting to loyalty oaths, participating in public rallies for the sale of bonds, and joining nationalistic societies became essential proofs of citizenship. Americans who chose not to flaunt their patriotism sometimes aroused mistrust.[7]

The American university did not escape scrutiny. In fact, professors became particular targets of suspicion, since, as the historian Walter Metzger wrote in 1955, they were "by trade and usually by disposition somewhat more detached from mass obsessions."[8] Across the country, boards of trustees, community members, even fellow faculty members "harassed those college teachers whose passion for fighting the war was somewhat less flaming than their own."[9]

Perhaps the best-known invasion of academic freedom during the World War I era occurred at Columbia. In March 1917, the Board of Trustees adopted a resolution that essentially imposed a loyalty oath on the entire university. It read:

Resolved—The unqualified loyalty to the Government of the United States be required of all students, officers of administration and officers of instruction in the University as a condition of retaining their connection with the University, and that the President have authority to exercise the disciplinary powers of the University to carry this resolution into effect.[10]

Many faculty members responded with disgust, calling the resolution "unjust and injurious" in a petition they sent to the trustees.[11] But President Nicholas Murray Butler accepted the authority that the resolution gave him. In his Commencement Day address in 1917, he declared that Columbia would not allow any opposition to the war effort. "What had been tolerated before became intolerable now," he said. "What has been wrongheadedness was now sedition. What had been folly was now treason."[12]

A rash of firings followed. Psychologist James McKeen Cattell sent a petition to three U.S. congressmen in August 1917 urging them not to pass legislation that would send American conscripts to European battlefields. He was dismissed in October. Politics professor Leon Fraser was summoned by the trustees for making critical remarks about a military training camp in Plattsburgh, New York, and was fired the next year. One of Columbia's best-known scholars, the historian Charles Beard, was investigated for condoning a speaker who had allegedly said, "To hell with the flag."[13] Beard was eventually exonerated—but he resigned his post in 1917, in protest of the dismissal of many of his colleagues. In his resignation letter, he explained his reason for leaving. He wrote: "The University is really under the control of a small and active group of trustees who have no standing in the world of education, who are reactionary and visionless in politics, narrow and medieval in religion." Beard went on to become one of the founders of the New School for Social Research—and not until 1919 did President Butler put an end to the trustees' investigations.[14]

The McCarthy era also posed significant challenges to academic freedom, and universities often yielded to the pressures of the day. James B. Conant, president of Harvard, said at one time that Communist Party members were "out of bounds as members of the teaching profession."[15] Many institutions fired faculty members suspected of Communist ties—in fact, the purges of the McCarthy era claimed the jobs of more than 600 professors and teachers nationwide. It is further estimated that 20 percent of all the witnesses called to testify before congressional and state investigating committees during the 1940s and 50s were college teachers or graduate students.[16]

At this point in history, significantly, the U.S. Supreme Court began to recognize academic freedom as part of the rights of free expression under the First Amendment.

Cases from the McCarthy Era, in particular *Sweezy v. New Hampshire* (1957) and *Keyishian v. Board of Regents* (1966), framed the liberty interest as one belonging to individual teachers. These early opinions set the groundwork for later cases in which a broad right to free academic decision-making was granted to the universities themselves. In cases like *Board of Regents v. Southworth* (2000) and the admissions cases *Regents of the University of California v. Bakke* (1978) and *Grutter v. Bollinger* (2003), the Court carved out a zone of freedom for universities, giving them wide latitude to determine how best to educate students.

The Court's first explicit mention of academic freedom was in Justice Black's dissent in *Adler v. Board of Education* (1952). Adler upheld the constitutionality of New York's Feinberg Law, which forbade the state from employing in its public schools any member of a group that advocated overthrow of the government. The Court held that dismissal from employment in the school system did not amount to a deprivation of the right to free speech. In his dissent, Justice Black predicted that the threat of investigation and possible termination "is certain to raise havoc with academic freedom" by turning the public school system into a "spying project" and "police state" where "there can be no exercise of the free intellect."

Five years later, in *Sweezy v. New Hampshire*, a plurality of the Court identified academic freedom as a core constitutional interest. In their concurring opinion, Justices Frankfurter and Harlan memorably identified the central role of academic freedom in a free society. *Sweezy* arose out of an investigation by the attorney general of New Hampshire into a series of lectures given by Professor Sweezy at the University of New Hampshire. When the professor refused to cooperate with the investigation, the attorney general sought to compel his testimony. The Court decided the case on due process grounds, holding that the attorney general had been given "a sweeping and uncertain mandate" such that the inquiry infringed on Professor Sweezy's constitutional rights. The opinion disapproved strongly of government interference with academic freedom, holding that "there unquestionably was an invasion of petitioner's liberties in the areas of academic freedom and political expression—areas in which government should be extremely reluctant to tread." The Court cautioned that "[s]cholarship cannot flourish in an atmosphere of suspicion and distrust. Teachers and students must always remain free to inquire, to study and to evaluate."

The concurring opinion in *Sweezy* used language that has been quoted, analyzed, and relied upon for nearly half a century. Justice Frankfurter warned of the "grave harm resulting from governmental intrusion into the intellectual life of a university." In its most celebrated portion, the opinion quoted with approval from a statement written on behalf of two "open" universities in South Africa that stated:

It is the business of a university to provide that atmosphere which is most conducive to speculation, experiment and creation. It is an atmosphere in which there prevail 'the four essential freedoms' of a university—to determine for itself on academic grounds who may teach, what may be taught, how it shall be taught, and who may be admitted to study.

This quick review of the origins, scope, constitutional basis, and vulnerability of the principle of academic freedom provides us with a helpful framework for approaching at least some of our contemporary issues. Given the regrettable violations of academic freedom, especially in times of war and threats to national security, that characterize the recent century, it is certainly understandable how universities now are feeling skittish and vulnerable. And, yet, we have more to resolve in our minds as we confront criticisms that we in universities are not living up to our own standards of intellectual integrity. It may well be that some of those critics have illegitimate and ulterior motives, claiming they only want diversity of voices when, in fact, they want to silence opposing views or to obtain their own platform within the university to propagate their political agenda. And it may well be that, assuming for the moment there is some merit to the criticisms, it is the proper business of the university and the faculty to remedy. In either case, we need to know what it is we are striving toward, our ideals and their social purposes, if we are to chart the right course, to defend meaningfully and persuasively our academic freedom against inappropriate interventions, and to speak authentically and persuasively to the broader society.

Do we believe there is a fundamental difference between what goes on in a classroom and what goes on in a political convention? What do we strive for in the university that academic freedom is supposed to protect, and how does that help improve our society? Are we saying that professors are completely autonomous in determining the content of their courses? Or are there some internal norms the community of scholars try collectively to live by?

I would now like to turn to that discussion.

II. THE IDEALS OF A UNIVERSITY

I think we should pause and take note of a few significant elements in the earlier review of academic freedom. First, note how academic freedom by most accounts, and in its origins, encompasses students' freedom to learn as well as faculty's freedom to teach. Academic freedom, in other words, is a freedom we share in the classroom. Second, note how the seminal "Report on Academic Freedom and Tenure" described the professor: namely, as someone steeped in "prolonged and specialized technical training" and about whom "no fair-minded person" would even suspect of speaking other than as "shaped or restricted by the judgment . . . of professional scholars." The idea of the "profession" of the scholar is, I think, one of the keys to understanding the ideals supported by the principle of academic freedom. What does it mean to be a "professional scholar?"

A

When you ask what our primary purpose is within a university, the typical answer would be that of preserving and advancing our understanding of life, the world, and the universe—of discovering truth. That is the typical answer, but some hold a different view. Some will say that a university is a time and place to find your identity, to discover who you are and what you believe. Some (Edward Said suggested this in one of his books on the role of the public intellectual) will say that, since the university is free of the interests of power, or money, or ideological party, interests which skew one's judgment, the academy is a place that identifies with those out of power, with the oppressed or the victims of injustice, and in that way naturally speaks truth to power. Some will say that the university is nothing more than a haven for the simple and pure pursuit of ideas, where curiosity is the only guide and the spirit of play is the governing motivation. Still, the most common explanation for the university is that it transmits as much of human understanding as it can from one generation to the next and adds as much new knowledge as it can to the existing store of human knowledge—a function that has, unquestionably, brought enormous benefits, practical and otherwise, to our society and to the world.

I certainly do not want to challenge that primary function of the university, but I do believe it incomplete. There is far more at work within a university than simply the search for truth. A significant additional function is that of nurturing a very distinctive intellectual character. It is often said of the academy that it is a place of deep skepticism, and I think that is true. But the qualities of mind emphasized go well beyond skepticism, and it is critical to understand what they are and how they relate to the broader society and to the political arena in particular.

I have now spent more than three decades of my professional life in the university, and of all the qualities of mind valued in the academic community I would say the most valued is that of having the imaginative range and the mental courage to take in, to explore, the full complexity of the subject. To set aside one's pre-existing beliefs, to hold simultaneously in one's mind multiple angles of seeing things, to actually allow yourself seemingly to believe another view as you consider it—these are the kind intellectual qualities that characterize the very best faculty and students I have known and that suffuse the academic atmosphere at its best. The stress is on seeing the difficulty of things, of being prepared to live closer than we are emotionally inclined to the harsh reality that we live steeped in ignorance and mystery, of being willing to undermine even our common sense for the possibility of seeing something hidden. To be sure, this kind of extreme openness of intellect is exceedingly difficult to master, and, of course, in a profound sense we never fully do. Because it runs counter to many of our natural impulses, it requires both daily exercise and a community of people dedicated to keeping it alive (which is why, I believe, universities as physical places will continue to thrive in a world of electronic communication). But we all know what I have just described from personal experience: the extraordinary, unique thrill of thinking about a subject one way until you feel there cannot possibly be another valid perspective, and then beginning with another line of thought and feeling the same certainty settle into our minds, all the while watching in amazement as it happens. Sometimes, of course, this yields new "truths," but that is not the only purpose for developing this mental capacity.

B

Different forms of government require different, and special, mental capacities of citizens. Just as with a market economy or a military, particular intellectual and emotional attributes are needed to make a successful democracy. It is not a simple matter to define these capacities, but it is almost certainly harder to build them up in a population. A democracy, in my view, poses the greatest challenge of all. Obedience to authority seems, at least, easier to inculcate and sustain than the intellectual flexibility of the give-and-take of perpetual conflict over multiple desires and beliefs that characterize life in a democratic system of government. When to share and embrace other views, when to insist on your own; when to compromise and when to resist; how to use reason and rhetoric, when even our most cherished and fundamental beliefs cannot be "proven" by logic—these are difficult to sustain in the best of times and, experience sadly shows, nearly impossible in the worst of times. I could go on at some length about this subject, having spent much of my scholarly life trying to understand—through the practiced lens of reflection and experience of the First Amendment and freedom of speech— what batch of social structures and qualities of mind are needed to support a democracy. I would just say this: The most thoughtful observers during the last century about the risks of totalitarianism (I'm thinking of people such as Oliver Wendell Holmes, Jr., Isaiah Berlin, and Hannah Arendt) all identified intellectual intolerance and certitude as the central cause of the failure of democracies and the shift to authoritarianism.

In the nineteenth century, John Stuart Mill argued that democracy is perennially at risk of being transformed into tyranny by the tendency of human nature to assume that our beliefs are true and, accordingly, to coerce opposing "falsehoods" into silence. Holmes offered a similar analysis of the normality of the roots of persecution: "Persecution for the expression of opinions is perfectly logical," he said. "If you have no doubt about your premises or your power and want a certain result with all your heart, you naturally express your wishes in law and sweep away all opposition."

In a volume of essays entitled "The Crooked Timber of Humanity," Isaiah Berlin speaks of how the 20th century was frequently devastated by great ideological storms sweeping across the landscape. In his essay "The Pursuit of the Ideal," Berlin identified two forces above all others that shaped human history in the twentieth century, the first being "the development of the natural sciences and technology" and the second the "great ideological storms that have altered the lives of virtually all mankind." Berlin senses the dangers of belief. "Happy are those," he says ironically, "who have, by their own methods, arrived at clear and unshakable convictions about what to do and what to be that brook no possible doubt." But, though happy, such people are a threat to human decency. "For if one really believes that [a solution to life's problems] is possible, then surely no cost would be too high to obtain it: to make mankind just and happy and creative and harmonious forever— what could be too high a price to pay for that?" Arendt, too, found the sources of totalitarianism in the self-inflating appeal of infallibility and its accompanying belief in one's own omnipotence.

In a speech to the Federal Bar Association, Learned Hand offered a simple parable about the kind of intellectual capacities required in a democracy, and why democracies fail when these capacities are absent. He compared a democracy to a group of children at play, confused about how to organize their games and deferring to an older, more experienced peer for direction. But that solution satisfies no one, as each child is unhappy to be bossed about by another, and eventually confusion reigns again—until, Hand wrote, "in the end slowly and with infinite disappointment they do learn a little; they learn to forbear, to reckon with another, accept a little where they wanted much, to live and let live, to yield when they must yield; perhaps, we may hope, not to take all they can. But the condition is that they shall be willing at least to listen to one another to get the habit of pooling their wishes. Somehow or other they must do this, if the play is to go on. . . ."

This is the intellectual capacity we teach ourselves and our students in the academy, a capacity that is useful in the search for truth but has many purposes in life beyond that. It characterizes the "scholarly profession." Perhaps we pursue this capacity to an extreme degree, but we're just one of many social institutions designed to contribute to the whole by nurturing the complex qualities of mind our complex modern societies need. The principle of academic freedom is the guardian of this enterprise, which ironically is to correct against the very intellectual impulses (both internal and external to the academy) that continually threaten to breach academic freedom (as we have seen in the opening discussion).

III. APPLYING THE FRAMEWORK

I now want to close the discussion by returning to the opening questions and offering some answers. I believe that there are four guiding principles that should shape our actions.

First, we need to realize that the health and vigor, which I believe is strong, of universities depends upon the scholarly professionalism I have described. This involves our commitment to the intellectual disposition of extraordinary openness of intellect and the self-restraints that entails.

Public life poses, as we have seen, constant pressures and temptations for the university. Within the academy, we always face the impulse to jettison the scholarly ethos and adopt a more partisan mentality, which can easily become infectious, especially in times of great controversy. As Raymond Aron observed in his book "The Opium of the Intellectuals" in the 1950s, the intellectual life is continually tempted by the "longing for a purpose, for communion with the people, for something controlled by an idea and a will."

I must say that every faculty member I have known is aware of this impulse and tries to live by the scholarly temperament, just as we expect judges to maintain a judicial temperament. In the classroom, especially, where we perhaps meet our highest calling, the professor knows the need to resist the allure of certitude, the temptation to use the podium as an ideological platform, to indoctrinate a captive audience, to play favorites with the like-minded and silence the others. To act otherwise is to be intellectually self-indulgent.

This responsibility belongs to every member of every faculty, but it poses special challenges for those of us who teach subjects of great political controversy. Given the deep emotions that people—students and professors both—bring to these highly charged discussions, faculty must show an extraordinary sensitivity to unlocking the fears and the emotional barriers that can cause a discussion to turn needlessly painful and substantively partial.

Some may wonder whether this is too much to ask of a classroom and, therefore, universities should forego these subjects altogether. I think this would be a grave mistake. Not only is this the only way our universities can offer insights into questions of great importance to the society, but, as I have described the broader role of the university in a democratic society, we would lose the ability to serve these societal purposes just when it's needed most.

Second, given the expectations of a scholarly profession, how should we deal with lapses, for surely we must expect there will be occasional failures? Let me answer by saying what we should not do and what we should do.

We should not elevate our autonomy as individual faculty above every other value.

We should not accept the argument that our professional norms cannot be defined and therefore transgressions must be accepted without consequences. We, as faculty, properly have enormous autonomy in the conduct of our teaching and our scholarship. Yet, it will not do simply to say that the professional standards within which that autonomy exists are too vague for any enforcement at all. Life, after all, is filled with drawing lines about highly elusive and difficult-to-define differences, and yet we do so because to shirk the task is to invite worse consequences.

We should not accept the argument that professors are foreclosed from expressing their opinions on the subject in the classroom, nor that because professors are free to do so in some contexts there are no boundaries involved whenever viewpoints are expressed. The question is not whether a professor advocates a view but whether the overall design of the class, and course, is to explore the full range of the complexity of the subject.

We should not accept the argument that we as teachers can do what we want because students are of sufficient good sense to know bias and indoctrination when they see it. This ignores the enormous differential in power between the professor and the student in a classroom setting.

We should not accept the idea that the remedy for lapses is to add more professors with different political points of view, as some would have us do. The notion of a "balanced curriculum," in which students can, in effect, select and compensate for bias, sacrifices the essential norm of what we are supposed to be about in a university. It's like saying of doctors in a hospital that there should be more Republicans, or more Democrats. It also risks polarization of the university, where "liberals" take courses from "liberal" professors and "conservatives" take "conservative" professors.

We should not say that academic freedom means that there is no review within the university, no accountability, for the "content" of our classes or our scholarship. There is review, it does have consequences, and it does consider content.

And this happens every day, every year, and it is properly lodged in the hands of the faculty of the departments and schools of our institutions. Every faculty member participates in such a process, as I have myself over many years, and it has, generally speaking, the highest integrity. In appointment, promotion, and tenure discussions, as well as annual reviews, we make professional judgments about the scholarly temperament, the originality of ideas, the development of students' understanding and capacities, the respect shown for students, the tolerance of mind displayed, the mastery of the subject, and many other qualities of mind.

This is what it means to be part of a scholarly community, as the seminal founding statement of the AAUP implied. It rests with the faculty, and the role of the university is to ensure that the system of local self-governance is enabled.

Third, we must respect what I would call the principle of "separation of university and state."

As I indicated at the outset, universities do not penalize faculty or students for comments they make as citizens in public debate. A corollary is that, while faculty and students are free to take whatever positions they wish on public matters, universities are not. We do not, as institutions, generally speaking, take positions on public issues.

The latter was a much-debated topic during the Vietnam War, as many pushed to have universities condemn the war. A well-known commission at the University of Chicago, chaired by the eminent First Amendment scholar Harry Kalven, issued a report saying that universities should not do so. The basic argument of the Kalven report was that to do so would chill debate on the campus. I think that is a problem, but I believe the opposite is also a problem. As I said before, the risk is always present that we will jeopardize the scholarly ethos and join the public sphere. We, therefore, need to maintain the line between the differing roles—the role of the scholar professional and the role of the citizen. The last thing we want to do is to turn the campus into a political convention.

My fourth point is that all of us, but universities in particular, must stand firm in insisting that, when there are lines to be drawn, we must and will be the ones to do it. Not outside actors. Not politicians, not pressure groups, not the media. Ours is and must remain a system of self-government.

To be sure, as we have witnessed throughout recent history, the outside world will sometimes find the academy so dangerous and threatening that efforts will naturally arise to make decisions for us about whom we engage and what we teach. This must not be allowed to happen. We must understand, just as we have come to with freedom of speech generally, that the qualities of mind we need in a democracy—especially in times of crisis—are precisely what the extraordinary openness of the academy is designed to help achieve—and what will necessarily seem dangerous and threatening when our intellectual instincts press us, to be single minded or, to put it another way, of one mind. In a democracy, that's what we must be wary of.

CONCLUSION

In closing, I want to note a deep irony of academic freedom, and its parent, freedom of speech. These freedoms, when they are at issue, often divert our attention from serious engagement on more substantive issues. When controversies erupt over something someone said, we often quickly find ourselves in a debate about whether that speech is protected or not, rather than expending our energy explaining why in our view the ideas are wrong and should be rejected.

With the broad perspective we've taken of the intellectual landscape, we can understand why this happens. Engaging with ideas, as it turns out, is actually a very hard thing to do. The demands it places on our powers of reason, of imagination, of tolerance often seem overwhelming. Indeed, as I said earlier, the more that our most fundamental beliefs are at stake the harder it is to defend them. Therefore, it is natural for all of us in a controversy to turn our attention to debating the narrower—and often seemingly safer—question of whether an idea is protected or not.

Yet, robustly engaging with difficult ideas is the basic purpose of academic freedom—a fact that makes this diversion a great pity as well as an irony. I've always felt that tolerance carries a responsibility to speak to the ideas tolerated. This is, moreover, a moment in American history, in world history, when difficult, painful, sensitive issues truly need our clear-eyed attention, and could greatly benefit from the academy's perspectives.

As I said at the outset, this is a time of high vulnerability and anxiety at our universities. Yet I am confident that what I have called the scholarly temperament is alive and well in our universities. I know it is at Columbia University. A handful of instances of inappropriate behavior within our nation's universities must not be permitted falsely to define the whole and foster a counterproductive climate of distrust. Our basic mission is still strong, our sense of unique purpose is still well placed, and the value that our universities continue to provide our students, our nation and the world is not exceeded by any other institution.

We do not need a new set of principles, tailored to the times. We need only to reaffirm the principles that have guided us for the past hundred years; that have seen our profession through times of great challenge and led us toward ever-expanding horizons of human insight and the building of democratic societies.

CHAPTER 7

COMMENCEMENT ADDRESS

Columbia University, Low Plaza, May 17, 2006

On behalf of Columbia's trustees and faculty, it gives me great pleasure to say congratulations to the Class of 2006. You began your journeys on Broadway at either 116th Street or 168th Street —and today you end it in the same physical places. And yet you've traveled great personal and educational distances to arrive at this day. There were the first, disorienting moments on campus; saying goodbye to family; putting together your dorm room or apartment; and looking into the faces of your fellow students as you wondered: "Who will be my close friends?" and (let's speak the truth) "Who's the smartest among us?"

You asked yourselves these questions, and you began the lengthy process of building your knowledge, sustained over long, long nights and late, late mornings, with procrastination so painful that work became a palliative. And then, finally, you raced to the end, looked beyond the horizon of the last exam, and glimpsed a life far less structured and, indeed, less protected.

But that horizon will wait until tomorrow. Today, Class of 2006, is your day!

Since Commencement is a day of reflection, I thought it would be interesting to turn back the clock to 1984, the year many of the undergraduates were born, to see how much has changed since then. A lot, I figured. But then I realized that in 1984, we had Donald Rumsfeld taking official trips to Iraq . . . Al Gore was said to be considering a run for the White House . . . And Tom Cruise was getting a lot of attention for dancing on furniture. Risky business, indeed.

For you, Class of 2006, today marks the end of a long personal journey. But it also marks the end of a family journey. This glorious academic space is usually the focal point of the educational values we stand for. Today, it's a focal point for the love and pride of your families. Indeed, for the parents, mentors, and friends who join us today, this is their graduation too. They've worked hard to send you here, worried every step of the way about your progress at Columbia, and called you constantly as if to prove it. Some of them have even learned to text message . . . unfortunately for you.

Parents, by nature, share a common bond: we want to do everything possible to ensure our children's education. It's always been this way. The great French essayist and philosopher Michel de Montaigne wrote five centuries ago about how, from birth, his parents had him cradled in the arms of a tutor who spoke nothing to him but Latin, so he could better learn the Classics, and had him awakened every morning to the dulcet tones of a musician so that his "tender brain" might be eased gently from sleep.

Talk about hyper-parenting.

Still, your families and friends have certainly done everything within reason—indeed, everything within their reach—to see you here this morning. This is, therefore, a momentous day for them as it is for you—so stand up and give them a round of applause.

Four years ago, many of you—along with your parents—made the difficult decision to attend Columbia. It was difficult not just because picking a college is a big decision, but for a far more momentous reason: you were among the first group of college students to arrive in New York after September 11. Your choice, in the aftermath of the attacks, must have seemed risky. But in choosing this city, at a time of such upheaval, you sent a very clear message. You said, in effect, "I want my education to be in and of the world."

Long before anyone had heard the term "globalization"—and long before this city was at the center of it—Montaigne wrote about the importance of such an education. He was skeptical that books alone could provide sufficient training for a life in this world. People who stuck to the printed word, he observed, developed an "uncontrolled avidity for learning"—so much so that it "brutalized" them and stimulated a "brooding disposition." . . . apparently he spent some time at the Hungarian Pastry Shop.

We recommend, therefore, that for the next three months, you stop "applying yourself immoderately to the study of . . . books," which, as Montaigne observed, is a major cause of dyspepsia.

So we urge you to ease off the books, at least for a while, and follow another piece of Montaigne's advice: to "mix with the world." But just saying that reveals a profound change between his world and ours. In his day, "mixing with the world" meant traveling to foreign countries, to discover, as he put it, "the characteristics and customs of the different nations, and to rub and polish your wits on those of others." You were an observer, an outsider, a fact-finder. Mixing with the world meant adding to your store of knowledge, collecting some interesting ideas and artifacts, and maybe getting into some interesting discussions along the way.

Today, things are far different. We mix with the world every day, almost without trying. Communications connect us to people oceans away in an instant. The ease of travel has caused distances to collapse. And more than ever, shared interests can unite us, across vast chasms of culture, wealth, and politics. All these changes and more make our relationship with people around the globe more immediate, more intertwined, and potentially more meaningful.

It's partly a phenomenon of an extraordinary increase in the volume of knowledge we have today, even at our fingertips. But the truly meaningful difference between our time and Montaigne's is not just the amount of knowledge that's easily available to us now, it's the breadth of knowledge that's relevant—actually, essential—to us. The imperative of our age is that we can no longer think of ourselves, or our ideas, or bodies of knowledge, as existing in isolation from one another.

In other words, we can no longer mix with the world simply because we are curious about it, or because it provides the foil against which to better understand ourselves. Today we learn about other cultures, other nations, and other views because we must do so, because our lives depend on one another.

We're all in the same boat, not in separate boats occasionally passing one another. We understand that disease or pollution in one place can spread everyplace; that poverty and hunger on one continent are our responsibility, just as they are when the desperate live nearby; and that a new discovery in one lab can spark innovation around the world.

What this means for you, Class of 2006—among other things—is that your education does not end today. That, of course, is the biggest cliché in the history of commencement speeches. As a former law professor, I can confirm this: there's some kind of law that requires every speaker to say this. It may even be in the Constitution.

But what's called for today is a particular form of learning and understanding, one that begins with the most elementary kind of self-education, the exploring of this vastly wider world of relevant knowledge. We need to step back and to think of ourselves as entering a new age of human exploration, as the modern counterpart of the age of world exploration in the time of Montaigne.

Despite the wealth of information now at our command, this is something most of us are ill-prepared for today.

For centuries now, we've created new knowledge through a process of specialization—a process to which universities are central. Indeed, virtually all of you will be specialists of some kind. And that's a good thing. The world needs more experts, and smarter experts.

But for some time now, we've recognized the limitations of a system which assumes that "groundbreaking" ideas occur mainly in the tiniest tributaries of knowledge. We've realized that even to understand our areas of specialty we must understand other fields, as well. We know that the problems of life don't always fit neatly within our categories of knowledge. If we want to serve good and humane ends, we need to work across areas of expertise.

But, beyond these recommendations for navigating between our expertise, there's a further great need today. For us to perform as citizens, as parents, as friends, or just to be fulfilled human beings, we must widen the scope of what I call our General Knowledge. We must find ways of expanding our knowledge and of making it whole again, not just subdivided by our chosen disciplines.

That's harder than you might think. To be perpetual students, we have to clear some psychological hurdles—and this is especially true as we grow older. Expertise gives us a sense of self-importance. Familiar areas become comfortable. And we can lock ourselves into intellectual cages of our own making that inhibit us from exploring fields outside our own.

This impulse serves us poorly in our new age. So, since we no longer have the power to live as individuals, or as a nation, in isolation, we need to think of ourselves, once again, as early explorers, setting out to rediscover the world for our time. And this requires an extraordinary openness of mind, a willingness to embrace unfamiliar knowledge, and, indeed, a humility.

The stakes are high. Think for a moment about the war in Iraq. As the conflict continues between Shi'ites and Sunnis, there's a profound sense of a missed opportunity. Before the war began, there was little meaningful public conversation in this country about how religious schisms, or the complex politics of the region, or the history of the Middle East and its relations with the West, might create the situation we now face.

Yes, experts spoke out on such matters. But were we as a society educated enough to have a truly democratic conversation about the potential risks and benefits of toppling Saddam's brutal dictatorship as a response to international terror?

Surely, that conversation would not have inoculated us against every possible problem. But it certainly would have given us a better understanding of the likeliest outcomes and what to do about them.

So, the stakes are high. But so is the potential to do good. The fact is we are on the verge of creating the largest marketplace of ideas the world has ever seen. An idea in one person's mind can, with amazing speed, be put to the service of all humankind. The solitary genius exists, to be sure, but for the most part good ideas come out of conversation and discussion, which can now occur on a global scale.

Some look at this emerging reality and see danger. When China comes up with a new way of doing business, or India makes a great leap in computer engineering, this tends to be seen as a gain for them and a loss for us—a zero-sum competition.

We can't deny that increased competition is a hallmark of our age and that our responsibility is to ensure our own citizens have the skills and opportunity to adapt and thrive. But I think we should be excited, not intimidated, by the participation of billions more people in this marketplace of ideas. It's the most hopeful thing for humankind I can think of at a moment when it is all too easy to see clouds on the horizon (but thankfully today, not over 116th Street).

And no one is better prepared to walk onto this stage than you. By your nature, and by your educational preparation from faculty who are among the best in their fields and unusually dedicated to teaching, you're ready to join this extraordinary and unprecedented new marketplace of ideas.

So while specialization in knowledge is part of the genius of the modern world, I ask you to think about all the basic things you don't yet know. Because that's what it will take to participate fully in this age of globalization: the willingness to be an explorer and the ability to approach knowledge without the inhibitions of expertise. But you should aspire for one more thing: to try as hard as you can to be one of those rare people who is able to transcend expertise and to see across boundaries, in full dimension, the great forces at work in their age.

To accomplish this, you must first be willing to put yourself in perspective. We know so much more about the human brain than people did in the time of Montaigne. We know that our minds are composed of some 100 billion neurons, and we can feel them fire up as we learn languages . . . or shut down as we listen to Commencement speeches.

But one thing we have long known and yet need to re-learn is that to see the whole we must diminish our sense of ourselves in the world. For people like you, who will reach the pinnacle of your chosen professions, imagining your achievements as small pieces of something much larger will not be easy.

But a little humility is in order. Montaigne understood this. He wrote: "Whoever reads in [Mother Nature's] face, her universal and constant variety; whoever sees himself in it, and not only himself but a whole kingdom, like a dot made by a very fine pencil; he alone estimates things according to their true proportions."

As you graduate, your challenge is to see yourself not as the center of things, but in relation to "everything." That is what it means to see the "whole kingdom." And that's the only way you might answer the great questions of our age.

And, so, I urge you to appreciate how the world is changing and vastly expanding the amount of things you must now try to know. I urge you to engage in that quest with the fervor of an explorer, to avoid being trapped within your field of specialization or intimidated by others unduly protective of their own, to devote some part of your lives to making knowledge whole again, to try to transcend the details of your knowledge and to grasp the great forces at work in our time, and to do that with the courage and imagination to see yourself as small in relation to the larger whole "like a dot made with a very fine pencil."

The world, however, can wait one more day. Today is your day at the center of things. Today you are the center of our attention; you are the center of our pride and celebration. And that is how it ought to be.

Congratulations, Class of 2006, on all of your accomplishments, and best of luck to you all.

CHAPTER 8

STATEMENT ABOUT PRESIDENT AHMADINEJAD'S SCHEDULED APPEARANCE AT THE WORLD LEADER'S FORUM

Columbia University, September 19, 2007

In 2007, Columbia's School of International and Public Affairs (SIPA) extended a speaking invitation to President Mahmoud Ahmadinejad of Iran, which generated widespread demand that President Bollinger cancel the event. Deciding not to do so garnered global media attention, and Bollinger explained that the rights he was defending were those of Columbia faculty to invite controversial guest speakers. Due to the event's scale and significance, Bollinger included it in the university's World Leaders Forum (WLF), emphasizing that, by prior agreement with Iranian representatives, his introduction of President Ahmadinejad would challenge him with pointed questions on highly charged issues—and that students would have the same opportunity to directly confront and debate him. The pieces that follow include Bollinger's advance public statement and introductory remarks.

On Monday, September 24, the President of the Islamic Republic of Iran, Mahmoud Ahmadinejad, is scheduled to appear as a speaker on campus. The event is sponsored by the School of International and Public Affairs, which has been in contact with the Iranian Mission to the United Nations. The event will be part of the annual World Leaders Forum, the University-wide initiative intended to further Columbia's longstanding tradition of serving as a major forum for robust debate, especially on global issues.

In order to have such a University-wide forum, we have insisted that a number of conditions be met, first and foremost that President Ahmadinejad agree to divide his time evenly between delivering remarks and responding to audience questions. I also wanted to be sure the Iranians understood that I would myself introduce the event with a series of sharp challenges to the president on issues including:

- the Iranian president's denial of the Holocaust;
- his public call for the destruction of the State of Israel;
- his reported support for international terrorism that targets innocent civilians and American troops;
- Iran's pursuit of nuclear ambitions in opposition to international sanction;
- his government's widely documented suppression of civil society and particularly of women's rights; and
- his government's imprisoning of journalists and scholars, including one of Columbia's own alumni, Dr. Kian Tajbakhsh.

I would like to add a few comments on the principles that underlie this event. Columbia, as a community dedicated to learning and scholarship, is committed to confronting ideas—to understand the world as it is and as it might be. To fulfill this mission, we must respect and defend the rights of our schools, our deans and our faculty to create programming for academic purposes. Necessarily, on occasion this will bring us into contact with beliefs many, most or even all of us will find offensive and even odious. We trust our community, including our students, to be fully capable of dealing with these occasions, through the powers of dialogue and reason.

I would also like to invoke a major theme in the development of freedom of speech as a central value in our society. It should never be thought that merely to listen to ideas we deplore in any way implies our endorsement of those ideas, or the weakness of our resolve to resist those ideas or our naiveté about the very real dangers inherent in such ideas. It is a critical premise of freedom of speech that we do not honor the dishonorable when we open the public forum to their voices. To hold otherwise would make vigorous debate impossible.

That such a forum could not take place on a university campus in Iran today sharpens the point of what we do here. To commit oneself to a life—and a civil society—prepared to examine critically all ideas arises from a deep faith in the myriad benefits of a long-term process of meeting bad beliefs with better beliefs and hateful words with wiser words. That faith in freedom has always been and remains today our nation's most potent weapon against repressive regimes everywhere in the world. This is America at its best.

CHAPTER 9

INTRODUCTION OF PRESIDENT MAHMOUD AHMADINEJAD OF THE ISLAMIC REPUBLIC OF IRAN

Columbia World Leaders Forum, Alfred Lerner Hall, September 24, 2007

I would like to begin by thanking Dean John Coatsworth and Professor Richard Bulliet for their work in organizing this event and for their commitment to the School of International and Public Affairs and its role in training future leaders in world affairs. If today proves anything, it will be that there is an enormous amount of work ahead of us. This is just one of many events on Iran that will run throughout the academic year, all to help us better understand this critical and complex nation in today's geopolitics.

Before speaking directly to the current president of Iran, I have a few critically important points to emphasize.

First, since 2003 the World Leaders Forum has advanced Columbia's longstanding tradition of serving as a major forum for robust debate, especially on global issues. It should never be thought that merely to listen to ideas we deplore in any way implies our endorsement of those ideas or our weakness of our resolve to resist those ideas or our naiveté about the very real dangers inherent in such ideas. It is a critical premise of freedom of speech that we do not honor the dishonorable when we open our public forum to their voices; to hold otherwise would make vigorous debate impossible.

Second, to those who believe that this event should never have happened, that it is inappropriate for the university to conduct such an event, I want to say that I understand your perspective and respect it as reasonable. The scope of free speech in academic freedom should itself always be open to further debate. As one of the more famous quotations about free speech goes, "it is an experiment as all life is an experiment." I want to say, however, as forcefully as I can that this is the right thing to do, and indeed it is required by the existing norms of free speech, the American university, and Columbia itself.

Third, to those among us who experience hurt and pain as a result of this day, I say on behalf of all of us that we are sorry and wish to do what we can to alleviate it.

Fourth, to be clear on another matter, this event has nothing whatsoever to do with any rights of the speaker, but only with our rights to listen and speak. We do it for ourselves. We do it in the great tradition of openness that has defined this nation for many decades now. We need to understand the world we live in, neither neglecting its glories nor shrinking from its threats and dangers. It is inconsistent with the idea that one should know thine enemies, to have the intellectual and emotional courage to confront the mind of evil, and to prepare ourselves to act with the right temperament. In the moment, the arguments for free speech will never seem to match the power of the arguments against, but what we must remember is that this is precisely because free speech asks us to exercise extraordinary self-restraint against the very natural but often counterproductive impulses that lead us to retreat from engagement with ideas we dislike and fear. In this lies the genius of the American idea of free speech.

Lastly, in universities we have a deep and almost single-minded commitment to pursue the truth. We do not have access to the levers of power, we cannot make war or peace, we can only make minds, and to do this, we must have the most fulsome freedom of inquiry.

Let me now turn to Mr. Ahmadinejad.

First, on the brutal crackdown on scholars, journalists, and human rights advocates. Over the past two weeks, your government has released Dr. Haleh Esfandiari and Parnaz Azima and just two days ago, Kian Tajbakhsh, a graduate of Columbia with a PhD in Urban Planning. While our community is relieved to learn of his release on bail, Dr. Tajbakhsh remains in Tehran under house arrest, and he still does not know whether he will be charged with a crime or allowed to leave the country.

Let me say this for the record, I call on the president today to ensure that Kian will be free to travel out of Iran as he wishes. Let me also report today that we are extending an offer to Kian to join our faculty as a visiting professor in Urban

Planning here at his alma mater in our Graduate School of Architecture, Planning and Preservation, and we hope he will be able to join us next semester.

The arrest and imprisonment of these Iranian Americans for no good reason is not only unjustified, it runs completely counter to the very values that allow today's speaker to even appear on this campus, but at least they are alive.

According to Amnesty International, 210 people have been executed In Iran so far this year, 21 of them on the morning of September 5th alone. This annual total includes at least two children, further proof, as Human Rights Watch puts it, that Iran leads the world in executing minors.

There is more. Iran hanged up 30 people this past July and August during a widely reported suppression of efforts to establish a more democratic society. Many of these executions were carried out in public view, a violation of the International Covenant of Civil and Political Rights, to which Iran is a party. These executions and others have coincided with a wider crackdown on student activists and academics accused of trying to foment a so-called "soft revolution." This has included jailing and forced retirement of scholars. As Dr. Esfandiari said in a broadcast interview since her release, she was held in solitary confinement for 105 days because the government believes that the United States is planning a velvet revolution in Iran.

In this very room, last year we learned something about velvet revolutions from Václav Havel, and we will likely hear the same from our World Leaders Forum speaker this evening, President Michelle Bachelet of Chile. Both of their extraordinary stories remind us that there are not enough prisons to prevent an entire society that wants its freedom from achieving it.

We at this university have not been shy to protest the challenge—and challenge the failures of our own government to live by our values, and we won't be shy about criticizing yours. Let's then be clear at the beginning. Mr. President, you exhibit all the signs of a petty and cruel dictator. And so I ask you, why have women, members of the Baha'i faith, homosexuals, and so many of our academic colleagues become targets of persecution in your country? Why, in a letter last week to the secretary-general of the U.N., did Akbar Ganji, Iran's leading political dissident, and over 300 public intellectuals, writers and Noble Laureates express such grave concern that your inflamed dispute with the West is distracting the world's attention from the intolerable conditions in your regime within Iran, in particular the use of the press law to ban writers for criticizing the ruling system? Why are you so afraid of Iranian citizens expressing their opinions for change?

In our country, you are interviewed by our press and asked to speak here today. And while my colleagues at the law school—Michael Dorf, one of my colleagues, spoke to Radio Free Europe viewers in Iran a short while ago on the tenets of freedom of speech in this country—I propose further that you let me lead a delegation of students and faculty from Columbia to address your universities about free speech with the same freedom we afford you today.

Secondly, the denial of the Holocaust. In a December 2005 state television broadcast, you described the Holocaust as "a fabricated legend." One year later, you held a two-day conference of Holocaust deniers. For the illiterate and ignorant, this is dangerous propaganda.

When you have come to a place like this, this makes you, quite simply, ridiculous. You are either brazenly provocative or astonishingly uneducated. You should know that Columbia is a world center of Jewish studies, and now in partnership with the Institute of Holocaust Studies.

Since the 1930s, we provided an intellectual home for countless Holocaust refugees and survivors and their children and grandchildren. The truth is that the Holocaust is the most documented event in human history. Because of this, and for many other reasons, your absurd comments about the debate over the Holocaust both defy historical truth and make all of us who continue to fear humanity's capacity for evil shudder at this closure of memory, which is always virtue's first line of defense. Will you cease this outrage?

The destruction of Israel. Twelve days ago, you said that the state of Israel cannot continue its life. This echoed a number of inflammatory statements you have delivered in the past two years, including in October 2005, when you said that Israel "should be wiped off the map," quote-unquote. Columbia has over 800 alumni currently living in Israel. As an institution, we have deep ties with our colleagues there. I have personally spoken out in most forceful terms against proposals to boycott Israeli scholars and universities, saying that such boycotts might as well include Columbia.

More than 400 college and university presidents in this country have joined in that statement.

My question then is, do you plan on wiping us off the map, too?

Funding terrorism: According to reports of the Council on Foreign Relations, it's well-documented that Iran is a state sponsor of terror that funds such violent groups as Lebanese Hezbollah, which Iran helped organize in the 1980s, Palestinian Hamas and Palestinian Islamic Jihad. While your predecessor government was instrumental in providing the U.S. with intelligence and base support in the 2001 campaign against the Taliban in Afghanistan, your government is now undermining American troops in Iraq by funding, arming and providing safe transit to insurgent leaders like Muqtada al-Sadr and his forces. There are a number of reports that you also link your government with Syria's efforts to destabilize the fledgling Lebanese government through violence and political assassination.

My question is this: Why do you support well-documented terrorist organizations that continue to strike at peace and democracy in the Middle East, destroying lives and the civil society of the region?

The proxy war against the United States troops in Iraq—in a briefing before the National Press Club earlier this month, General David Petraeus reported that arms supplies from Iran, including 240-millimeter rockets and explosively formed projectiles, are contributing to, quote, "a sophistication of attacks that would by no means be possible without Iranian support." A number of Columbia graduates and current students are among the brave members of our military who are serving or have served in Iraq and Afghanistan. They, like other Americans with sons, daughters, fathers, husbands and wives serving in combat, rightly see your government as the enemy.

Can you tell them and us why Iran is fighting a proxy war in Iraq by arming Shi'a militia targeting and killing U.S. troops?

And finally, Iran's nuclear program and international sanctions: This week, the United Nations Security Council is contemplating expanding sanctions for a third time because of your government's refusal to suspend its uranium enrichment program. You continue to defy this world body by claiming a right to develop a peaceful nuclear power, but this hardly withstands scrutiny when you continue to issue military threats to neighbors. Last week, French President Sarkozy made clear his lost patience with your stall tactics, and even Russia and China have shown concern.

Why does your country continue to refuse to adhere to international standards for nuclear weapons verification, in defiance of agreements that you have made with the U.N. nuclear agency? And why have you chosen to make the people of your country vulnerable to the effects of international economic sanctions, and threaten to engulf the world in nuclear annihilation?

Let me close with a comment. I close with this comment frankly and in all candor, Mr. President. I doubt that you will have the intellectual courage to answer these questions. But your avoiding them will in itself be meaningful to us. I do expect you to exhibit the fanatical mindset that characterizes so much of what you say and do. Fortunately, I am told by experts on your country that this only further undermines your position in Iran, with all the many good-hearted, intelligent citizens there.

A year ago, I am reliably told, your preposterous and belligerent statements in this country, as at one of the meetings at the Council on Foreign Relations, so embarrassed sensible Iranian citizens that this led to your party's defeat in the December mayoral elections. May this do that and more.

I am only a professor, who is also a university president.

And today I feel all the weight of the modern civilized world yearning to express the revulsion at what you stand for. I only wish I could do better. Thank you.

CHAPTER 10

COMMENCEMENT ADDRESS

Columbia University, Low Plaza, May 21, 2008

O n behalf of Columbia's trustees and faculty, it gives me great pleasure to say congratulations to all of the Classes of 2008.

On this day alone, with this majestic ceremony, in this magnificent space, the incredible array of Columbia's extraordinary schools and campuses is made visible. We come together and are truly one. All of you—the graduates, your families and friends—are an amazing sight. Welcome to everyone.

It is, of course, you, our graduates, who bring us all here together. We recognize your hard work. Your commitment. Your achievements. You deserve to enjoy
the moment, to savor it, and to remember it always.

And though we would like to take credit for all your impressive qualities and
accomplishments—and reserve the right to do so once you become renowned in
your fields—we readily admit today that the people who had the most to do with
you getting to this point in life are your parents and families. They supported you,
they believed in you—and they dreamed of this day for you long before you
dreamed it for yourself.

So before we go any further, let's hear it for the people who truly made this
day possible: Your parents and families.

On behalf of everyone at Columbia, I, too, would like to thank all the parents
and grandparents in the audience. It has been our pleasure to teach your children, to learn from them and with them. We share your pride in them . . . and
we share in their gratitude for your love and support.

And now, to our graduates.

For most of you here today, your current journey at Columbia ends when you
march out those gates at 116th Street. In that brief walk, it will be natural to think
only about the life ahead. I know your minds are focused—to the extent they are

focused at all after your activities of last night—on simply getting out (as if you had been imprisoned within these gates). It may surprise you, but in the flash of a moment I (and I'm sure others) can relate to that feeling. Thirty-seven years ago, about this time, I left my wife's and my apartment on West 96th Street and took the bus up Amsterdam Avenue to the Law School with only one thought in my mind—that this would be the last stupid exam I would ever take for the rest of my life. And it was. So, I know the feeling—the relief at being done, the excitement of experiencing life without thinking what part of it is going to be on the final.

Let me quickly add, however, that your final final exam will never be your final test, because, fortunately or unfortunately, all life is one big test, just like all life is one big curriculum. It all just comes in different versions, different forms, and usually with a lot more hanging in the balance. But, if that's true, then what is it about the experience you've had over the last two, four, or seven years here at Columbia that is distinctive from life beyond these gates—other than in the formal sense of curricula and tests?

To answer that we must go back in time to when you entered these academic walls. Look back and ask how is the person you are today different from the one who arrived here?

There are some obvious answers: There are many things you know now that you didn't know then. You've read new books, considered new theoretical approaches, and acquired new critical thinking skills. What we like to call "learning how to think." There are friendships and memories that you will carry with you for life, and will carry you through life. "When I was at Columbia . . ." is a phrase you'll repeat so often in the years ahead that you'll be forced to keep your friends from here if only because they're the only ones who will tolerate your stories, which will be retold with greater and greater frequency—and embellishment—the older you grow.

But, my suggestion to you today is that the most important thing you have experienced at Columbia, and will remember in the years ahead, isn't captured in your transcript or your photo album. It is rather a completely unique experience in life, a sustained and concentrated immersion into a life of the mind that calls on you, first, to suspend your beliefs, even your very identity, and then to deploy your imagination to absorb, as much as you can, the full complexity of any subject—the multiple perspectives, the manifold interpretations and explanations, the new possibilities, and the paradoxes the mind cannot yet unravel.

This is immensely hard to do, and it only becomes possible with repeated practice. Something in us resists going there. To hold multiple, even opposing, perspectives in your mind simultaneously, to hold another viewpoint as if it were your own (because that's the only way it can be truly understood), is to stand face to face with the utter complexity of life and the limits of our powers of thought. Yet, the words "But have you considered . . .?" ring out across this campus every hour of every day, and they will hopefully ring in your minds for the rest of your life.

This is what universities uniquely do, great ones anyway. As our illustrious predecessor at Columbia, historian Richard Hofstadter, said on this platform 40 years ago, the university "marks our commitment to the idea that somewhere in society there must be an organization in which anything can be studied or questioned—not merely safe and established things but difficult and inflammatory things, the most troublesome questions of politics and war, of sex and morals, of property and national loyalty."

Often I have referred to this special intellectual character of universities as the Scholarly Temperament.

Now, to be sure, this is not all a university is. Coupled with this extraordinary commitment to inquiry and reflection is also the university as a forum, where everything under the sun can be debated and discussed. In this dimension of the university, we don't enter by suspending our beliefs, we instead stand on them, we take ideas seriously, and we engage with those who look at the world from a different angle. In the Forum, beliefs are put to the test. More like the world outside, here is the clash of views in the marketplace of the mind, where ideas fight for supremacy, because in the real world ideas really matter.

Now, these are two states of intellectual being—the suspension of belief and openness on one side and the engagement with beliefs in the public forum on the other. Two states, about which there are several things to be noted. Three, in particular I want to address.

First, these two states are always in tension. Each calls upon distinct capacities, one sets the imagination free and we lose ourselves in the complexity of things, while the other involves the courage to step forward into life and to meet—as philosopher Mortimer Adler put it—the responsibility of making up your mind. Each side is doubtful about the other. Reflection, reveling as it does in complexity, is embarrassed by belief's tendency to oversimplify things, especially as belief does in the heat of battle. The politician's clever rule to only give answers to the questions you prefer to be asked is incomprehensible in the book of the Scholarly Temperament—an intellectual sin. For its part, the mind in engagement can sometimes disdain the life of luxury that permits intellectual roaming when the needs of the moment seem to call for decision and action. And reflection's clichéd critique at the "shallowness" of public debate is too often just an excuse to take the easy way out and remain on the sidelines.

Second, the two states, though in tension, are absolutely necessary for each other. The extraordinary openness that is the core of the university experience prepares us to better understand and meet the arguments of others, to experience empathy, to compromise, and to moderate the natural tendency of belief to mutate into authoritarianism. Standing up for our beliefs, on the other hand, provides us with the raw material for a life in reflection. And it makes us feel and be part of our time.

In constant tension and yet mutually dependent and beneficial, these two different places in the universe of the mind make us feel unstable at times, confused, disconcerted. But, once we understand what is happening and then do it well, it can be thrilling. This is the stuff of life, and I wish I could say more about it but, even after all these years, I can't.

My third point brings me to a major caution. When you leave these gates, the positions in the mental universe are reversed in how they're weighted. The battle over beliefs is increasingly dominating and threatens the possibilities for a reflective mind. Busyness is the first problem. Multi-tasking is the arch-enemy of reflection. Technology gives us too much information too much of the time. Even the much-maligned sound bite is suffering, dropping (we're told) from 42 seconds on average in 1968 to four seconds today.

You don't depend, as we did, on a handful of nightly network news shows. As every political candidate and public figure has painfully learned, the democratizing power of the web is matched by the danger that minutes, hours and years of human experience can be reduced to just a few select seconds that get posted and endlessly replayed the world over. The kind of open exploration of a university cannot be downloaded in a few megabytes of digital video or reduced to fit on the head of a flag lapel pin, which only indicates again how important and vital universities are and how privileged you are to have been here.

But by far the biggest threat to both reflection and engagement is the innate, almost primal, impulse to censorship. The Censorship Impulse is alive and well in every one of us, some more than others, of course. We think of it mostly as manifesting itself in law, but its reach into our own minds and into human affairs is far more pervasive. At its core, the Impulse will always prefer a world in which speakers and ideas are excluded rather than confronted and answered. Naturally, our impulse is to make the world safe for our own beliefs. And the impulse is ingenious in its ability to mount reasons to that end.

There are so many reasons, for so many contexts. It is said: A speaker will persuade people to think bad thoughts and do bad things; will offend some and make others angry and resentful; will ruin the minds of our youth; will lead others to think we approve the message or don't care enough to oppose it; will bring instability, divert us from other more important tasks, and make it more difficult and perhaps even impossible for experts to handle the situation. We limit speakers in other ways, too, when claiming that others will be "chilled" and thereby diminish speech overall or that it will reflect badly on the rest of us.

Now, here's the interesting point: All these arguments about the costs of openness are very often true—in the sense that they point to consequences that are real. Indeed, that's why freedom of speech and academic freedom are continually under siege, even in a nation that says it places this value at its core, because "reasonable people" can always make freedom seem foolish and foolhardy.

Yet, time after time in our history the better side of America—indeed, part of its genius—has declined to be "reasonable" in this sense and instead has chosen the path of extraordinary tolerance, willing and even eager to live with seeming disorder and very real risks for a higher—albeit highly elusive—life in which we entrust our fates to matching idea against idea instead of to a policy of silence and exclusion.

Take the famous case of the Pentagon Papers. Both the *Washington Post* and the *New York Times* had illegally received these classified documents about the history of the Vietnam War and were about to publish them while the war continued to rage. For the government, and those who sided with the government, it was unthinkable that the press could freely publish official documents that would, it was credibly said, make conducting foreign policy substantially more problematic. The Court conceded the point but said it was not the goal of the First Amendment to make diplomacy easier but rather to make informed public debate possible. The press is an institution with a special role to play in that higher process, and that's true of our universities, too.

Or take another example of how we bear the risks of speech: What about falsehoods? Should we have to tolerate speakers who say things that are not true? Yes, we should, said the Court in the *New York Times v. Sullivan*. We must gird ourselves for national conversation that is "uninhibited, robust, and wide open." Because, as Brandeis said some decades earlier, "The fitting remedy for evil counsels is good ones . . ." Or, as I've put it less eloquently, because it's incumbent upon us to meet and defeat bad words with better words.

Whether you're a society or a university or an individual person, being committed both to a life of reflection and engagement (each informing and moderating the other) that is "uninhibited, robust, and wide open," will seem disorderly, messy, and even at times chaotic. But it is certainly invigorating and makes the future possible. From the wilderness that is the human mind, with all its untamed dangers and magnificent potential, we daily build our lives, idea upon idea. The Censorship Impulse would rather deny us that future. In its extreme form, it would even sacrifice the lives of thousands as is now tragically happening in Myanmar. But, as I've said, the impulse to suppress rather than to confront comes in many versions.

I want to close with a word about you. This is probably not a good time to be assigning grades, but on all matters I've talked about this morning I give you an A+. (I'm sure the faculty agrees.) You have exhibited the capacity to suspend your beliefs and to feel the world's complexity, and you have seized the corollary responsibility to stand up and be counted on your beliefs. We've seen it in our courses, and we've seen it most vividly in your thoughtful reactions to controversies, some of global dimensions.

In this anniversary year of 1968, there are some who have said that students today are not as active and engaged as we were at your age. Not for a moment should anyone dare to question your capacity to integrate all these different ways of being and to find your own ways to advance the public good.

Yours is a generation of hands-on engagement, of service and giving. In every college and school, on every campus, the habits of generous and open-hearted citizenship have been evident to those prepared to look and admirable for its lack of concern with being visible. Your extraordinary curiosity about the bigger world and about how to have an impact on it is heartening to all of us who realize we are handing over a planet desperately in need of fresh thinking.

My only concern for you as you exit these gates today is that you keep alive in your hearts and minds the special kind of mind that is uniquely nurtured here. I've already warned you that life's busyness, technology's intrusion, the Censorship

Impulse and a world that insists increasingly on quick answers and strong opinions untempered by periods of reflection will make you too one-sided.

The only remedy now is to make your own university, your own Columbia, inside yourself. Since life doesn't come in semesters with five courses and an exam, you will have to create your own curriculum. Reading books is just one way, but there are others. Montaigne, for example, preferred conversation as a mode of learning to books (the study of which he thought a "languid and feeble process that gives no heat"). For Montaigne conversation was "the most fruitful and natural exercise of the mind" because, he said, "If I converse with a strong mind and a rough disputant, he presses upon my flanks . . . his imaginations stir up mine; jealousy, glory, and contention, stimulate and raise me up to something above myself."

So, make it a point to have good conversations. Promise yourself to ask two questions for every statement you make. And if you have enough of these conversations and manage to sustain the precarious balance between periods of reflection and active engagement, which you've had the chance to develop here at Columbia, if you can avoid on the one hand, the Censorship Impulse and, on the other, the irresponsibility of indecision, then you will continue to help the world have good conversations—and a better future—too.

For, in the end, we all seek, as Montaigne said, to rise up to something above ourselves. As you pass through these gates for the last time, good luck and do well on that final test.

Congratulations, Class of 2008.

CHAPTER 11

GLOBALIZATION AND FREE PRESS

David Baum Memorial Lecture on Civil Rights and
Civil Liberties, University of Illinois College of Law, 2011

Published in 2010, President Bollinger's book Uninhibited, Robust, and
Wide-Open: A Free Press for a New Century *outlined his advocacy for
applying American First Amendment principles to a global public forum. In the
following two lectures presented that year, Bollinger stressed the importance of
developing an international consensus regarding the vital role of an independent
and professional global press not constrained by the financial limits of the free
market. He also addressed the problems of censorship, access to quality information in the age of the internet, and the contraction of international coverage by
the American press.*

I t is always difficult in the midst of an era to know its defining characteristics. But I would be surprised, if in future decades, people did not say
that the period from the end of the twentieth century to the beginning of
the twenty-first century was the period in which the shape of the modern world
was determined, and that the primary forces that caused this new world were
twofold: the spread of capitalism and free market economies throughout the
world and the invention of new technologies of communication (principally the
Internet, the World Wide Web (which is only about fifteen years old), and satellite communications). We live, as never before, in an interdependent and integrated world economy. Nearly half of the revenues of the S&P 500 corporations
are generated from business conducted outside the United States;[1] developing
countries now provide roughly half of the manufactured goods bought by developed countries (up from fourteen percent in 1987);[2] and, on a more personal

scale, a not insignificant portion of many Americans' retirement fund or 401(k) is invested in foreign enterprises. At the same time, the ability to communicate and have access to information, knowledge, and opinion has taken a giant leap forward. Billions of people across the planet have some degree of access to the Internet.[3] Global media outlets are proliferating, with newer entrants such as Al Jazeera, CCTV, and France 24 joining traditional international institutions such as BBC and CNN.[4] Meanwhile, the websites of the *New York Times*, the *Washington Post*, and the Associated Press and Reuters are garnering tens of millions of "visitors."[5] As The Associated Press reports, when they "publish" an article it can reach several billion people.

The consequences of globalization are both good and bad. Certainly, the most notable benefit is lifting up hundreds of millions of lives destined for poverty and sickness and creating a diffusion of basic wealth and well-being that all humans deserve.[6] This effect is, by any measure, a great good, and we should all rejoice in this extraordinary development in human history. We also have some very practical reasons for being happy about this phenomenon. For the fact is that our prospects for a full recovery from the recent Great Recession over the next five to ten years depend significantly on the creation of new wealth in emerging economies, which is necessary to make up for the decline in aggregate demand caused by the protracted period of excessive spending and borrowing by the American consumer.[7] The positive facets of globalization are far more extensive than economic benefits, affecting as they do our broader appreciation of the vast variety and intrinsic interest of the human condition.

Yet we also know that globalization does not spread its consequences only benignly over humanity and the natural world. We face a host of problematic and vexing issues as a result of globalization. Many are notorious: the rise of violent extremism among populations threatened by modernity, the potentially catastrophic consequences of climate change, the extreme shortage or depletion of the earth's natural resources, the degradation of the environment,[8] the periodic and extraordinary breakdowns in the world economy,[9] the spread of disease, the loss of cultural sites and artifacts, the growing divide between rich and poor, the problems of dealing with increasing multicultural societies, and the list continues.[10]

To realize the enormous positive potential of globalization—to channel it, regulate it, and encourage it in the right ways and to grapple with its manifold problems—will require many things. Among the most important is ensuring that the world has the institutions necessary to accomplish what we need. Institutions—political and civil—are central to the structure of any society, including an emerging global society. Two such institutions that we have invented and relied upon now for centuries are universities and the press.

In my recent book[11] and in this lecture, I am concerned with the latter, but I link the two because doing so helps to make an important point about the press. Both of these institutions are concerned with providing objective and accurate information, ideas, and analyses that we need in order to both understand and act in our world. There is a deep kinship between the academy and the press. The press is more concerned with grasping the here-and-now of the world, the current state of things. We in universities are generally more concerned with taking our time and thinking a bit more deeply about things, trying to see matters in a larger context. Obviously, there are differences, but the journalist and the scholar are more similar than not, and, importantly, both are motivated in their hearts by a desire to serve the public good according to certain professional standards.

This comparison helps to highlight those features of the press that are so important and relevant to the new world of globalization. In the United States, the Supreme Court has played a major role in articulating the special role a free and independent press can play in society. These theories have primarily focused on the political and social benefits we derive.[12] The press is part of the marketplace of ideas through which we seek to understand our world and to find truth. It also serves the needs and interests of citizens in exercising their sovereign responsibilities. It does this by not only exposing the misdeeds and errors of government, but also by informing us more generally about the issues we must face and resolve. Collectively, the press is our national public forum, the place we turn to (many hours a day for many of us) to participate in, and be educated by, the ongoing discussions of matters that are of immediate interest. All in all, therefore, a free press serves the public good in many ways. It is not just a "business" like General Motors or Goldman Sachs. In fact, sometimes we even say the press is the "fourth branch" of government with its own distinct powers and semi-official responsibilities.[13]

Now, with the phenomenon of globalization well underway, it is imperative that we begin to think much more systematically about how we will build and develop the concept of a free press for a new global public forum. This is part of a much larger historical process that has been underway for centuries. Authority and structures related to authority have to shift as human activity changes. This happened throughout the last century in many areas of society. The U.S. economy went from a collection of mostly local and regional affairs to a national system. Policy making and regulation had to shift accordingly. Just one among many examples is our central banking system. Established in 1913, the new Federal Reserve System was organized to provide twelve regional banks with the authority to deal with what was then a set of regional economies.[14] But in the ensuing decades, as the economy became national in scope, a more centralized banking authority was needed, and the powers of the Federal Reserve Bank in Washington, D.C. grew accordingly.

We can see the same process unfolding over the twentieth century with respect to the First Amendment and the constitutional rights of freedom of speech and press. As the issues faced by the nation became more national in reach, in part because of the growth of a national economy, and as the technologies of communication facilitated a national discussion (especially with the introduction of radio and television broadcasting), the power of local communities to set the balance between a free press and other societal interests (like personal reputation, privacy, offensiveness, and so on) became intolerable. Censorship anywhere effectively constituted censorship everywhere, since speakers in the new national forum would naturally be inhibited by censorship anywhere in the system. This was one of the great insights of the Supreme Court in *New York Times Co. v. Sullivan*, which nationalized the rules with respect to defamation laws throughout the country.[15] Remember that *Sullivan* involved a libel lawsuit brought by a public official in Alabama against the *New York Times* for an advertisement that allegedly injured the official's reputation.

This is exactly the process that must now unfold at the international level as the phenomena associated with globalization necessitate the creation of a forum suitable for handling the information we need and the issues we must resolve. Fortunately, we have the technological capacity for a very effective global discussion led by a vibrant press. What we do not yet have, however, are two critical elements. First, we do not have sufficient international consensus about the vital role of an independent and professional global press with appropriate levels of access and limits on censorship. Second, we do not really have the capacity for high quality, professional journalism on a global scale. I want to take up each of these areas for discussion.

Virtually no nation—even those with a commitment to a vibrant press such as the United States—is presently structured to embrace a global free press.

Certainly, many nations in the world today actively fear an independent press and see journalism more as an instrument of governmental policy than as a key source of objective information and analysis for their society. In these countries, there are very serious restrictions on press access to information and newsworthy events and debilitating censorship. The important point to realize is that the problems such restrictions on the free flow of information and ideas create are not limited to speech in those nations. What happens in a system of global communication is the same thing that happens with local censorship in a national system: namely, censorship chills speakers wherever they are. If what I say from the United States brings a criminal or civil action against me in another country, as is happening today and will happen with greater and greater frequency as communication becomes ever more global, such legal action will matter, and I will adjust my expression to take account of that potential reality. Therefore, as I have said, censorship anywhere becomes censorship everywhere. Furthermore, we must recognize that a lot of what we will need to know about the world will come through the efforts of "local" journalists. When "local" journalism is suppressed, therefore, our interest in hearing and knowing are similarly curtailed. In other words, because issues within countries are now often global in significance (that is, after all, what globalization amounts to), censorship in China, for example, is as significant or at times even more significant to us as censorship in California.

This difficulty is the heart of the problem we have to solve, and it promises to be one of the great debates of the century, one that may well replicate the debates internal to our own country over the limits of free speech and free press during the last century. We need to be both patient and humble as we enter this process. Our own experience in the development of a vibrant free press principle was not by any means a straight line to robust protection. We only began interpreting the First Amendment (at the level of the Supreme Court) in 1919,[16] and our approach was neither consistent nor, I would say, wholly admirable. We too sent people to jail (including, it should be noted, a candidate for president of the United States) merely for giving speeches or publishing commentary that the government claimed would undermine good public order or threaten national goals.[17] We too tried to enjoin the press from publishing official secrets.[18] We too denied the press access to newsworthy events and information.[19] And we too set up an administrative system for licensing part of the press (broadcasting and cable) and regulating it—including its content—in order to promote the "public interest, convenience, or necessity."[20] In other words, our own recent history by our own current standards is checkered in character and complex in its implementation.

In many places throughout the world, what we ended up discarding is currently accepted. China, in particular, appears to be struggling with a commitment to a more or less open economic system and a relatively closed communications system.[21] Understanding China is one of the great tasks of the modern day, and I would be among the first to say that we are not—in neither the academy nor in the press—devoting anything close to enough intellectual resources to that purpose. With respect to the U.S. press, apart from the financial press employed by Bloomberg News, we may only have two dozen full-time foreign correspondents covering all of China. That clearly is not in our national interest. I will, in a moment, come back to that issue of capacity, but now I want to focus on two contrasting interpretations of contemporary China. One view surmises that the very sophisticated leadership of China understands and accepts that the changes in Chinese citizens through capitalism will inevitably result in greater demands for intellectual openness.[22] It is just a matter of time according to this view. But another view, and one I am hearing increasingly from serious China observers, is that the leadership believes quite the opposite—namely, that they can have both sustained economic growth and a closely controlled society intellectually.[23] They see these not as inconsistent or in tension but as complementary. I hear people in many countries saying they are watching to see how this great debate will now unfold.

We need to give very serious attention to how we might persuade the Chinese over time that it is a mistake to choose a closed over an open society. Obviously, this will not be easy, assuming they take the position many are fearfully positing. Up to this point in our history, the dialogue about matters such as this has generally taken the form of principles of fundamental human rights.[24] Clearly, the concept of human rights has been one of the great advances in human civilization, and we should continue to aspire to these ideals. But one of the key aspects of what we call globalization and the emergence of a global society, with increasing interdependency among peoples and with all the potential and the problems that are beyond the reach or solution of any one nation, and with the corresponding need for a global public forum, is that now all of us are directly and adversely affected by the suppression of information in any one nation.[25] We have, therefore, additional reasons for objecting to censorship beyond our noble concern that all people possess basic human rights. Coming to grips with this new reality is what undoubtedly motivated Secretary of State Hillary Clinton, shortly after China announced that it would continue to monitor and censor Google, to give a landmark speech discussing Chinese actions that could threaten not only the rights of Chinese citizens but the rights and interests of the rest of the world and therefore had to be taken up as a matter of U.S. foreign policy.[26] Secretary Clinton did not go on to say what might follow from this new realization, but we can begin to imagine a number of consequences.

One thing we might say is that we can no longer continue building a trade relationship with China unless it begins to allow the free flow of information to match the free flow of goods and services. It is simply too dangerous to American interests to become dependent and intertwined economically without a parallel openness.[27] If we want to actually persuade China, which after all always ought to be our primary goal, are we ready and able to make the case to them that they and we will be better off if they choose a path of openness for an independent press? Our own arguments for robust free speech and press, as I indicated earlier, have tended to center on the political and social ends of truth, Madisonian democratic self-governance, and tolerance.[28] These ideas probably will be more difficult to develop persuasively for China. What we do know about China is that it believes in the national benefits of a free-market economic system.[29] I think our best opportunity, therefore, is to make the case that openness over time is critical (necessary if not sufficient) for sustained economic growth.[30]

The argument might go like this. Right now you are able to grow economically, at a rate never before witnessed in human history, because you have a natural base in manufacturing and exporting of goods, which notably does not require a high level of societal creativity and innovativeness (what my colleague Ned Phelps calls dynamism).[31] At some point in the not-too-distant future, however, maybe five or twenty years hence, you are going to lose that advantage in the world market, and your continued success will then depend upon a culture and social character that thrives on independent thinking and creativity.[32] There is, moreover, a direct link between the commitment to a vigorous free press (as well as free speech) and that kind of character.[33] You would be wise, therefore, to begin to cultivate that shift.

While I believe the argument I have just made to be true, and it certainly fits well into our (the United States') perspective on life, I have to admit that we have precious little study, analysis, and data to support it. It is, as I have said, a different tactic from the one we have successfully employed in this country to develop our own commitment to a free press. We would be wise to expand our under-standing of freedom of the press and its relation to all the things we value (includ-ing a vibrant economy) in order to be better able to make the case for greater openness in the global debate about that principle. In the new global society, we need to be prepared to make new and different arguments, as well as to listen carefully to the ways others conceive of organizing themselves collectively to get the information and knowledge we need.

That brings us to the importance of developing a set of legal norms, as the First Amendment has served in the United States, to guide us on these issues of access and censorship. In fact, international law and the jurisprudence of the United Nations have such a norm, embodied principally and originally in Article 19 of the 1948 Universal Declaration of Human Rights[34] and then incorporated into the International Covenant on Civil and Political Rights.[35] Some 192 nations[36] have signed on to the Declaration by becoming Member States[37] and 72[38] on to the Covenant. Article 19 of the Covenant declares, in forceful language, "Every-one shall have the right to hold opinions without interference."[39] It is worth not-ing that, from the standpoint of comparing it to the First Amendment, there is a strong endorsement of the right of citizens to have access to information, a demand that freedom of speech and press be respected by nations for all world citizens, and an application of these principles to all forms of media. The language that might cause pause (again, taking the First Amendment as a benchmark) is the third paragraph of Article 19, which restricts these freedoms "[f]or the respect of the rights or reputations of others" and "[f]or the protection of national secu-rity or of public order . . . or of public health or morals," and then language in the following Article 20, which speaks of limitations on the basic principle, not-ing, "any advocacy of national, racial or religious hatred that constitutes incite-ment to discrimination, hostility or violence shall be prohibited by law."[40] This language is the source of the major current controversy involving the argument of many Islamic nations that so-called "defamation of religion" be condemned and prohibited through an international convention.

I do not have time in this context to discuss in depth the prospects of Article 19 becoming substantively a powerful force for press freedom in the world. But I would make several key points. First, the general problem with Article 19 is the lack of any provision for effective enforcement. As with so many international legal norms, the substance may be good but the implementation is weak or even nonexistent. Investigations and reports, which are largely all that is currently allowed, are not insignificant, but they do not take us far enough towards the desired goal. Here, the unwillingness of nations to forego any degree of independent sovereignty to the collective good will, if not corrected, seriously impairs our chances of creating a sound and workable global society. The United States must at some point take the lead here. It is in our long-term national interest to do so. Second, the text of Articles 19 and 20 are potentially consistent with our current First Amendment doctrines. The question before us, therefore, is not whether the legal text is congruent with our own perspective, but whether we should and will commit ourselves to a process that may yield a good interpretation over time. Third, there are more hopeful signs in this regard when one turns to certain regional conventions where the incorporation of the substance of Article 19 is accompanied by a system of effective judicial enforcement. A notable instance is the Inter-American Court of Human Rights.[41] Some dozen or more decisions respecting press freedom have begun an important jurisprudence of freedom of the press. Fourth, there are other international legal structures, more effective than the International Covenant on Civil and Political Rights (ICCPR), to which freedom of the press might be meaningfully and logically attached. The most promising is the system of the World Trade Organization (WTO). There are now some cases in the WTO in which censorship and restrictions on the press and media are objected to on the ground that they constitute an unfair trade practice, most recently Google's accusations that China's censorship of their site was an "unfair barrier to trade."[42] These are promising developments. Some experts in the international trade community do not think it would be a good idea to incorporate the interests of freedom of the press into the law and policies of free trade.[43] While more effective as an international legal system than nearly every other attempt to create a legal system for the international community, the WTO is always fragile and every interest (labor and environmental concerns are two prominent examples) can arguably become "free trade" issues, with the unhappy outcome that the entire system will collapse because too much has been added together. I would contend, however, that information has a far closer nexus to the evolving economic system—a necessary condition for it to thrive—than other related, albeit also important, interests. Fifth, and the last point I would make here, is how imperative it is for the First Amendment community to begin devoting more attention to these issues. This is a highly talented, creative, and deeply informed group of professors. Over the past fifty years, the scholarly analysis of the First Amendment has contributed enormously to its development.[44] Yet today there is strikingly little attention paid to what is happening and needs to happen on the global stage. I hope this trend will change.

I want to move beyond the problems of censorship in the global public forum and take up the other important question, namely, what do we need to do to make sure we are getting the information and ideas—the quality as well as the amount—we need to deal with this new global society? Both are closely related— indeed, perhaps the best way to overcome censorship is for people to experience the highest quality journalism so they will know what they are missing. In any event, as is always true, we can have all the freedom in the world and yet fail because we do not use that freedom wisely. So, what issues are the issues involved in building up our journalistic or press capacity to produce the journalism we need?

Let me begin with two observations. First, there has been a very significant and distressing contraction in the coverage of the world by the American press since the onset of the financial crisis that has overwhelmed the profession.[45] The story of sharply declining revenues of the major press due to the migration of readers and viewers and advertisers to the Internet is by now well told.[46] Along with the inevitable shrinkage of newsrooms has come the elimination of foreign bureaus and foreign correspondents.[47] Reporting of foreign news is, naturally, down as well. So, at the very moment when we need an expansion of journalism, there is a contraction. Second, a separate and very interesting parallel development is the rise of national media designed to have a global presence. BBC World and BBC World Service have been and are leaders here, but we now find other major entrants into this arena—notable examples being Al Jazeera of Qatar, Xinhua and CCTV of China, and France 24 of France.[48] Third, it is a reasonably debatable question whether the proliferation of expression via the Internet will naturally provide the kind and quality of information we need in the new global society. People often point to the rise of "citizen journalists" as an offset to the declining fortunes of traditional press.[49] I am among those who believe that this is not an even exchange, and therefore, we will need to do more than adopt a laissez-faire attitude here. I believe, as I indicated at the outset, that institutions are extremely important to the success of journalism, just as they are to scholarship. Fourth, I believe that, while the free market is extremely useful and effective in promoting good journalism, it is not enough to get us where we want to be. The press, as we have come to define its role in public life, is a public good, and public goods never completely thrive in a free-market environment.[50] Hence I favor, and have argued for, a substantial commitment of state funding for the press, and I favor a commitment to establishing a U.S. press with a broader global reach and footprint.

Before saying how that might happen, let me provide a more complete answer to those who believe that public funding is inconsistent with our free press traditions and a break with our very successful experience in creating probably the most vital system of free press in the world today.

We need to start with a simple fact: our press today is the result of a highly mixed and complex structure designed over the course of the last century. It has not been only private ownership operating in a completely open and free market as many people seem to assume. Newspapers have, indeed, largely been under private ownership, but by the middle of the twentieth century, it was clear that certain features of the daily newspaper business were leading to monopoly status in virtually every city across the country. Within a decade or so, nearly all towns and cities had one daily newspaper (or one owner, as amendments to the antitrust laws allowed so-called joint operating agreements between formerly competing newspapers).[51] I will come back in a moment to the consequences of this development, which was not by any means all bad.

Broadcasting, meanwhile, was designed (under the Radio Act of 1927 and then the Communications Act of 1934) to be a special combination of private owners licensed by the government and regulated according to the "public convenience, interest, or necessity."[52] That system included the regulation of content, not censorship in the sense of forbidding the expression of certain ideas (with the notable exception of "indecency"), with regulations intended to expand the range of voices the "public" needed to hear yet would not if the "licensees" could just follow their "business" interests. Hence the government devised policies to promote coverage of "local" news, "fairness" in the discussion of public issues, and "equal time" in the coverage of candidates for public office—all, by the way, upheld by the Supreme Court as constitutional under the First Amendment.[53] What is most significant about this branch of the U.S. press and how it was structured is that it would have been possible to utilize an entirely free-market approach, namely by auctioning off the airwaves and leaving its development thereafter to private decisions in the market. This, however, was not the course chosen or demanded by the First Amendment. Lastly, in this very brief overview of the history of the press in this country, we need to take note of a third branch of the U.S. media, namely the system of public broadcasting which was designed in the 1960s with direct public funding.[54]

Overall, then, we must conclude that the "press" as it has evolved in the United States is not the product of the system of private property operating in a completely free market. (Of course, one can take the position that the press, as it now exists, would be much better had these government interventions not occurred; but personally, I do not find that persuasive and one rarely hears it made.)[55] Let me say that I do believe that the market is a powerful system for a strong free press and must be the dominant model. But just as there is no reason in experience to conclude that a free market alone will yield the press we need, so is there no reason in theory. For a free press, as we have conceived of it and as I observed at the outset, is really a public good, with an important systemic and public service role to play, and, just as with scholarly research and universities, you simply cannot expect serious journalism or basic research to flow only from a free market. It will always require some other element of motivation besides maximizing profits. Even daily newspapers became better (in the sense of elevating their capacity to inform their readers and the public) by not pocketing their monopolist profits but instead by investing the money in hiring more specialists—economists, scientists, lawyers, foreign correspondents, etc.—to deepen their coverage of news.[56] This began in the 1970s and continued until recently, when under major new pressures from the market and the loss of their previous protective monopolistic moat they have begun shedding this journalistic capacity.[57]

Now, again, my point is not that in order to sustain a high-quality institution of the press you must rely on monopolies and public funding and regulation. It is rather that we need to be realistic about how we got to the point we are at in terms of creating a very high-quality press, realizing that it will not happen only with a free market operating alone, and continually assessing and considering what might be done to enhance opportunities for the press to meet the very high public purpose we have appropriately assigned to it. To that end, and in the new context of the need for high quality journalism in a global public forum, I would make one very specific and concrete suggestion.

I noted at the beginning of my talk how other nations are using their state-sponsored and funded media to establish a broad global presence and through that to advance their national agendas. CCTV and Al Jazeera are two of the prime examples of newer entrants into this area, where historically BBC World Service has led the field. We in the United States cannot take it for granted that this will just naturally evolve into the quality of journalism both we and the world will need. With retrenchment underway in the capacity to cover international news, and with the serious challenge to a vibrant global flow of information that censorship around the world presents—for which (as I said earlier) one of the best antidotes may be a clear demonstration to the world of what a free and independent press can offer—we would be very well advised to plan for a stronger publicly funded system of international public broadcasting.

As it happens, we already have an excellent government-funded (partially, to be sure, at about $500 million annually[58]) system of NPR and PBS. Like the BBC, these are highly regarded journalistic enterprises. While they have some capacity to engage in world-wide reporting, it is not anything close to the scale of either what is needed and possible or what peer systems have to work with in other countries.[59] In fact, a significant part of the reporting of world news, for NPR, happens by broadcasting programs of BBC World and BBC World Service (ironically, paid for by British citizens).[60] For reaching global audiences, we have a series of government-sponsored broadcasting entities set up primarily during the Cold War with a purpose of combating Communist propaganda by communicating the position of the United States.[61] Voice of America and Radio Free Europe are the legendary institutions of this group, which also now includes Radio Free Asia, Radio Martí (for Cuba), and Alhurra (for the Middle East).[62] Interestingly, because these were established as communications media of the U.S. government, and therefore were seen as having the potential to spread our own government propaganda, which could be used by the government to infect the American marketplace of ideas, Congress under the Smith-Mundt Act of 1948 forbade these media from rebroadcasting back into the United States.[63] Even in the new era of the Internet, where these media have very active and readily available websites, this prohibition remains in place and seems to me constitutionally suspect.[64] The more interesting problem is why we (the United States) would continue to maintain this dual system of respected journalism in NPR and PBS on the one hand, and the international propaganda media on the other, with each receiving approximately the same amount of funding, when what we and the world need more than anything is truly global journalism capable of reporting the news in an independent, objective, and professional manner. That is why I have recommended an American World Service, a media institution with sufficient funding and a guarantee of editorial autonomy capable of bringing the highest quality American journalism to the global public forum.

It is, of course, absolutely necessary that editorial autonomy be secured. Many people seem to find state funds and high-quality journalism as utterly incomprehensible. I have already noted that this ignores both our history and our theory of the role of the institution of the press in society. It is worth re-emphasizing that both NPR and PBS have achieved a status of highly respected journalism (as has, I would submit, the BBC). Experience demonstrates that it is possible to have high-quality journalism while also having relatively few instances of improper government intrusion into the editorial process. It is also worth noting that every system of funding for the press, including the free market, carries risks of funders (whether the state, foundations, or advertisers) trying to exert undue and inappropriate influence over the content of the press. We, therefore, cannot escape the problem of improper interference by abandoning the idea of public funding. Also, there is the fact, which I think is devastating to the doubts about state funding, that universities—which I indicated at the outset, are parallel institutions with the press serving the public need for information and ideas—are and have been for many decades recipients of massive state funding, both federal (especially in the case of scientific research) and state (with our public universities). We care as much about our academic freedom as the press cares about journalistic autonomy, and we have been able to make this work, primarily through vigorous monitoring of, and resistance to, inappropriate government intervention, supported by a claim under the First Amendment that funding does not permit censorship. This last point deserves further analysis, but we have good cases (both for academic freedom and for journalistic autonomy) on which to build a strong and robust constitutional principle protecting that autonomy. In the end, what we want is what we have had—namely, a vibrant mixed system using multiple systems—mostly free market with some publicly supported institutions, to achieve our overarching goal, which is to receive the information we must have to forge both an understanding of, and a consensus about, what kind of world we want to create for ourselves.

Here, then, is the summary of the argument I have presented. Globalization is the great change of our era, of this new century, wrought of economic forces forging connections throughout the world and of new technologies making human communication far easier. We need institutions designed to help us understand, tame, and channel these largely positive forces, and a free and independent press is one such institution. Just as we came to understand how beneficial a free press is to the ends of life we seek in this country, so we must do so now on the world stage. To do that we must focus our attention on two fundamental matters: one is to secure the right of access to information and the freedom to publish (i.e., to realize that censorship anywhere is now effectively censorship everywhere and that all the press is our press), and the other is to ensure there is the capacity for high-quality journalism once access is available and censorship contained. For each of these areas I have offered suggestions. We need to develop the right arguments to make in global discussions about a free and independent press. Among other things, this means developing the case for why such a principle is integral to creating the kind of social culture capable of the creativity needed for a mature and dynamic economy. We need to set about establishing global legal norms for a strong free press. Article 19, in its international and regional forms, offers a fair shot at being the kind of legal text that might work. The system of legal obligations under the WTO also offers important opportunities to make the link between commitments to free trade in goods and services and free trade in ideas. At some point, perhaps not for a while, but the time will surely come, when sacrificing some sovereignty by committing ourselves to the process of interpretation and general enforcement will be a risk worth taking. We also need to begin examining the many ways in which our borders are used as barriers to the freedom of press we value so highly, including such areas as visa policies for foreign journalists and restrictions on foreign journalistic entities from entering our media (broadcasting and cable, in particular). With respect to the issue of capacity of professional journalism to report to the world and from the world to us, I have argued for the creation of an American World Service, which could arise naturally out of the restructuring of the now anachronistic system we have of a national public media and an international propaganda media.

More than anything, however, we need a change in consciousness—to envision the problem we must solve as not only a matter of securing human rights for peoples around the world but also securing the information and ideas we need to govern effectively an increasingly integrated world. This is the ultimate stage of a progressive shift from the local to the national to the global, which began at least in the last century and is represented by the evolution of the First Amendment—most strikingly embodied in the decision of *New York Times v. Sullivan*—into a set of doctrines protective of a national public forum suitable for a national political and economic society. What we need now, therefore, is a clear-sighted understanding of the broad chilling effects of censorship and its impairment of our collective ability to create the world we might, if we only had the information to make the right choices.

CHAPTER 12

A FREE PRESS FOR A GLOBAL SOCIETY

American Academy of Arts and Sciences Induction Symposium, Cambridge, MA, October 10, 2010

The American Academy of Arts and Sciences, founded in 1780, is a nonpartisan research center that "convenes leaders from every field of human endeavor to examine new ideas, address issues of importance to the nation and the world, and work together 'to cultivate every art and science which may tend to advance the interest, honor, dignity, and happiness of a free, independent, and virtuous people.'"[1] President Bollinger, who is a member of the academy, was invited to provide the keynote address at the annual induction ceremony regarding issues at the forefront of new technology and the public good.

The need to build a system of free press that is suitable (from both U.S. and global perspectives) to the conditions of globalization is a subject of intrinsic importance. It is also an example of how the extraordinary forces of globalization are reshaping intellectual fields. (Universities, in my view, should be thinking much more systematically about this challenge, but that's a larger subject for another day.) Today, the system of free press that prevails in the United States blends constitutional law, public policy, the specific conditions of markets—with respect to daily newspapers, in particular—and the development of journalism as a profession. All these elements emerged in the twentieth century. Like universities, the press is one of the central institutions of a democratic society. At its best, the press serves the public good by disseminating information and analysis and by functioning as a public forum for discussing issues of importance to society. Perhaps its greatest contribution lies in its capacity for calibration: that is, the ability to judge what is important and why.

In the twentieth century, the nation became less an assemblage of states and regions and more a national entity. The structure and institutions of the society shifted accordingly. The growth of the economy; the rise of issues with national scope, such as civil rights; and the development of new communications technology—broadcasting, in particular—that enhanced national discussion: all contributed to the need for a free press that could function on a national level and was appropriate for a rising, robust, and dynamic national society. To that end, a complex ecology of First Amendment public policy and journalism evolved. The Supreme Court initiated a series of landmark decisions that ultimately provided a unified national approach. Those decisions pushed the boundaries of free speech and press beyond what any nation in history had done before. They also articulated the important public role performed by the press, locating the rationales for extraordinary protection in the political and social interests of democracy, reason, and tolerance.

Meanwhile, public policy intervened in the new broadcast media. With the Supreme Court's blessing, the federal government organized a blend of private ownership and public-interest regulation to expand the range of voices. It also launched a public broadcasting system with guarantees of editorial autonomy. Finally, the print media used its revenues, especially the monopolistic profits of daily newspapers, to deepen and expand its expertise to cover the news. Journalism began to look more and more like a profession, with standards of behavior that transcended interest, profit, and partisanship. Private enterprise, market conditions, state policy, and constitutional cases—none of which could have given rise to a free press all on its own—combined to create the best press in the world.

In our current century, the conditions undergirding the system have shifted. Free markets have gone global, driving changes of enormous significance throughout the world. Some changes are good, such as improved standards of living and better health for hundreds of millions of people; others are bad, like climate change, or problematic, like the fragility of the international economy, the tensions of multiculturalism, or conflicts between modernity and other ways of life. Ours is a world driven by business and finance, aided as always by new communication technologies; in this case, the Internet and satellite broadcasting are especially influential. It is a world that moves with extraordinary rapidity and that often resists the sunshine provided by a responsible press. It is a world in desperate need of the kind of information that only institutions of journalism can provide. We therefore need a system of free press suitable to this new world.

I fear that the United States does not grasp the full degree to which we are becoming integrated and interdependent with other countries. Half of the revenues of S&P 500 companies are generated outside the United States. Half the goods consumed by wealthy nations are manufactured in emerging economies. Half of U.S. government debt is in foreign hands. What happens to this world? How does it evolve? What choices do we need to make to create the best of all possible worlds? At the least, we should think carefully and systematically about what kind of press system will provide us and others with the journalism we need to address these questions. As form is sometimes said to follow function, so free press follows issues—and the issues are increasingly global.

Three major areas require particular attention. First, the balance of interests that produced our First Amendment jurisprudence is starting to shift. For example, when the *Washington Post* obtains classified documents or information, we can count on its journalists and editors to feel the force of patriotic considerations in deciding what to publish; this is not the case for those behind WikiLeaks. Today, when an unknown pastor in Florida threatens to burn the Koran, the hostile audience that will be aroused, and the violence that might ensue, is not within the same control, or on the same scale, as the threatening mob in Illinois that prompted one of the Supreme Court cases of the last century. For these reasons, the Pentagon Papers case may not look quite the same today. One thing is for sure: the Secretary of Defense's call list will get very long. My point is not that the case law should change, but rather that the resolution we have reached will to some extent need to be reconsidered.

Second, to design this system of free press on a global scale, our basic perspectives and assumptions must change. To the extent that we need information about what is happening in the world, the working distinction in our minds between domestic and foreign press must recede; indeed, much of what we need to know will come from the foreign or international press. This reality has implications for policy. For example, access for members of the press is crucial. Restrictions on foreign journalists that exist today in virtually all countries, including the United States, and are justified on grounds of foreign policy or sovereignty become problematic. Visa and travel restrictions on international journalists, or decisions by cable companies not to carry certain international media, will need rethinking.

Censorship on a global scale is a third matter of enormous concern. Nations throughout the world have very different ideas about the role of the press and the scope of freedom it should be afforded. In a world of global communication, the reality increasingly is that censorship anywhere is censorship everywhere. In the United States during the twentieth century, state laws restricting speech and press eventually gave way to a set of national norms, with *New York Times Co. v. Sullivan* being the primary case in point. A similar transformation must unfold globally.

A speech or essay in the United States can get its speaker or writer in trouble in Italy, Turkey, China, or Britain. Again, our fundamental perspective must change. This is no longer a matter of nobly securing human rights for the rest of the world; rather, it is a practical matter of securing the basic flow of information and ideas required to accompany and complement the free flow of goods and services.

We seem hardly prepared for this new world, and our shortcomings will not be corrected by advances in technology alone. Those of us who believe in the virtues of a very open and free press system must develop new rationales and arguments to persuade those who do not share our intuition. For example, we might emphasize the relationship between openness and sustainable and stable economic growth, the latter being something nearly all societies now seem to want. We will have to work toward stronger international legal norms. Texts such as Article 19 of the Universal Declaration of Human Rights, the International Covenant on Civil and Political Rights, World Trade Organization guidelines, and other regional treaties provide a place to begin.

Finally, besides problems of access and censorship, we must focus on the capacity of the press to cover the dynamic, fast-moving, and somewhat secretive forces of globalization. It is unfortunate that at the moment we need more and better international press coverage; the current financial crisis has caused budgets for foreign bureaus and correspondents to contract. Even without this troubling state of affairs, however, we would benefit from a more focused discussion of the role public policy might play in bringing more independent and objective journalism to the world—and more of it back home to us.

The American population must be better educated than we are about global issues. Other nations, certainly, are engaged in international events. New public service broadcast systems are reaching out to the world from France, Russia, the Middle East, and China, joining the traditional institutions such as the BBC World News and BBC World Service. I believe the world would benefit from more

American-style journalism and I have suggested the formation of an American World Service modeled on the BBC.

At present, the United States has a dual system of publicly supported broadcasting. On the one hand, there is an editorially independent press with a domestic mission, namely NPR and PBS. On the other is a government press with an international mission, which includes Voice of America, Radio Free Europe, Radio Free Asia, and several other news organizations. In yet another example of how the world has changed while our policies lag behind, a 1947 statute bars these government propaganda outlets in the international arena from rebroadcasting back into the United States. Whatever one thinks of these media, they will always be viewed as the voice of the American government. The best of free and independent American journalism needs to join these and other institutions, many of them private, in the new global public forum. A good method to achieve such integration, for example, would be to augment the funding and mission of NPR.

For Americans who are skeptical about public support for the press, I should reiterate that neither theory nor experience suggests that a free market alone can create the conditions necessary for an independent, global press to arise. Certainly, editorial autonomy is essential to any free press. There are ways to establish that reality in practice and in First Amendment law. By comparison, at universities, where we care as much about academic freedom as journalists do about editorial freedom, we have long maintained our autonomy in spite of significant state and federal funding. Journalism, I believe, can do the same. The world is undergoing momentous changes through the forces of globalization. We need a free press that is suitable to this new world. To achieve that goal, we must change our basic concepts and develop our laws and policies to deal with the serious issues of access, censorship, and the capacity of the press to provide the information we need. Only then can the press do its part to help shape a world that will work for ends we believe in.

QUESTION: Could you comment on online journalism and whether you believe that a robust, open, and balanced forum could be Internet-based?

LEE BOLLINGER: This is a very large subject. The Internet is bringing enormous amounts of new information, opinion, and analysis to discussion of global and national issues. I think this development is a huge plus. However, the Internet will not replace the institutions that are devoted to the spread of information and analysis on an independent and objective basis. That is the domain of journalism. While it is typically thought that the citizen journalist is one of the great new advances of the Internet age—a view that I share—I do not think it replaces the need for large organizations that have a unique range of capacities to go out and report on the world. I think the other point to be made, which I offer up tentatively, is that the type of "journalism" that is not of the traditional media tends to contain more opinion than objective reporting. Journalism is a profession, just as scholarship is a profession, meaning that professional journalists are committed to certain norms in the way they pursue information and truth. By the same token, we might ask, could the courses, discussions, or sources of information that we have access to at universities be replaced by Internet alternatives? Taking a basic economics course online does not connect a student to an institution devoted to the development of knowledge about economics or laws. I think that is a huge loss.

QUESTION: Previously, newspapers could hire robust editorial staffs because they had the revenue. How will we replace that capacity in the Internet age? How will we accrete enough mass, gravitas, and editorial staffing to supplement at least the blogosphere?

LEE BOLLINGER: The answer I'm giving in op-eds, essays, speeches, and my book is: through public funding. We have a mix that balances private institutions, publicly funded media, and hybrids that incorporate some public policy. I would shift the nature of that balance to devote more public funding to journalism, in part to make up for the economic losses we are experiencing. Where we are is completely unsatisfactory. From informal conversations with members of the American press, I understand that, apart from the financial press employed by Bloomberg News, we may have only two dozen full-time foreign correspondents covering all of China. A handful has been there long enough to have acquired a deep knowledge of the society. Perhaps five or six journalists have a sense of how China evolved, what is going on in China, what the leadership is really like, and China's views on topics we care about, such as openness. Do they believe that the emergence of a free press is inevitable, or do they believe that a closed society is consistent with sustained economic wealth? Those kinds of questions are immensely significant to the United States and the world. It seems that we would want to have many more journalists trying to understand them, as well as more university faculty and student investigators. We in the universities have not adjusted our fields and our array of expertise to really try to understand what is going on in the world, China being a particular example. Again, I would use public funding.

I have followed the press for many decades, and I have asked editors of major daily newspapers to give me a sense of the history of the press in this country. Leading newspapers started making substantial profits in the late 1970s and early 1980s, when they came to dominate the market. That's when they hired economists, lawyers, scientists, and other experts to cover subjects like the court or the economy. Today, newspapers are in the process of losing a good deal of that range of expertise. Allowing it to unfold without a careful public policy review is a mistake.

QUESTION: My impression is that the First Amendment was originally intended to provide freedom of speech to the press so that it could criticize the government. But in the course of the last two hundred years, it seems we have morphed that right into the freedom for individuals to express themselves in a variety of ways. The Internet offers a megaphone for a good deal of objectionable speech. Is it your sense that the intent has morphed, or do you believe that freedom of speech originally was meant to apply not only to the press but also to individuals?

LEE BOLLINGER: I think the provision was intended to apply to individuals, but we know stunningly little about how the First Amendment was interpreted by the people who drafted it. There has been very little effort to unravel that mystery. The first Supreme Court case to interpret the First Amendment was in 1919. Thus, freedom of speech and press as we know them today are an invention of the twentieth century.

And as I point out in many places, it was not an auspicious beginning. Oliver Wendell Holmes wrote for a unanimous court in three early decisions, upholding convictions against people who had protested for various reasons prior to World War I. One of the individuals whose conviction was upheld by the Supreme Court was presidential candidate Eugene Debs. He gave a speech in Ohio in which he praised people who resisted the draft. That was held to be a crime sufficient for a presidential candidate to go to jail. While he was there, he received a million votes for president in the 1920 election.

Then the law changed. Holmes oversaw a ruling on the First Amendment and religion that resulted in strong protections for individuals. During the McCarthy period, however, as people were jailed for speaking about overthrowing the government, the court fell victim to the traditional notion that in a new period, threatened by international conspiracy, the government must be allowed to take action.

In the 1960s, everything changed again, with cases like *New York Times Co. v. Sullivan* and *Brandenburg v. Ohio*. Our current jurisprudence really derives from that period, rooted in some fine decisions of the 1920s and 1930s. None of those cases is based on an understanding of what the framers wanted, largely because, as I mentioned, there has been virtually no historical analysis of what the framers' exact vision might have been. Yet we should not readily accept the idea that the framers had a vision that we have altered over time.

Why do we take freedom of speech so far in the United States? Why were neo-Nazi speakers allowed to march in Skokie, Illinois, in 1977? Four thousand Holocaust survivors lived in that community, and half the population was Jewish. We take free speech further than any other society in the world, and that includes neighbors such as Canada, and Britain. We are now in a position where our exercise of free speech rights are not just domestic issues; they are published globally, and an American can end up being prosecuted, as has happened, in Italy or Turkey.

This is the beginning of a whole new era, a whole new century. *New York Times Co. v. Sullivan* was pivotal in recognizing that Alabama could not have a rule that allowed people to sue freely for libel; it undermined the *New York Times'* ability to publish a national edition because it could face libel cases in the least protective areas of the country. Now, we are facing that problem on a global scale. For most of my professional career, I have struggled with the question of why we have such extreme protection. I think it is rooted in a strategy to test our limits of tolerance in the area of speech as a lesson or symbol of the need to bring tolerance to every area of social interaction. I think we bend over backward to be tolerant because that's the kind of character we want to have. But other societies have reached very different judgments about what individuals can say publicly. Germany, for example, does not allow neo-Nazi speech; we can understand why certain societies might establish different rules. We are now in a global discussion about defining the parameters of free speech on an international scale.

QUESTION: Liberty is inseparable from responsibility. How can we institutionalize responsibility and protect the citizen from slander and libel?

LEE BOLLINGER: I think we look to universities. Quality journalism is a major responsibility of universities and journalism schools. Under Nick Lemann, Dean of the Graduate School of Journalism, Columbia is working closely on these projects and others, strengthening the journalism school as a place for professional development. I also think the participation of people who exhibit the best qualities of a professional journalist, to serve as a kind of model or example for how we should speak and behave, is extremely important.

We should value enormously the quality of the free press that has been achieved in this country; it's an astonishing institution. Nurturing it, helping reshape it through this difficult period, and building a free press on a global scale are great goals. In these efforts, we can work toward a culture in which debate is conducted on the highest possible levels.

CHAPTER 13

THE PENTAGON PAPERS

Learned Hand Lecture in Honor of Judge Wilfred Feinberg,
U.S. Court of Appeals for the Second Circuit, June 22, 2011

---

*After graduating from Columbia Law School in 1971, President Bollinger served as
a law clerk for Judge Wilfred Feinberg of the U.S. Court of Appeals for the Second
Circuit, followed by a clerkship with Chief Justice Warren Burger of the U.S. Supreme
Court. The following lecture, in honor of Bollinger's mentor and friend, reflects on
the significance of the landmark First Amendment case known as "The Pentagon
Papers" (New York Times Co. v. United States). When the Second Circuit decided
the case, ruling against the New York Times, Judge Feinberg dissented, advocating
that the newspaper should not be enjoined from publishing classified information, a
position that later prevailed with the Supreme Court.*

I t is a great honor to be invited to give this lecture, named after one of the
great American judges, of this distinguished Court, about a subject—the
Pentagon Papers case—that is of immense significance to this nation and,
indeed, the world, and, finally and personally most significantly, in celebration
of the 91st birthday of a man—Bill Feinberg—who has over half a century on the
bench carried forward the highest judicial standards set by Learned and Augus-
tus Hand and who is a mentor and dear friend (along with Shirley, his wife) to
every one of us here this afternoon. There are themes within themes and inter-
connections large and small running through this occasion. Generation after
generation of law students are every year introduced to the First Amendment—
the problems of its theory and reach—through the mind of Learned Hand in
the *Masses* case of 1917. On June 23, 1971, as the Pentagon Papers case coursed
through the 2nd Circuit, Judge Feinberg voted (in dissent) not to enjoin the *New*

York Times, which shortly afterwards would be the courageous decision of the Supreme Court, in a landmark case that altered history. Less widely observed, understandably, is the fact that two months later I would enter Judge Feinberg's chambers as his new law clerk, beginning one of the most important years of my professional life; or the even more important fact that some three decades later my daughter, Carey, would also serve as a law clerk to the judge. So, let me just say, to Bill Feinberg directly, without extracting every level of meaning from this moment, how grateful and admiring everyone in this room is for your remarkable service to this Court and to the law and for your friendship over these many decades.

The subject this afternoon, thus, is the Pentagon Papers case, a decision of iconic status in First Amendment jurisprudence and widely known in American society. Every society, certainly every democratic society, must decide what balance to strike between the legitimate interests of the government in working in private (secret) and the legitimate interests of the citizens in knowing what the government is doing. One of the contexts in which this issue arises is when the press comes by classified information leaked by government employees. Should the press be free—protected by the First Amendment—to publish that information? That, of course, is the question the Pentagon Papers case posed and, to some extent, resolved.

I want to make three general observations about the Supreme Court's decision and then offer two broader comments about where we are today with respect to the issue of publication of classified information and about the revolutionary changes the phenomenon of globalization creates for the First Amendment as we have come to know it.

Pentagon Papers is one of the most well-known, least understood decisions in the jurisprudence of the First Amendment. Interestingly, the issue it addressed is almost never litigated but it is iconic. Pentagon Papers is the culminating case in that seminal period of the 1960s and early 1970s when the Court essentially created the framework for free speech and free press in America, the framework that still exists and that is the most speech protective system in the world today and perhaps in human history. Pentagon Papers stands with *The New York Times v. Sullivan*, *Cohen v. California*, *Brandenburg v. Ohio*, *Red Lion Broadcasting Co. v. FCC*, and several other cases as the bedrock of the American approach to freedom of speech and press. These opinions drew from the classic opinions of First Amendment jurisprudence—notably Hand in *Masses*, Holmes and Brandeis in

Abrams and *Whitney*, and a few others—that date from earlier in the twentieth century. It is a surprising fact—virtually unknown by people outside the law, and often underappreciated even by people within the law—that the Supreme Court never spoke about the meaning of the First Amendment until 1919. And, when it finally did speak, it was more about the virtues and necessities of censorship than the glories of liberty of expression. (It was more about how you can't yell fire falsely in a crowded theater than about how the best test of truth is the power of a thought to get accepted in the marketplace of ideas.) While our country seems unaware of how recent our First Amendment jurisprudence really is, we as a people seem even more blissfully ignorant of the fact that our national behavior towards dissent has often been disturbingly more like the repression of authoritarian regimes we regularly condemn today than the image we carry around with us that in America you can say just about anything you want with the full protection of the Constitution. It may be true today, but it has not by any means always been so. (We all know the story of Eugene Debs.)

Pentagon Papers is certainly part of that favorable pro-free speech self-image. Yet it is interesting that it has achieved that iconic status given that the decision in favor of protecting publication was narrowly achieved (6 to 3, with 3 of the 6 highly qualified) and, even more importantly, that the decision was arguably very limited. When I teach Pentagon Papers, one of my standard hypotheticals is to assume I am the editor of a major newspaper in possession of classified documents leaked to one of our reporters by a government employee in clear violation of the law and who likely will go to jail if discovered and prosecuted. I seek assurances from my general counsel—the unfortunate student called upon for that day— that Pentagon Papers will keep me from ever wearing an orange jump suit. Citing Pentagon Papers, my general counsel usually affirms that publication would be protected, but then gradually backs away from that position as the discussion proceeds to reveal how the majority opinions seem to only talk about prior restraints and may not speak to subsequent punishments, and also seem to say the outcome might be different if Congress were to authorize the Executive Branch to take action against publishers, or if the government could just provide some actual proof of genuine harms to national security. I point out how disappointed I am in a "landmark" free press decision that protects my freedom to publish harmless information but not my right to avoid prosecution afterwards for doing so. (In candor, I've never completely understood the rationale for the very strong presumption against all "prior restraints," at least when they take the form of injunctions. From the standpoint of the editor, I imagine him or her saying: Look, if you really are concerned for me, which I very much appreciate, I'd rather have a very strong presumption against going to prison than one against being ordered by a judge not to publish.)

Yet Pentagon Papers is a prime example of how the specific limits of judicial decisions do not reflect the real significance of a case. It is a very notable fact that Pentagon Papers is the only instance in our history (other than the less well-known case involving the Progressive Magazine and its announced intention to publish plans for building an atomic bomb) when the U.S. government has sought to enjoin or punish the press for publishing classified information. The average person may be forgiven for believing that the Pentagon Papers case stands for the much larger proposition that in America, even in the face of an assertion by the President of the United States that publication will make our foreign policy more complicated and difficult, the Supreme Court will side with the press and its role in informing the public about the actions of our government. Along with *Times v. Sullivan*, that is no small victory for the ideal that in a Madisonian democracy it is the citizens who are the ultimate sovereign and not the other way around.

There is, I believe, an even bigger point to be made here. When you stand back and look at the decision in Pentagon Papers, and some other related cases, and at the way we have lived with that decision, it is a remarkable portrait of pragmatic American solutions to conventional societal problems (i.e., disclosure of classified government documents). As Alexander Bickel observed at the time, the upshot of Pentagon Papers is this: Under the First Amendment, the government is free to withhold as much information from public view as it chooses, despite the fact that we know from experience that the government will be far more secretive than it should. It may enforce this secrecy by criminally punishing officials who leak any of this information to the press, no matter how valuable to citizens that information may be. The press, on the other hand, may freely take information from leakers and freely publish that information (unless the government can prove grievous, irreparable and imminent harm to the national interests), even though that may significantly injure the ability of the government to do the public's business, domestically or in foreign affairs. To many outside observers this system seems incomprehensible and chaotic. It appears to be unreasonably messy, risky, and oddly non-judicial in resolution. And, yet, from almost any perspective, it seems to me, it has worked well, very well in fact. Governments learn to live with leaks (indeed, even learn to use them to advantage), rarely prosecute leakers, and classify information with abandon. The courts avoid the seemingly immensely complex task of being the final arbiter of what information should remain secret and what public. And the press, following professional journalistic standards and acting with a sense of responsibility to the nation, on balance publish what citizens should know and exercise self-restraint towards the rest.

This, I believe, is a system that reflects a civilized society. Rules that on the surface appear to invite risks and disorder may in fact work brilliantly because they work within a social context where people and institutions behave responsibly, provided there are checks and balances in place. Freedom is often greater when we do not want or need to use it to the maximum. This is the one of the great lessons of the magnificent set of cases from the era of the 1960s and 70s, which began with *Sullivan* curbing the law of defamation to avoid discouraging citizens from speaking under the threat of legal liability for falsehoods. The most interesting and significant thing about the American system of freedom of speech and press is not that it is the most protective of any society (now or before) but that the risks of that commitment have not materialized. This means the First Amendment stands as a continual reminder, a national teaching moment, about our capacities to function successfully in a highly pluralistic, diverse society, with a myriad of viewpoints and perspectives about how to live.

The Pentagon Papers case was the crest of these remarkable decisions, and we have been living off of them ever since.

The big question today, in light of the extraordinary event of Wikileaks' possession and disclosure of millions of U.S. government documents, is whether Pentagon Papers can survive the new realities of this new century. Allegedly, the source of these leaks is a mere private in the Army who had computer access to this huge body of classified information and chose, with the click of the send button, to transmit them to an organization based outside the United States and led by a man not a U.S. citizen who asserts a mission in life of achieving total transparency, no matter what the consequences. Thus far, only a fraction has been released, primarily through established news media, such as the *New York Times* and *The Guardian*. There is an ongoing debate about the extent to which this has resulted in or threatened harms.

There are at least two or three factors that raise concerns and relate to the continuing viability of the approach of Pentagon Papers. The first is the ease of leaks in the era of computers and the Internet. A vast amount of government information is presumably now readily accessible by large numbers of employees, who, with the most minimal effort, can disseminate it broadly and instantly. The risks of very high-cost leaks seem far greater than in a world in which the Xerox machine was the primary available technology. The second is the reality that the array of individuals able and likely to receive leaks is infinitely broader than the group of professional reporters working for established (and largely monopolistic) news outlets. Inevitably, recipients will include people with little, no, or adverse interests in the welfare of the United States. When the editors of the *Washington Post* or the *New York Times* were in possession of classified information, you can be sure they would listen to official pleas for restraint in publication and actually practice restraint themselves in the face of a good faith case of very serious harms. Not so with someone who disdains secrecy and proudly professes disinterest in the bad consequences of publication. The question, in a way, is how many Julian Assanges will there be in this new world, as compared to the number of Abe Rosenthals or Ben Bradlees.

At this point, I think the most we can say is that experience will inform our judgment whether to maintain the course with Pentagon Papers or move in a different direction. I do not have the time in this lecture to consider alternatives, but I will say that it has seemed to me that it is a more reasonable option than many have heretofore assumed for the courts to insist on a general responsibility of the government under the First Amendment to make reasonable efforts at openness, the contours of which would be decided over time on a case-by-case basis (essentially building on the right of public access upheld in *Richmond Newspapers*). I also believe, again contrary to the current ways of thinking, that courts should recognize a special set of stronger protections under the First Amendment for the "press," difficult as it may be to delineate the boundaries of that segment of society (essentially building on the approach once outlined by Justice Stewart and implicitly reflected in several First Amendment cases). A principle of higher protection for the press would help secure both the public interest in appropriate levels of government secrecy and good and aggressive disclosure to the public. Either or both of these options would alleviate the pressure of Pentagon Papers to protect the publication of nearly everything anyone can get their hands on.

Whether we are living through a transitional period, needing updated and recalibrated rules governing disclosure is debatable. But we are seeing inconsistent and sometimes inequitable outcomes. How else to make sense of the aggressive—and ultimately, failed—prosecution under the Espionage Act of Thomas Drake, the National Security Agency employee who claimed he was acting patriotically when he leaked information to a *Baltimore Sun* reporter about government overspending on a telecommunications program. In this case, the actions of a whistleblower who made possible the kind of investigative, accountability journalism we expect from a robust free press were targeted by the Justice Department; the same Justice Department that is struggling to contain the wholesale leaking of classified documents that could result in real harm to sources and military personnel.

As the *Washington Post*—in full disclosure, on whose board I serve—said on its editorial page:

"This newspaper is not a disinterested party and maintains an interest in obtaining information that sheds light on the inner workings of government. But we also recognize the government's obligation to hold accountable those who breach agreements, especially ones that touch on national security interests. The question is whether the action taken is proportionate to the alleged crime. In Mr. Drake's case, it was not."

Let me turn, finally, to some thoughts about Pentagon Papers and what I think of as a still larger set of changes at work in the world today, with very significant implications for the First Amendment. The era of *New York Times v. Sullivan*, that culminated in Pentagon Papers, can be thought of as a response of a nation undergoing a tectonic shift from local control of local issues to national control of national issues. The economy was increasingly national in scope, and issues like civil rights, the environment, and criminal justice called for national solutions, along with matters of war and peace. This change was aided, perhaps created, by new communications technologies, which were inherently national in character (television and radio in particular). *Sullivan* was one of several major Court decisions that found local law (i.e., the tort of defamation) in conflict with the need for a national public forum for debating national issues. Pentagon Papers further protected the American press in its efforts to inform an American public about a raging national debate. It followed the traditional approach of extending deference to the government in defining national security and foreign policy interests at stake, but in the interest of robust national debate, the Court at least insisted on some concrete proof of intolerable costs.

Today, with globalization, I believe we are entering the next stage of this process of issues calling for a wider public forum, which will have important implications for the First Amendment. The fundamental characteristics of change are the same. Economies are less national and increasingly global and integrated. Nearly half of the revenues of the S&P 500 corporations are generated from business conducted outside the United States; developing countries provide roughly half of the manufactured goods bought by developed countries (up from 14% in 1987); approximately half of the U.S. government's debt is in foreign hands; and on a more personal scale, a significant portion of everyone's retirement fund is invested in foreign enterprises. And gone are the days when America's demand for energy was so large, relative to other nations, that it determined the price of oil we consume. This all means, in turn, that the challenges we face as a nation have expanded to become global in dimension—from mitigating climate change, and rebuilding the foundations of the global financial system, to preventing the spread of infectious disease, and addressing widening disparities in personal income and wealth. The new technologies of communication (the Internet and satellite, in particular) are forging this inter-connectedness while making a global public forum necessary and possible. We are rapidly approaching an environment in which all that we say, whether we intend it or not, is global in reach and has global significance. This means we are exposed to censorship laws all around the world. Just like Alabama's libel law became an intolerable limitation on national discussion, the new reality is that censorship anywhere is censorship everywhere.

Because we will live in a world in which our issues are global issues and cannot be solved except by discussion with citizens around the world, we will have a direct interest not only in our own capacity to receive information from and about the rest of the world and to speak to the rest of the world, but also in how the rest of the world receives information and participates along with us in the global public forum. This new context has a number of implications for the First Amendment; essentially, we will have to ask more and more what limits should the Constitution put on actions by the U.S. government that might adversely affect that global public forum? Questions arise that didn't appear to be questions before, or appear in a new light, such as: What restrictions on participation in our public debate by foreign individuals and entities (media or corporations) should be protected under the First Amendment? (I'm thinking of visa restrictions, or rules about foreign media and access to cable broadcast, or campaign finance laws.)

In a recent Supreme Court decision in *Holder v. Humanitarian Law Project*, a majority of the Court held that advice provided by a U.S. group to a designated "foreign terrorist organization" about international law and about how to work within international organizations like the United Nations, constituted "material assistance" under the federal statute and could accordingly result in criminal prosecution. The Court said this expression was not protected by the First Amendment. The government's claim that national security concerns justified the prohibition on speech because support for legitimate activities of the foreign organizations could be expected to result in support for their criminal terrorist activities was accepted by the majority, with the explanation that courts must defer to the judgment of the government on such matters. Chief Justice Roberts, writing for a six-Justice majority, argued:

"In this context, conclusions must often be based on informed judgment rather than concrete evidence, and that reality affects what we may reasonably insist on from the Government."

These are difficult questions to be sure. But at what cost do we rely on conclusions based on informed judgment, not evidence, which lead to infringements on speech? To my mind, the Chief Justice's reality is inconsistent with the spirit of Pentagon Papers in insisting that when First Amendment rights are at stake the government at least has the obligation of demonstrating—not just claiming—very serious harms. But the lessons of Pentagon Papers, and the source of its landmark status, I believe, go further than that. Pentagon Papers was a great decision because it was highly sensitive to the value of speech and press in a forum that needed information. The animating spirit was that, if at all possible, that discussion would be protected. Not to the point of unreasonableness or complete disregard of every other value. But that, at least, would be the starting point, not the other end of the speech spectrum where the burden is on the speech to prove its value (as happened in *Schenck* with the starting point that yelling fire falsely in a crowded theater was not protected).

That spirit now needs to be transferred to thinking about protecting speech in the global public forum, which is where we are going to live for at least the rest of this century.

A great case like Pentagon Papers offers endless facets of meaning, new and old. It exists in the great tradition of the First Amendment that begins with Hand, weaves its way through the decisions of great judges—like Bill Feinberg—and brings us to the doorstep of a new century with new conditions and new demands for fresh thinking. Thank you for inviting me to reflect on these matters, and Happy Birthday, Judge Feinberg.

CHAPTER 14

THE REAL MISMATCH

Slate, May 30, 2013

In the spring of 2013, the U.S. Supreme Court reconsidered the constitutionality of affirmative action in university admissions in the case of Fisher v. University of Texas. *President Bollinger and colleagues at thirteen universities submitted an amicus brief to the Court emphasizing the proven educational benefits of racial and cultural diversity. Some opponents argued that affirmative action created a "mismatch" between "less qualified" applicants and the most academically demanding schools, compromising the students' educational outcomes. Bollinger argued that the real "mismatch" would be between the purported gains of dismantling affirmative action and the actual outcome of a more divided—and diminished—America.*

The distance the United States has traveled in overcoming racial discrimination reflects one of our nation's greatest achievements. Our long struggle toward redeeming the country's founding ideal of equality has been embraced for decades by virtually every institutional sector in American society. But we still have a long way to go. And with an imminent Supreme Court ruling in *Fisher v. University of Texas at Austin*, a case in which a white student has challenged the school's affirmative action policy, we are at risk of historical amnesia, of unraveling a heroic societal commitment that we have yet to fulfill. This is occurring amid a public debate too often framed by a false choice about diversity in higher education.

On university and college campuses, the educational benefits of racial and ethnic diversity are not theoretical but real and proven repeatedly over time. This is a conclusion embraced both by the Supreme Court in its definitive 2003 ruling on the matter, *Grutter v. Bollinger* (as University of Michigan's president at the time,

I was the named defendant), and by my colleagues at 13 schools which, along with Columbia, jointly submitted a brief in the *Fisher* case asserting that "diversity encourages students to question their assumptions, to understand that wisdom and contributions to society may be found where not expected, and to gain an appreciation of the complexity of the modern world." Empirical studies have demonstrated that exposure to a culturally diverse campus community environment has a positive impact on students with respect to their critical thinking, enjoyment of reading and writing, and intellectual curiosity. Indeed, there is a nearly universal consensus in higher education about these benefits.

For many years now, the value of diverse backgrounds and viewpoints has been embraced as essential to the fabric of our major institutions, from the military services to private corporations. Yet there is evidence that, particularly in the private sector, the commitment to racial diversity is eroding. A change in the law at this moment making it harder for colleges and universities to supply racially diverse professional talent could be devastating.

Yet, today, we are hearing the argument that higher education's historic commitment to racial diversity must be replaced by efforts to enroll more children of low-income families at top universities—as though these are mutually exclusive goals. The obvious reply is that the right course is to pursue both. Certainly, at Columbia we take great pride in an undergraduate student body with as high a percentage of low- and moderate-income students as any of our peer institutions and the largest number of military veterans, as well as the highest percentage of African American students among the nation's top 30 universities. Over and over, our students tell us that they come for the intellectual excitement produced by the various kinds of diversity on our campus. In fact, last week at commencement when I addressed Columbia's class of 2013, the loudest applause from the graduates came in response to my suggestion that encountering the diversity of their talented classmates was the most influential part of their experience on campus.

Many other universities and colleges are equally committed to creating educational communities that reflect the widest possible ranges of talent, background, and human experience. For those of us whose job is to preserve and enhance the quality of higher education, the new insistence on choosing either socioeconomic or racial diversity makes no more sense than deciding that we can dispense with exposing our students to Alexis de Tocqueville's *Democracy in America* because they've already read Adam Smith's *Wealth of Nations*. To view them in the alternative is willfully and unnecessarily to impoverish the educational mission.

How, then, has this binary choice, at once voluntary and wrongheaded, come to inform the latest round of American society's recurring discussion of race, discrimination, and diversity?

To start, there is widespread discomfort in this country with government or institutional policies that factor race into decision-making. One concern, a legitimate one, is that this door swings both ways: By opening it in order to use racial identity for benign purposes, such as overcoming past discrimination or promoting diversity, we also make ourselves vulnerable to institutionalized prejudice and bias.

The real challenges intrinsic to gaining diversity's many benefits must not be conflated, however, with the very different and erroneous idea that the United States in 2013 has become a post-racial society, for that surely is not the case. According to the Civil Rights Project at UCLA, the nation's population of African American and Latino K–12 students is more segregated than at any time since the 1960s. One-third of black students and almost one-half of white students attend a primary or secondary school where 90 percent of their classmates are of their race, a trend that shows no signs of abating. Particularly for these students, a college experience of immersion in a diverse student body will be essential if they are to thrive in the multi-racial society they will inhabit as adults.

Another familiar argument for ending affirmative action in higher education, cloaked in new data and rhetoric, is that such efforts put African American and Hispanic students in educational environments where they are over their heads and bound to fail. However well intended, this "mismatch theory" has been widely criticized by scholars for employing flawed methodology. Indeed, if there is one thing that respected studies have shown, it is that both minority and low-income students who went to top-tier colleges do better later in life than equally smart students who did not.

Finally, it is understandable that public concern about high tuition costs and growing student debt has focused attention on maintaining socioeconomic diversity. But let's be candid. The source of increased tuition is not too much racial and cultural diversity; nor will the problem be solved by ending affirmative action in admissions. The real culprit here is the foolish decision of too many state governments to slash investment in public universities, like the one I graduated from, where the vast majority of students in the U.S. receive their college education and find a ladder of opportunity.

America's race problem was centuries in the making and is far from solved. This is not the moment for reversing our collective progress by limiting the ability of institutions of higher education to achieve racial diversity along with class diversity, and other forms as well.

If we were to reverse course, we would find ourselves living in a changed and diminished America, where the number of black and Latino students admitted to the nation's top schools would be much smaller. At California's flagship state universities, UCLA and Berkeley, the percentage of admitted undergraduate students who are African American is still 40 percent below what it was 17 years ago when the state adopted a referendum banning any consideration of race in the admissions process. The figures for admission of Latino applicants are better only because of the huge increase in the proportion of California's high school graduates who are Latino. Make no mistake: This outcome hurts all students on campus by robbing them of the skills learned through exposure to diverse people and perspectives, the very skills needed to succeed in today's global marketplace.

Should the Supreme Court make it impossible or difficult for colleges and universities to continue their affirmative action efforts, many will wonder why we saw fit to abandon our commitment to racial diversity in higher education. At that point the real mismatch will be painfully apparent—the one between the supposed gains brought about by banishing race from college admissions, and the reality produced by such a change.

CHAPTER 15

TO MOVE FORWARD,
WE MUST LOOK BACK

Chronicle of Higher Education, June 27, 2013

On June 24, 2013, the U.S. Supreme Court issued its ruling in Fisher v. University of Texas. Although the Court did not overturn precedent that had established the constitutionality of race-conscious admissions, it remanded the case to the U.S. Court of Appeals for the Fifth Circuit, holding that courts must apply strict scrutiny when analyzing the constitutionality of such admissions policies.

In the immediate aftermath of the Supreme Court ruling in *Fisher v. University of Texas at Austin,* the decision has been understood as upholding the principles underlying affirmative action to create a diverse learning environment, opening the door to a still unknown level of judicial review of admissions practices at colleges and universities, and generally sidestepping the most fundamental questions about diversity and race in America. I want to suggest that this decision, despite its seeming moderation, should also serve as a call to action.

Alone among the justices, Clarence Thomas tied the *Fisher* case to the larger historical and societal context in which affirmative action was born, albeit in a way that I find to be profoundly wrong. In his passionate concurring opinion, Justice Thomas reminded us of what is at stake and of the need to offer a countervailing view. His provocative claim that there is "no principled distinction between the University's assertion that diversity yields educational benefits and the segregationists' assertion that segregation yielded those same benefits," deserves to be fully considered. For there is a very real principled distinction between the two, and it explains why colleges must be allowed to assemble diverse student bodies if we are to fulfill our educational mission in American society.

Ask any faculty member or administrator of an American college why we are committed to diversity, and the swift and certain reply will be that our students learn better in educational environments that confront them with people who are, or whom they perceive to be, different. Ask the same question of students, as I did at Columbia University's commencement in May, and they will tell you that encountering the diverse backgrounds and experiences of their talented classmates was among the most influential part of their experience on campus.

Probe further as to why, for this purpose, a racially diverse learning community is so valuable, and the answer will be that the past history and current reality of race in America continue to shape experiences and perspectives in powerful ways. To enter into this conversation about the importance of diversity is to contemplate our nation's unique history and its enduring effects on the present. It is a shame that the Supreme Court's deliberations and opinions—and, too often, our own discussions—seem no longer able to reflect on those historical and contemporary realities.

What, then, to make of Justice Thomas's argument that just as "no court today would accept the suggestion that segregation is permissible because historically black colleges produced Booker T. Washington, Thurgood Marshall, [and] Martin Luther King Jr.," it must also be the case that no court today should validate race-conscious admissions policies based on the rationale that they "produce better leaders?"

The first thing to say is that the formulation raises the question of whether the absence of diversity was the source of Washington's, Marshall's, and King's immense intellectual accomplishments.

But more to the point, for the past 35 years, since the *Bakke* decision held that the use of race in admissions was permissible to obtain the educational benefits of diversity so long as it was not in service of a quota system, society has sought to promote the intellectual growth and greater open-mindedness that occur when college students are exposed to classmates different from themselves. And since *Brown v. Board of Education*, in 1954, we have recognized the link between the way we educate our children and our struggle to overcome two centuries of slavery and another hundred years of Jim Crow laws. The nation has a forceful and undeniable interest in this objective. The suggestion that there is no difference between this multilayered societal commitment and the benefits to be derived from segregated environments is divorced from historical reality.

And our great system of higher education does not stand alone in this view. Virtually every institutional sector in the nation concurs with what higher education has done to assemble racially and culturally diverse enrollments. Reprising what they had done a decade earlier in *Grutter v. Bollinger*, the nation's leading corporations submitted an amicus brief in *Fisher* in support of the University of Texas. The companies identified the ability to hire graduates from diverse campus environments as a "business and economic imperative." Obviously, they will not be able to achieve their own goals if we do not produce graduates with the capacity to work across perceived and real divides within our institutions.

The altered legal landscape established by *Fisher* raises consequential questions about what is required by the Supreme Court when it holds that lower courts must be satisfied that "no workable race-neutral alternatives would produce the educational benefits of diversity." Will courts demand that race-neutral plans first be implemented and found wanting? (I suspect not.) What data must be analyzed by universities in reaching these judgments?

As the answers to those questions emerge, we will continue to hear the arguments made prominent in recent months by the critics of affirmative action. Chief among those is that we should dispense with race-conscious affirmative action in favor of preferences for the children of low-income families.

This, of course, is a false choice, because we should and do embrace both kinds of experiences and because, in truth, unless we pursue both independently, we will not succeed in getting either one. At Columbia, as at most of our peer institutions today, admissions officers value a kaleidoscope of talents and nontraditional backgrounds, including those possessed by military veterans, artists, and individuals who have overcome the obstacles of geography or family circumstance. We are proud that we have been able to achieve high levels of both socioeconomic and racial diversity.

To be sure, at a time of growing inequality in our society, we all should acknowledge legitimate concerns about the high tuition costs and growing student debt that are responsible, at least in part, for the attention to socioeconomic diversity. But as both a graduate and a former president of a public university, I know that the source of increased tuition is not the pursuit of racial and cultural diversity, as some argue. It is, at least in large part, the fact that too many state governments have, for too long, slashed their investment in the public universities that are the ladders of opportunity in our society.

Two months from now, all of us in higher education will welcome new and returning students to our campuses. I suspect that the most common message we convey will be about the opportunities for learning that are available because of the diversity of the students and the faculty who will teach them.

But few, if any, of us will go on to describe the origins of that diversity and the social context in which it arose and exists today. Fewer still will explain the connection between the educational benefits we rightly extol and the legacies of racial and other injustices that mar our ability to say we live by the ideals we subscribe to in the Constitution. If we want our educational institutions to retain their distinctive and irreplaceable value to society, it is essential for us to make that connection.

With *Fisher* we have achieved a further cementing of Supreme Court precedents for the constitutionality of affirmative action in higher education. What we have not achieved, and need desperately to have, are more decisions with heart—conveying the essence of why it matters to the broader moral and social needs of the nation.

CHAPTER 16

SIXTY YEARS LATER,
WE NEED A NEW *BROWN*

New Yorker, May 16, 2014

On April 22, 2014, in its ruling on the case of Schuette v. Coalition to Defend Affirmative Action, *the U.S. Supreme Court upheld the right of Michigan voters in a 2006 referendum to enact a constitutional amendment prohibiting "all sex-and race-based preferences in public education, public employment, and public contracting." This state ban effectively ended the University of Michigan's affirmative action policy that the Court had upheld in its 2003* Grutter v. Bollinger *decision.*

Sixty years ago this Saturday, on May 17, 1954, a unanimous Supreme Court held that state segregation of black schoolchildren was unconstitutional. *Brown v. Board of Education* marked a signal moment in American history—not only constitutional history. In the turbulent years that followed, the nation struggled to come to terms with the legacy of centuries of mistreatment of African Americans and other minorities. But, while race was at the core of *Brown*, the decision affected virtually every aspect of American life: the criminal-justice system, the meaning of citizenship and democracy, and even freedom of speech and freedom of the press. The decision was not just about schools; it was about the nation living up to its own professed ideas. By addressing, and dealing with, racial injustice, the Supreme Court spoke to every sector of society—and every sector responded.

By the nineteen-seventies, almost all selective colleges and universities in the United States had adopted policies of affirmative action, and began to consider applicants' race or ethnicity, in order to achieve a "critical mass" of African Americans, Hispanics, and Native Americans in their student bodies. These efforts, which took place at around the same time that the doors of academe were more fully opened to women, radically changed the composition of student bodies. Other institutions, including the military and businesses, made similar efforts to diversify their personnel. The effect on modern American life was spectacular, and one of the most consequential transformations was a new and shared acknowledgment of America's racial history, and the pervasive and lingering impact of that history right up to the present day.

But, as the third post-*Brown* generation comes of age, there are reasons to be alarmed that this shared understanding no longer exists—and reasons to fear that the noble dream expressed in *Brown*, of creating an inclusive and integrated society, is on the precipice of being forgotten.

The beginning of that dream's decline can be traced to 1978, and Justice Lewis Powell's famous opinion in the Supreme Court's *Bakke* decision—the first case to consider the constitutionality of affirmative action. The medical school at the University of California, Davis, had set aside a specified number of seats for historically disadvantaged minorities. The policy was successfully challenged, with the Supreme Court holding that a system of "quotas" was impermissible. Powell's opinion, which provided the controlling guidance about the legality of admissions policies, made a fateful distinction. If the goal of such policies was to help "certain groups . . . perceived as victims of 'societal discrimination,' " they would violate the Constitution, because this "imposes disadvantages upon persons . . . who bear no responsibility" for earlier discrimination.

Powell's opinion forbade polices that helped members of "relatively victimized groups at the expense of other innocent individuals." On the other hand, he said, universities could consider race and ethnicity to create "a diverse student body" and an atmosphere of "speculation, experiment and creation" for the purpose of training leaders "through wide exposure to the ideas and mores of students as diverse as this Nation of many peoples."

Every university dean and president knows Powell's distinction and follows it scrupulously; every university general counsel stands ready to insure they do. Rather than linking considerations of race in admissions to the ongoing effect of centuries of mistreatment, we speak vaguely—but passionately—about the educational benefits of diversity in every speech, publication, convocation, and commencement ceremony.

By de-coupling "diversity" from the realities of race past and present, the rationale for these admissions policies sounds hollow and banal—a shortcoming that is not lost on the young people we educate or the broader public we should inspire.

Where university presidents fear to tread, public officials are even less bold. Very few politicians will incur the political risk perceived to accompany outspoken statements on these issues. Since his election, President Barack Obama has spoken infrequently enough about race that we can quickly catalog the times he has done so with true passion: the "beer summit" after the controversial arrest of Henry Louis Gates; his response to the recent racist comments made by Donald Sterling, the owner of the Los Angeles Clippers; and, most notably and most powerfully, his unscripted remarks after the acquittal of George Zimmerman in the killing of Trayvon Martin.

As a result, our public debate on affirmative action—and, more broadly, on race in America—now consists of bloodless legal pronouncements disconnected from history, aberrational constitutional law, vague claims that we live in a "postracial" society, and unsupportable scholarship. In *Grutter v. Bollinger*, the first Supreme Court decision upholding the constitutionality of affirmative action in higher education, Justice Sandra Day O'Connor added a qualification unseen in any other major constitutional interpretation. Noting that, in the preceding generation, "the number of minority applicants with high grades and test scores has indeed increased," she went on to say, "We expect that 25 years from now, the use of racial preferences will no longer be necessary to further the interest approved today." (I was president of the University of Michigan and led the legal and public defense of the university's policies.) The close, 5–4 decision was a substantial victory for colleges and universities across the country. Unfortunately, O'Connor's time limitation, completely foreign to constitutional jurisprudence and built on a suspect scaffolding of wishful thinking, made clear that *Brown*'s legacy was in serious jeopardy.

Of late, an appealing fiction that aids and abets our amnesia about race in America has taken hold among some progressives: on this view, our greatest social problem today is inequality of wealth and income, and so admissions to colleges and universities should take this as their focus. It is further believed, wrongly, that this would produce racially diverse student bodies without requiring us to consider race and ethnicity. While we should indeed make special efforts to admit the children of low-income families, those efforts alone, given the demographics of the United States, would favor white students over minorities. In states where affirmative action has been banned, evidence shows that consideration of income alone cannot approximate the critical mass of black, Hispanic, and Native American students able to benefit a student body. It should also be pointed out that there is important value in having students from all sectors of American life, not just those from low-income families. We value geographic, international, and experiential diversity, too, and no one ever suggests that university student bodies would be well served in those respects by limiting our concern to a population of financially needy applicants.

The cost of this unwillingness to acknowledge the continuing centrality of race in the United States is pervasive and dispiriting. Look at the facts on the ground. Six decades after *Brown*, forty percent of black and Hispanic children attend severely segregated primary or secondary schools—those in which ten percent or fewer of their classmates are white. The reality of effective segregation is, of course, deplorable. But what makes one's heart sink is the fact that so often things are worse today than a generation ago. In 1988, there were two thousand seven hundred and sixty-two schools in America with white populations of less than one percent; today there are six thousand seven hundred and twenty-seven.

As Pro Publica's recent story "Segregation Now," about Tuscaloosa, Alabama's Central High School, made devastatingly clear, "the city's schools have seemed to move backwards in time" since a federal judge, in 2000, released them from a court-ordered desegregation mandate. A black teenager like D'Leisha Dent, who is featured in the article, today no longer attends the kind of racially integrated high-quality school that her mother did—but a separate, struggling school serving the poorest part of the city. It is ninety-nine percent black, effectively as segregated as the one her grandfather attended a half century ago. As the writer, Nikole Hannah-Jones, reported:

"Tuscaloosa's schools today are not as starkly segregated as they were in 1954, the year the Supreme Court declared an end to separate and unequal education in America. No all-white schools exist anymore—the city's white students generally attend schools with significant numbers of black students. But while segregation as it is practiced today may be different than it was 60 years ago, it is no less pernicious: in Tuscaloosa and elsewhere, it involves the removal and isolation of poor black and Latino students, in particular, from everyone else. In Tuscaloosa today, nearly one in three black students attends a school that looks as if *Brown v. Board of Education* never happened."

While public primary and secondary schools are becoming resegregated, we have seen the rise of various methods within states, primarily ballot initiatives, to end affirmative action in higher education. Popular referenda on important public issues are a strange form of democratic decision-making under the best of circumstances—but, when you take a highly charged issue such as affirmative action, and you ask whether "racial preferences" should be disallowed, we know the outcome in advance. This is what happened in California with Proposition 209, in 1996, and in Michigan after the *Grutter* decision. Four other states (Washington, Nebraska, Arizona, and Oklahoma) have also amended their constitutions in this way.

Last month, in *Schuette v. Coalition to Defend Affirmative Action*, a majority of the Supreme Court held these popular referenda constitutional. The decision sparked a widely noted debate between those in the majority and Justices Sonia Sotomayor and Ruth Bader Ginsburg, who, in dissent, argued forcefully that to single out particular policies that help disadvantaged minorities and make those policies more difficult to adopt is inconsistent with earlier civil-rights precedents involving fair-housing ordinances and school-busing policies designed to integrate public schools. In her personal and candid opinion, Sotomayor suggested that refusal to recognize the reality of race only reinforces the discrimination that continues to afflict American life.

Now these six states, along with four others banning affirmative action through executive order and legislation, have provided an end-around method of opposition that surely will be seized and exploited. As this happens, experience shows that the gains for minorities in higher education are quickly lost. In both 2011 and 2012, not long after the Michigan constitution was amended through popular referendum, African American students made up only 2.8 percent of the University of Michigan Law School graduating class. This marked a sixty percent drop from the average proportion of black Law School graduates prior to the state's constitutional amendment, and it represented the lowest percentage at the University of Michigan since the late nineteen-sixties. In the University of California system, only 5.3 percent of business-school students enrolled in 2012 were underrepresented minorities, less than half the national average at business schools, despite California's notably diverse population.

The first step to reversing this tide is to bring context to the issues at stake: there are countless policies, attitudes, and persistent practices in American life that had their genesis in an earlier era, and yet still remain partially or fully intact, prolonging the evils of the past. They are largely invisible yet powerfully shape our society. Consider, for example, the funding of our public schools through local property taxes. This foundational reality of American life could be different, but in 1974, by a 5-4 vote, the Supreme Court declined to hold the system unconstitutional. The same general critique applies to the way we establish metropolitan boundaries, determine zoning ordinances, and plan roads, highways, and public transportation.

At the time *Brown* was decided, the United States was in the process of implementing one of the largest government-led social transformations in human history, transferring "more than $100 billion to create a modern middle class . . . a sum more than six times the amount spent on Marshall Plan aid in war-torn Europe." In his extraordinary book, "When Affirmative Action Was White," my colleague Ira Katznelson documents and explains how multiple policies of the mid-twentieth century, from Social Security and the G.I. Bill to new labor laws and home-mortgage assistance, promoted the modern American middle class. But, by design, "most blacks were left out" and, Katznelson concludes, the "Gordian Knot binding race to class tightened." Katznelson leaves us with an unassailable directive: "Without attention to this history today, it is hard to know how to proceed."

So here we are, sixty years after *Brown*, and fourteen years away from Justice O'Connor's wishful ending point: popular referenda have become a favored shortcut to terminate affirmative-action programs; we have a constricted and decontextualized manner of discussing race and diversity in higher education; there is a leaderless public debate about these issues; and primary and secondary education is growing more segregated.

This is a bleak and tragic picture, and it should be a reminder that we urgently need a more serious, realistic, and open discussion about race in the United States today. Along with it, we need a new movement like the one that led to *Brown*—before it is too late, and the issue vanishes beneath another cycle of inattention.

This movement, we know from past experience, can be led from the middle of the political spectrum. During the *Grutter* lawsuit, as the University of Michigan faced wide public skepticism and I struggled to enlist effective allies, it was former President Gerald Ford, a proud Michigan alumnus, who responded to my request that he write about affirmative action, and who first stood up for our case. Ford appealed to the common decency of most Americans from his own personal experience. Writing in the *Times*, Ford recalled an incident from his days as a college football player, when his close friend Willis Ward, one of the best players on the Michigan squad, withdrew himself from a game at Georgia Tech after the opposing team "reputedly wanted [him] dropped from our roster because he was black." Ford continued: "I have often wondered how different the world might have been in the 1940's, 50's and 60's—how much more humane and just—if my generation had experienced a more representative sampling of the American family." President Ford then quoted his Democratic predecessor, Lyndon Johnson: "To be black in a white society is not to stand on level and equal ground. While the races may stand side by side, whites stand on history's mountain and blacks stand in history's hollow. Until we overcome that history, we cannot overcome unequal opportunity."

Together, Johnson and Ford understood what a current majority of our Supreme Court does not. And, in their different ways, they communicated to the American people what a university president cannot.

The nation's struggle with race may be tiring, but it is not behind us. We need voices from all walks of American life to be raised, urging us to stand together on higher ground, to avoid regressing back to an era of more segregated and more unequal education.

CHAPTER 17

COMMENCEMENT ADDRESS

Columbia University, Low Plaza, May 21, 2014

On behalf of the Trustees and the faculty of Columbia University, it is my very, very great pleasure and honor to welcome all of you to this ceremony to celebrate the graduation of the Class of 2014. Every year we gather in this magnificent academic forum, at this moment unmatched in beauty anywhere in the world, to affirm the achievements of our extraordinary students and to reaffirm the intellectual bonds that connect us to those who have passed through these gates for 260 years and to those who will do so for centuries to come. Sixteen different schools are represented here today, along with our affiliate institutions of Teachers College and Barnard. In a time when life can seem increasingly fragmented and solitary and technological, this glorious ritual, in this utterly unique spot on the planet, seems all the more remarkable and thrilling.

This is a day that is all about the graduates and about what you've earned—earned through endless and mostly foggy hours of study; earned by overcoming again and again your natural inclination for procrastination, following the principle of just-in-time, which means waiting until the last moment to study for exams and write papers (although it's a well-known fact that the smarter you are the more you tend to procrastinate); you have earned all this through sacrifice of something we call sleep, not to mention nutrition and personal hygiene; and earned by carrying on in those inevitable moments of low self-doubt.

While this occasion is about you, there are also a few people here today who've contributed mightily to your getting to this delightful point in life and whom you'll never be able to thank enough. I can assure you that nothing focuses the mind like the successes and disappointments of one's own children. And, as much as we, your faculty, feel deep affection for you, nothing can compare to the pure adoration of your parents and families. Please, take this opportunity to thank them.

Today we mark, and we celebrate, what in all likelihood you will come to see as one of the defining experiences in your lives—your years of education here at Columbia. I hear this from alumni all the time—how their Columbia experiences were transformational for them. In a surprising number of instances, they also add how this is where they met their spouses, partners and best friends in life, typically right here on the steps of Low under the bewitching eye of *Alma Mater*.

By tradition, Columbia does not have an outside speaker at this grand occasion, when we officially confer your degrees, only the University President. So, let's just get one thing clear, getting disinvited isn't an option. And it shouldn't be on any other campus either.

Today I want to talk to you about the world to come and about the role of universities in that world. As we naturally take stock of what you've accomplished, think about the relationships you've formed, the talents you've discovered, it's also a moment to imagine what your future will hold and what the world will be— both of which intersect, because what we will be always depends to a significant degree on what reality calls on us to be.

Commencement has a magical quality of lifting up our line of sight and letting us view our lives across a wide swath of time. When we imagine what your world will be like, over the next half century or so, we get a better view of what our own world has been like, and then we see better the worlds of our parents and grandparents and families. When you see it that way, you realize that you can better grasp the course of history and its discrete eras through the people you have actually known, across a span of about two centuries—a long time, indeed. Commencement, in other words, vastly expands our vision of where we have come from and where we are going.

Now, as I think of the world ahead for you, it would appear that the defining element will be the exponential increase in the intimacy, the inter-relationships—of all of humanity. We seem to be becoming closer by the day. All across the planet, people are congregating and meeting in massive cities, the things we make and consume are made and consumed everywhere, we now exchange information and ideas simultaneously on the first ever truly global communications system, and we are always flying about to see one another. Everyone, of course, wants to come to New York City, and, as reflected in our admissions data, wants to enroll in Columbia University in the City of New York.

While many of our grandparents started out in small towns and on farms and occasionally sent telegrams, our parents traveled around in cars and listened to the radio and then later, television. My generation lived in multiple places in the United States, had more television channels and toured the world. Your world is wondrous in comparison. Basically, as far as I can tell, you will live everywhere, know everything, and talk to everyone. Yours will be the biggest world ever invented—and yet also the smallest. And, like it or not, your fates will be more intertwined with those of all humanity than ever before—for good or ill, depending on how you handle it.

There are already many momentous issues that come with this trajectory of integration—environmental changes and threats, economic instability, unfairness in the distribution of wealth, privilege and the conditions of work. But our biggest challenge, by far, is overcoming our massive ignorance about each other, about the histories we bring into the present, the cultures that sustain our societies over time, about the values we hold dear. The integration of the world is moving rapidly beyond the mere transactional and becoming very personal, putting us exactly at the point where understanding each other is imperative. And we're unprepared for that encounter.

Now, there are many, many reasons why great universities are important in the world. But none is more important than helping us develop the skills and capacities of understanding other peoples, other perspectives. Every part of the university does this, but here the humanities and our great undergraduate curriculum stand out. Listening carefully, putting aside one's preconceptions, always being on the lookout for when you're suddenly puzzled because that's often where insight is to be found, building up through continuous practice our imaginative strength to pretend actually to be someone else, if just for a moment—all these and other capacities are so hard to do well and yet so essential now.

Too much of the world is organized around a goal of simply maximizing the collection of competing self-interests—international organizations are built around the nation state each with its self-interest, corporations are built around maximizing profits, and so on. This is normal and to be expected. Cooperation is good, but sharing your lives together is better. And, in your more intimate world, nothing will ever work well without, first, a deep and sympathetic awareness of the needs, desires, values, aspirations, and the ever-present, ever-elusive sense of dignity that together play out so differently with peoples around the world and, second, a commitment to finding a life together structured around deep mutual understandings and shared values wherever they can be found. This is the prime skill-set of universities, especially Columbia.

Let me give an example. The Edward Snowden case marks your time here at Columbia, in the same way that the Pentagon Papers case marked that time for my generation. Recently, *The Guardian US* and the *Washington Post* received the Pulitzer Prize (awarded right here at Columbia) for their news reports using some of Snowden's trove of classified information detailing the massive system of NSA surveillance within the United States and in foreign countries. As we know, this has become a major national and global firestorm, which followed not long after Private Manning released classified information to Wikileaks and then to several major newspapers. Snowden (who is about the same age of many of you here) has asylum in Russia, and our graduate Attorney General Eric Holder has indicated Snowden may face criminal prosecution for taking and then disclosing secret government documents to persons not entitled to receive them. (Our other alumnus, President Obama, hasn't ruled out a prosecution.) There have been no threats, however, of similar actions against the newspapers.

Now, this affair raises a classic and perennial question for every society: namely, how do you balance the interests of the public in having a well-functioning government, in which some degree of secrecy is obviously necessary, and the interests of the public in knowing about what its government is doing so that the public can decide whether it likes it or not?

The answer in the United States is very complex and messy. It is basically this: The government can classify information and operate in secret as it wishes. It has no constitutional obligation to inform the press or the public about what it's doing, even though we know for a fact it will over-classify information and exceed all reasonable needs of secrecy. Government employees may choose to leak information they think the public should know about, but, if they do, and are found out, they may be fully prosecuted, even though they may be absolutely right about the public interest in having this information.

The press, on the other hand, may knowingly receive this information and publish it, and the government may not stop it from doing so (absent proof of extraordinary harm to the nation). This is the holding of Pentagon Papers. However, it has not been decided whether the government may prosecute the press after the fact of publication, an ambiguity in the constitutional interpretation of the First Amendment that clearly leaves journalists with at least some sense of jeopardy. As a matter of historical practice, however, two facts are important:

established news organizations have almost always consulted the government in advance of publication about potential national interests at stake, and refrained from publication when persuaded, and, second, the government has never pursued a prosecution of the press to test its powers under the First Amendment.

To some, this system seems pure madness and dangerously chaotic, too risky for government secrets or too un-protective of leakers and the press. To others, it shows the utility of experience over logic and the genius of disorder and ambiguity. But one would, I think, have to say that up to now this unruly system has worked reasonably well, in the sense that there have been no major breaches of national security and the public has been kept reasonably informed.

But now there are three points to raise:

The first is a question, whether you will need to change this system because the facts on the ground have changed. The amount of government secrets is growing exponentially; leakers can do more harm because computers make it a lot easier for them to leak; and the recipients of leaked information (like Wikileaks) do not in any sense have a stake in the well-being of the nation. Whether these are material facts calling for a different constitutional and policy accommodation will be for your generation to decide.

The second is an observation about how this very major issue fits in the new world. Until recently, this has been largely a matter of internal national dilemma. Now, it's a global issue to be discussed and resolved globally. Leaks of the Snowden variety, of which there will be more in the years ahead, involve secrets of other societies too. That means their laws and policies may be invoked against leakers and the people and organizations that publish the leaks. Moreover, we now have a keen and growing interest in other governments and their secrets because their actions, like ours, affect everyone. So, as with climate change, economic regulation, and a host of growing global challenges, this issue demands that we understand each other better and find workable resolutions.

The third point emerges from this realization. Nations all around the world, including those closest in general character to ours, like Britain, have given very different answers to the classic problem of balancing government secrecy and public knowledge. As you see, it is not by any means a simple matter to explain our system. And, surprisingly, it is relatively new, in fact. Our grandparents were the first generation to ever see a Supreme Court decision on the First Amendment, in 1919, and the Supreme Court upheld the very law the government now applies when it prosecutes leakers and would apply against the press if it chose. Our parents saw the evolution of a different understanding of freedom of speech and press. But it wasn't until 1971 and Pentagon Papers that the current system was conceived. Most of our own history, therefore, actually looks more like a lot of other countries do now.

And to explain our system you have to dig deep into our culture, to the remarkable idea that all power should be limited and opposed, in practice as well as in principle; to the radical idea that the public is the true sovereign in a democracy; and to the fundamental belief that a more open, uncontrolled, uninhibited, even at times seemingly chaotic and risky system for freedom of thought and expression will yield insights, creativity, long-term stability, and a life worth living better than any other system.

But now think this: If it's hard to explain our system, with its own mixed history, complex structure, and connection to our deepest values, none of which can be proven in any sense of logic, just think how hard it is going to be for us truly to understand the history, structure and deeper values of other societies on this, or almost any other, issue. Yet, that's where we and you are going to have to do, far better than we can right now.

Let me say this to you finally. You have made our work at Columbia a joy and a privilege. I feel—and I hear this all the time from others—every time I have the opportunity to interact with you, inside and outside the classroom, I feel how extraordinary you are and how proud you make us feel to be part of your educational adventure. I envy the opportunities you will have to shape a world that has so much promise and potential, with huge problems, to be sure, but not like those that brought the world to near collapse and mass destruction as happened over the course of the last century.

It's just a fact that you will be the people to lead in this era. You may now doubt your powers to influence the world's course, but to your parents, classmates and friends, to your teachers and mentors, and to a nation and a world that desperately awaits your arrival, you do have the power and, I hope, understand your great responsibility precisely because of what you've been able to discover here together at Columbia.

Please, also, bear in mind always what a special and unique place Columbia is, in such a great city, and appreciate the role it has to play, not only in the world, but in your own minds throughout your lives.

Congratulations and my very best wishes to you, the Class of 2014.

CHAPTER 18

HOW TO FREE SPEECH: AMERICANS ONLY FIGURED OUT FREE SPEECH FIFTY YEARS AGO. HERE'S HOW THE WORLD CAN FOLLOW OUR LEAD.

Washington Post, February 12, 2015

From 2014 to 2016, President Bollinger launched several Columbia University ini-tiatives to advance the jurisprudence supporting freedom of expression both within the United States under the First Amendment and around the world. These included Columbia Global Freedom of Expression, directed by international human rights leader Agnès Callamard, which established the first online international database of case law on freedom of expression; and later the Knight First Amendment Insti-tute, led by former ACLU deputy legal director Jameel Jaffer, which promotes free speech and press through strategic litigation and research.

W e have been negotiating between the new and the old, the for-eign and the familiar, tolerance and censorship forever. But digital communications and global commerce are remaking the world: Last year, there were more than 1 billion international travelers. Some 2.7 billion people around the world are online. Smartphones and satellite dishes are the symbols of our time, pushing people everywhere to demand more control over their futures, greater openness and more responsiveness from governments.

These trends draw previously separate cultures into contact with one another: Turkish soap operas are popular in the Balkans, and Taiwanese animators skewer Scottish secession efforts. But technologies that convene different cultures do not always help them interact peacefully, as the Paris attacks on *Charlie Hebdo* and the kosher grocery show.

As those tensions rise, governments and reactionary groups resort to nationalism, victimization and suppression to keep foreign or offending speech at bay. The Pew Research Center found that, as of 2011, nearly half of the world's countries punished blasphemy, apostasy or defamation of religion. Russia has just legislated harsher punishments for those guilty of offending religious sensibilities, and violent protests in Pakistan halted attempts to soften anti-blasphemy laws. China employs more than 2 million people to monitor online activity and support government censorship, according to the BBC. And last year, the ownership of Venezuela's oldest daily newspaper, *El Universal*, changed hands under mysterious circumstances, a move accompanied by a much softer editorial stance toward the government. These salvos against freedom of speech and the press force the question: Can the global society emerging today also be a tolerant one?

To Americans, that debate can feel very foreign, especially when it results in Paris-style violence. After all, our respect for First Amendment freedoms is one of the few values that still rises above partisan politics.

In truth, though, the protections for uninhibited expression that prevail in this country are just a half-century old. They were not attained quickly or easily, nor were they simply a product of judicial edict. They became fixtures of the American legal and cultural landscapes because they emerged from larger forces that are visible again today around the world: expanding economic markets, quantum leaps in communications technology and a set of urgent social problems solvable only through previously unavailable levels of concerted action. The way that Americans learned to adapt to changing times, and to tolerate discordant views, shows how others can, too.

Contrary to what most people think, our modern conception of freedom of speech and press is a relatively recent phenomenon—one not fully formed until the 1960s. The first Supreme Court decisions about the meaning of the First Amendment did not come until 1919, and in its debut the amendment did not fare well. World War I and the emergence of Russian communism had spread fear and intolerance in the West: A prominent Socialist, a German-language newspaper editor and Eugene Debs, a frequent candidate for President of the United States, were convicted of crimes for speech that today would certainly be protected. In the opening case, *Schenck v. United States*, Justice Oliver Wendell Holmes, Jr. authored a unanimous decision upholding Socialist Charles Schenck's conviction and gave voice to the memorable (if inapt) analogy that "the most stringent protection of free speech would not protect a man in falsely shouting fire in a theatre and causing a panic."

But this was only the beginning of America's halting evolution into a far more tolerant society. A repentant Holmes and his brilliant new colleague, Justice Louis Brandeis, wrote eloquent dissents in later cases that began to steer our jurisprudence in a different direction, leading eventually to *Near v. Minnesota*, a 1931 decision banning government censorship in advance of publication and establishing the doctrine of "prior restraint," which later allowed this newspaper to publish the Pentagon Papers. In 1940, *Cantwell v. Connecticut* held that an anti-Catholic message was shielded from state interference intended to protect perceived religious sensibilities from offense.

Progress stalled in the 1950s, amid the Cold War and the witch hunts of McCarthyism. In *Dennis v. United States*, the court upheld the convictions of 11 Communist Party leaders for advocating the overthrow of the government. In *Beauharnais v. Illinois*, the court allowed the state to punish the distribution of a leaflet by a white supremacist on the grounds that Illinois' troubled history provided ample reason for alarm about racial violence. A powerful culture of "states' rights" preserved a constitutional policy of deference to local control.

All this was about to change. It was common at the time for judges to elevate state libel protections above the Constitution's guarantee of freedom of speech and the press, inhibiting what many newspapers were willing to publish. In 1964, the Supreme Court overruled one such decision out of Alabama, in *New York Times v. Sullivan*, and declared the "central meaning" of the First Amendment to be the right of citizens to discuss public issues, including criticism of public officials. In this case involving the civil rights movement and one of our national newspapers, the justices unanimously committed America to a realm of expression in which debate would be "uninhibited, robust, and wide-open." *Sullivan* was widely understood, right away, to have established a national norm, and it was followed by numerous decisions expanding on this new sensibility.

But in a broader sense, the court was ratifying sweeping changes already working to turn the United States into a truly national American society (foreshadowing the transition to a global society occurring today). By the time of the *Sullivan* ruling, 90 percent of U.S. families owned televisions, which had been novelties just a decade or so earlier. The government had constructed an interstate highway system, and air travel was becoming much more common. Regional disparities in per capita income fell, reflecting the emergence of a national commercial marketplace. Uninvolved white Northerners contended for the first time, thanks to TV news, with the graphic bigotry of Jim Crow, helping to forge a cohesive national culture that contained a growing moral conscience. Traditionally local issues suddenly became national ones. And Americans needed a set of standards to govern the exchange of information and ideas. *Sullivan* and its progeny were merely the capstone to this process, yet the ruling had a huge effect: It gave the United States the strongest freedom-of-expression jurisprudence in the world, perhaps in history.

Of course, the extraordinary protections here did not signal the end of our debates over the First Amendment. Nor do they mean that intolerance and suppression are now alien to American society. In my own world, for instance, protesters pushed a number of colleges and universities to disinvite admirable public servants who were scheduled to deliver commencement addresses last spring. So we should tread cautiously before casting judgment on foreign governments and their people. Still, these are footnotes to a profound, far-reaching ethos that embraces freedom of thought and expression.

The collision of forces we faced (and mostly sorted out) is now evident all over the world. Issues that until recently were matters of local prerogative, such as representations of the prophet Muhammad, are often geographically unconfined. With unrestrained exposure and access, emboldened individuals are making common cause with their fellow citizens, and governments are feeling besieged by their unexpected demands. For now at least, a chief effect of the global forum is to generate resistance from those who perceive the new world as a threat.

Governments whose authority is ebbing have been increasingly brazen in their attempts to silence critics. Turkey used charges of tax fraud and massive fines against a conglomerate of newspapers and TV stations critical of President Recep Tayyip Erdogan's policies. Hungary's government established a media authority to impose restrictions on content deemed inappropriate.

To counter these regressive trends, it is critical that we nurture the norms, laws and institutions needed to support free expression globally. There is a sound foundation on which to build. Article 19 of the Universal Declaration of Human Rights, adopted by the U.N. General Assembly after World War II and subsequently reaffirmed by the nations of the world, unequivocally asserts the freedom of expression and the right to "receive and impart information and ideas through any media and regardless of frontiers." Just as, over the past century, the

First Amendment moved from the periphery of America's civic consciousness to its center, Article 19 must gain a similar familiarity, globally.

The surest way to make this happen is to harness the prevailing international commitment to free markets and a global economic system, which demands the open sharing of information. For example, Washington should signal the economic importance of ideas by developing a new international trade regime that protects journalism, academia and digital information. The administration has already gestured in this direction by urging the World Trade Organization to investigate how Chinese censorship blocks commerce and not just speech.

Next, the U.S. government should insist that regional and bilateral trade pacts commit all parties to the free flow of information and ideas integral to trade and investment. The Trans-Pacific Partnership agreement being negotiated by the U.S. trade representative, for instance, should contain not only provisions concerning the environment and labor standards, but also vigorous protections for freedom of information and expression. Columbia's own Global Freedom of Expression and Information project is cataloguing international legal precedents on freedom of speech, and next month it will present the first awards for legal attempts to strengthen international norms.

Given the breadth of attacks on speech and the press around the globe, this approach may appear to elevate hope over experience. Yet as tragic and worrisome as setbacks such as Paris are, they are small impediments to titanic forces that must ultimately lead to greater and greater openness. It will, no doubt, take a long time. But the American experience shows that the backlash to new ideas and cultures, now evident in many countries, can be overcome. The yearning for freedom of expression is universal. There is nothing uniquely American about it at all.

CHAPTER 19

WHAT ONCE WAS LOST MUST NOW BE FOUND: REDISCOVERING AN AFFIRMATIVE ACTION JURISPRUDENCE INFORMED BY THE REALITY OF RACE IN AMERICA

Harvard Law Review Forum, April 12, 2016

In June 2015, the U.S. Supreme Court announced an unusual decision: it intended to re-hear the Fisher v. University of Texas *affirmative action case in its upcoming 2015–2016 term. The case was argued before the Court in December 2015, and a ruling was expected before the end of June 2016.*

This academic year has seen college and university students across America calling on their institutions to do more to create campus cultures supportive of African American students and other underrepresented minorities. There have been demands to increase faculty and student diversity, change curricular requirements, and adopt mandatory cultural sensitivity training. There have been efforts to rename buildings, remove images, and abandon symbols associating schools with major historic figures who were also proponents of slavery, segregation, or other forms of racism. As in all tumultuous periods for higher education, these events have provoked useful discussions about fundamental principles and brought to the fore some essential truths.

First, freedom of speech must remain a core value on our campuses, even as it inevitably causes offense. If we believe, as I do, that colleges and universities are defined by their capacity to ensure uninhibited debate and to promote critical thinking, then we cannot abandon that belief in times of controversy.

Second, our pursuit of diversity would benefit from a greater collective awareness of the relationship between today's concerns and historic events recent
enough to have occurred during my lifetime, for without that awareness it is difficult to understand the complexity of race in America.

It would be reasonable to look to the Supreme Court for such guidance: after
all, the modern struggle for racial equality in this country traces back through
judicial pronouncements that forced a rethinking of constitutional principles and
social attitudes. *Brown v. Board of Education* did more than reject over a half century of enforcement of the "separate but equal" doctrine in the context of public
schools. Embracing a construction of equal protection infused with the fundamental ideals and values embedded in the Constitution and the Bill of Rights,
the Court explained to the nation that the promise of equality requires a collective effort to achieve integration. *Brown's* call to end racial discrimination reverberated across both the private and public sectors and reshaped our conceptions
of our communities and our families. And while jurists and legal scholars wres-
tled over defining the particular contours of the Court's reach in directing the
nation toward its goal, *Brown* provided a foundation essential to the civil rights
movement: a powerful acknowledgement of this country's legacy of slavery and
racism and of the lingering and pervasive effects of that past. Yet for many years
now, Supreme Court jurisprudence has conspired to turn our attention away
from our history—and erode our shared understanding—with decisions that
assume the existence of the very colorblind society that we have yet to achieve.
I want to review how we arrived at this place and to begin a discussion about
the consequences.

Readers of this Forum well know that until *Brown* was decided on May 17, 1954,
Plessy v. Ferguson was the law of the land, constitutionally sanctioning discrimination in language that is difficult to read today. With a unanimous decision,
Brown finally abandoned *Plessy's* holding, recognizing that separate was inherently
unequal in a racially stratified society. Federal courts across the nation then set
about doing the work of enforcing desegregation measures. But courts went well
beyond striking down race-based school assignment policies: they supported
voluntary government efforts affirmatively designed to integrate the nation.

Then, on June 28, 1978, in *Regents of the University of California v. Bakke*, Justice
Powell, announcing the judgment of the Court, rejected U.C. Davis's presumed
and historically grounded construction of the Equal Protection Clause as
allowing racial classification by the state to remedy the effects of "societal

discrimination." He favored instead a construction that focused on the Fourteenth Amendment's "universal terms, without reference to color, ethnic origin,
or condition of prior servitude." The medical school admissions policy at issue
was constitutionally impermissible, said Justice Powell, because it gave preferences to "members of relatively victimized groups at the expense of other innocent individuals." Race and ethnicity could be considered, however, to the extent
necessary to achieve an alternate goal rooted in the First Amendment: the creation of "a diverse student body" composed of "students who will contribute the
most to the 'robust exchange of ideas' " for the purpose of training leaders of "this
Nation of many peoples." At its best, Justice Powell's ruling was wrapped in the
idealism of colorblindness and in the concern that, regardless of a corrective or
benign purpose, any race-based classification is "likely to be viewed with deep
resentment." Its effect, however, has been to constrain all that *Brown* aspired to in
this consequential respect: advocates for an integrated America have to content
themselves with talking about the utility of "diversity" and allowable ways to
achieve it. In court briefs and oral arguments, America's historical racism is off
limits.

No jurist will ever have a more acute understanding of the cost of the Court's
ahistorical decision in this matter than Justice Marshall. Having led the litigation strategy producing *Brown*, he witnessed the Court's turn away from those
ideals from within its chambers. Justice Marshall's opinion in *Bakke* expressed
utter disbelief that against a backdrop of nearly two centuries of constitutional
interpretation permitting "the most ingenious and pervasive forms of discrimination," the same Constitution would now be interpreted—only one generation
after *Brown*—to forbid State action aimed at "remedy[ing] the effects of that
legacy of discrimination." Justice Marshall did not mince words in his warning
that the failure of the Court to recognize remedial actions as "a state interest
of the highest order" will "ensure that America will forever remain a divided
society."

The impulse to push our history and its continuing consequences into a more
distant past—and advert to reasoning divorced from present reality—runs deep
in our jurisprudence and across our society. It is almost always expressed affirmatively, passionately, and in high-minded language. Just two decades after the
Emancipation Proclamation itself, the Supreme Court declared in the Civil Rights
Cases that it was time for African Americans to "take[] the rank of . . . mere
citizen[s], and cease[] to be the special favorite of the laws." In 2007, Chief Justice

Roberts offered a similar refrain with his admonition that "[t]he way to stop discrimination on the basis of race is to stop discriminating on the basis of race." That statement, authored in a case considering integration plans in the Seattle and Louisville public school systems, was supported by the Chief Justice's suspect assertion of moral equivalency: "Before *Brown*, schoolchildren were told where they could and could not go to school based on the color of their skin. The school districts in these cases have not carried the heavy burden of demonstrating that we should allow this once again—even for very different reasons."

The "very different reasons" behind the Topeka School Board's insistence on separate but equal and the efforts in Seattle and Louisville decades later to achieve racially integrated school systems were treated by Chief Justice Roberts as an afterthought—a caveat worth noting—rather than the heart of the matter. The symmetry championed by the Chief Justice has a legalistic resonance, but the consistency demanded by the Court is otherwise asked to bear too heavy a weight. Why is the genius of our Constitution inadequate for recognizing the difference between Topeka and Seattle? And why must we look for that answer through an ahistorical lens?

Justice Marshall properly understood that the Supreme Court's change in direction in *Bakke* would sideline the Court from confronting our "sorry history of discrimination and its devastating impact" and that public debate would be diminished without this crucial context. Framed as group-based racial preferences disconnected from any recognition of the deep origins of structural racism in this country that endure through our policies and practices, affirmative action has been increasingly rejected not only by the courts but also by state referenda, legislation, and executive orders. The Equal Protection Clause has become a sword in the service of maintaining the status quo of racial stratification and is no longer a shield protecting the less powerful and the historically oppressed. And the resentment and outrage that Justice Powell sought to avoid engendering has instead festered and grown within those disenfranchised groups. All of these factors are reflected in the persistent claim that we live today in a post-racial society, notwithstanding the familiar scenes from our city streets and college campuses that say otherwise. Were the nation governed by constitutional rulings that continued to recognize as worthwhile the goal of an integrated society identified in *Brown*, it is fair to speculate that misguided assertions of a post-racial America would find much less traction.

The second hearing of *Fisher v. University of Texas* provides the Supreme Court the latest opportunity to review the constitutional rationale for allowing college admissions offices to consider race "holistically" among several factors when assembling a diverse student body. The case was argued last term and, because of the vacancy left by Justice Scalia's death and Justice Kagan's recusal in the matter, now awaits decision by a panel of seven Justices. It is a moment to broadly consider the shape of an alternative jurisprudence neither subservient to popular views nor cabined by damaging precedent—an exercise that need not rely solely on imagination. We can look to a line of concurring and dissenting opinions that run from Justice Marshall in *Bakke* to Justice Sotomayor in *Schuette v. Coalition to Defend Affirmative Action, Integration & Immigrant Rights & Fight for Equality by Any Means Necessary (BAMN)*. Indeed, it is Justice Ginsburg, in her opinions in the companion cases *Gratz v. Bollinger* and *Grutter v. Bollinger*, decided in 2003, who gives us the clearest glimpse of such an alternative.

In her dissent in *Gratz*, Justice Ginsburg cast an unflinching eye on our nation's history and demanded that our Constitution have the flexibility to be both color-blind and color-conscious for the purposes of achieving the integrated society envisioned by *Brown*. And much like the Court did in *Brown*, she flatly rejected the dictates of ever-growing precedent that the same standard of judicial review must apply to all race-based classifications. For Justice Ginsburg, a one-size construction of the Constitution "would be fitting were our Nation free of the vestiges of rank discrimination long reinforced by law. But we are not far distant from an overtly discriminatory past, and the effects of centuries of law-sanctioned inequality remain painfully evident in our communities and schools." Her logic is rooted in the disheartening facts that are evident to anyone willing to take a hard look: in the years since *Brown*, segregation in our public school system, and concomitant disparities in educational opportunities, have not only persisted but have also grown.

Justice Ginsburg was moved to write a separate concurring opinion in *Grutter* to address the unusual twenty-five-year expiration date that Justice O'Connor imposed as a "logical end point" to race-conscious admissions programs. This date was calculated to place *Grutter* at the expected halfway mark between *Bakke* and the elimination of consideration of race in its entirety. Noting the remarkable brevity of the same twenty-five-year time period between the *Bakke* decision and *Brown*'s "end to a law-enforced racial caste system, itself the legacy of centuries of slavery," she argued that an appropriate endpoint cannot be measured in years. Instead, Justice Ginsburg stressed that measures implemented to bring about an integrated society must necessarily be left in place until equal treatment and opportunity are achieved in fact.

Who can say with any certainty how Supreme Court case law would have differently evolved if Justice Ginsburg's opinions had been written on behalf of a majority of Justices? This much, though, seems clear: It is very unlikely that the Court would have twice chosen to hear a case (*Fisher*) where the defendant is a state university system with an admissions policy that, because of extreme resegregation at the secondary school level, primarily relies on a neutral criterion (finishing at the top of your high school class) to achieve diversity. Nor is it likely that a jurisprudence informed by Justice Ginsburg's views and continuing on the path of *Brown* would have featured a virtually unbroken string of white plaintiffs claiming injury from state-sanctioned policies dedicated to greater equality. And while the search for narrowly tailored means and race-neutral alternatives could be expected to be among the issues at stake in a given litigation, those concerns would not have come to define the entire legal playing field in case after case after case. Instead, the Court's jurisprudence might have embraced Justice Sotomayor's sharp counter-position that "[t]he way to stop discrimination on the basis of race is to speak openly and candidly on the subject of race."

The Supreme Court is at its best when it articulates and explains the fundamental values of the nation as embedded in the Constitution, and the Bill of Rights in particular. The path suggested by Justices Ginsburg and Sotomayor reaches for this aspirational role in a way that controlling case law on affirmative action does not. Great decisions, such as *Brown*, elevate a specific controversy into a framework that explains the larger ideals we hold dear as a country. The significance of the Court raising its sights to focus on larger societal interests and enduring values is nowhere more evident than in the evolution of the First Amendment over the course of the last century. Constricted holdings in *Abrams v. United States* and *Whitney v. California* eventually gave way to the minority views of Justices Holmes and Brandeis as fully realized several decades later in *New York Times Co. v. Sullivan*, where we were told that public officials must endure even negligent falsehoods injurious to their reputations because citizens cannot be constrained when exercising the rights and responsibilities of self-government. Viewed from this perspective, the question becomes not whether Justice Sotomayor's call to speak "openly and candidly on the subject of race" leads inevitably either to the stigmatization of African Americans or to greater resentment from whites, but rather whether those concerns should be subordinated to the higher goal of creating an integrated society that has fully come to grips with its history of racism.

To reject Justices Sotomayor and Ginsburg is to contribute to the forces of forgetfulness and amnesia—including disregard for the very real successes achieved through affirmative action thus far—which taken together already function to shield us from the underlying reality of segregation and discrimination that continue to exist. And therein lies what may be the decisive shortcoming of an approach that understands the value of racial diversity only in terms of its educational benefits, without acknowledging the persistent reality of race in America. Such an approach leads, on balance, to what we have today: a greater sense of injustice that comes from the feeling that injustice is being ignored or slighted or denied. In the end, if one set of damages based on perception (stigma or resentment) is being remedied at the cost of creating another set (feeling ignored or slighted), then isn't the better course to insist on a discussion that is uninhibited, wide-open, and fully accountable to the past?

For the moment, at least, the prevailing culture favors individual achievement over collective advancement; it does not help matters that government action is rarely celebrated and market outcomes always are. In such an environment, college admission is seen to be a zero-sum game; preferential treatment is equated with injustice; and thus, there is an unsurprising yearning for achieving the goal of diversity by focusing only on family income. The reality is different. America's demographics combined with the persistence of structural impediments and lingering discrimination mean that focusing exclusively on socioeconomic diversity in admissions is certain to be inadequate.

As we live through a period of dramatic political conflict over filling Justice Scalia's seat and await the results of a frequently unrecognizable presidential election, it is anyone's guess as to whether we are on the cusp of a changed environment, one more hospitable to the values and constitutional interpretation that prevailed from 1954 to 1978. Also uncertain is how the current round of *Fisher* will be resolved by the Supreme Court.

In light of that uncertainty, I want to conclude with a personal observation. I believe deeply that the highest levels of excellence in post-secondary scholarship, teaching, and research exist only in a diverse university or college community. I was proud to lead the University of Michigan in its litigation resulting in a landmark Supreme Court decision recognizing the state interest in promoting these specific educational benefits. As Columbia University's president, I have been asked to steward one of the longest standing commitments to these values in all of higher education. The value of a marketplace of ideas is widely appreciated now, and we generally embrace the mysterious ways in which a diversity of beliefs and perspectives yields better ideas than would emerge from a single vantage point.

Every college admissions committee vigilantly observes the bounds of Justice Powell's diversity rationale for considering race and ethnicity in assembling a class; and every university president and general counsel stands ready to ensure their compliance. We all are sincere when we say we value diversity. But because *Bakke* forced a decoupling of the value of diversity from the realities of race past and present, we are consigned to hollow and banal discussions of its educational benefits in every speech, publication, convocation, and commencement ceremony. The failure of our institutions and of our leaders to continue to remind us, with the passion of the Court in *Brown*, of the larger context for why we must all commit to the value of racial and ethnic diversity robs it of its meaning and, I fear, some of its beneficial effect. Obscuring history and its present-day consequences does not bring us any closer to the ideals of a truly integrated nation. Higher education and all of American society would benefit immeasurably if the Court were to unite in leading a more meaningful discussion of diversity and to rediscover the constitutional basis for this endeavor that was embraced all too briefly in *Brown* and then abandoned in *Bakke*.

CHAPTER 20

COMMENCEMENT ADDRESS

Columbia University, Low Plaza, May 18, 2016

O n behalf of the Trustees and the faculty of Columbia University, it is my very great pleasure and honor to welcome all of you to this ceremony to celebrate the graduation of the Class of 2016. It is our tradition to gather in this magnificent setting, surrounding *Alma Mater*, to affirm the knowledge acquired by our extraordinary students and to recognize their remarkable achievements. You are now intellectually and loyally connected to all those who have been here before you over the past 262 years and to all those who will come for centuries ahead. You represent sixteen different schools, along with our affiliate institutions of Teachers College and Barnard. And each of you here today is forevermore linked to one another through a scholarly bond that is now forged in this very special place at this precise point in time.

While this occasion is about you, there are also a few people here today whom you'll never be able to thank enough. I can assure you that nothing focuses the mind like the successes and disappointments of one's own children. And, as much as we, your faculty, feel deep affection for you, nothing can compare to the pure adoration of your parents and families. Please, take this opportunity to thank them.

Though there is certainly a reassuring and pleasing familiarity in the rituals and trappings of this grand ceremony, it is also the case that each Commencement is distinct—informed by its specific time and the unique features of the world graduates will find upon leaving Columbia. This year, it is fair to say, we gather at a moment when several of the tectonic forces that for decades have shaped modern life for billions of people around the world appear to be shifting, and perhaps abruptly. It is these potential human, societal earthquakes, happening or potentially about to happen, that I want to speak about this morning.

For those who care about freedom of mind, of speech, and of expression; for those who believe the best life is one lived amidst a broad array of beliefs and ideas that make possible a collective quest for human truth; and for those who seek to develop their intellectual capacities for any number of important reasons—to deploy reason for good ends, to appreciate the complexity of life, to know as much as possible what humans have learned over the millennia, to master the art of conversation and civil discussion, to expand tolerance in a world that can never be as we would want it to be—for those who care about these things, this is a disconcerting time.

The continuing appeal of intolerance and the persistent attraction of authoritarian rule are sobering facts of contemporary life. When this mentality prevails in countries with histories of dictatorship, that's one thing. Deplorable as it is, we at least know what we're dealing with. But when it takes hold in established democracies—as it is right now in several democratic nations, perhaps even including our own—we are, by turns, unnerved, mystified, and even shocked. At this moment and in this place, as we come together to celebrate thousands of graduates dedicated to the quest for learning and wisdom—how can we escape asking where the world is truly headed?

The most obvious causes of these trends toward so-called illiberal democracies—a term reflecting democracies being self-destructive—are often said to be tied to the defining realities of modern society: an unstable and rapidly shifting balance of power among nations; globalization of markets, of communications, and of populations; and differential consequences across and within society, enhancing the welfare of some, but undermining the employment, incomes and expectations of others, who are now expressing their frustrations and angers in public forums and at the ballot box. To be sure, these are all important contributors to the state in which we find ourselves.

But what if these warning signals are the product of something still deeper and more profound—a consequence of the changed structure of public thought and discussion itself? What if the very foundation of democracy—a commitment to hearing every voice and viewpoint, and a belief that from the resulting clash of ideas the truth will prevail—what if that core idea is not only no longer valid but actually, and ironically, abetting the abandonment of democracy? The arguments for this disturbing perspective, which we can expect to hear with increasing frequency, are not without force: online social platforms have made it easier for people to insulate themselves from opposing views by providing an inexhaustible supply of opinions corroborating what they already believe. This process of steady reinforcement makes us self-righteous, less tolerant and, eventually, angry when we are confronted by contrary positions.

There is also the technology-enabled habit of skimming news for headlines, which thins out our knowledge and perniciously makes us superficial without realizing we are. But even worse, we are losing the basic norms of civilized behavior. Falsehoods are circulated without correction or consequence, individual privacy is disregarded, and bullying and cruelty towards others seems normal.

These criticisms—taken together and in the context of the rise of authoritarian political movements, where extremes seem to be crowding out the moderate and sensible, the serious and intelligent—cast doubt on our entire system of public discussion. For the moment, it appears that democracy is falling victim to a downward spiral of anemic debate providing fertile soil for intolerance and repression, which, in turn, does further damage to meaningful public discourse, ultimately leading to its collapse.

As powerful as this critique is, there are strong reasons why it is not yet time to despair.

First, it is important to understand that every new communication technology—beginning with the printing press, in the 15th century, and then, in the last century, radio, television and movies—has been greeted not with enthusiasm and protection but with guarded fear and regulation. Virtually all the criticisms being leveled at the Internet are echoes of forecasts of great harm that were made when these earlier technologies suddenly appeared on the scene. There were worries of moral degradation, sedition, opportunities for propaganda and manipulation of public opinion, and all of these fears led to regulations that subsequently were found to have been excessive. Of course, the fact that these fears proved to be unfounded before does not necessarily mean they are false now, in this potentially different context; nonetheless, our history and this consistent overestimation of the harms of new methods of communication, at the very least, ought to make us hesitate and think very carefully before acting to impede the development of still newer innovations and the discussions they facilitate.

Second, the principle of freedom of speech has become perhaps the most widely-embraced civic value in our nation, existing beyond partisanship, precisely because the courts, and then the public, infused this constitutional guarantee with a sophisticated appreciation of human nature. There is nothing naïve about America's conception of this basic right. We champion freedom of expression while recognizing that, for human beings, intolerance is often the very first impulse, but we choose to push ourselves to a higher ideal of what life can be.

Almost one hundred years ago, Oliver Wendell Holmes set forth the first modern articulation of the world we have come to know. To a nation gripped by widespread intolerance and censorship arising from the fears of World War I and the new ideology of Communism, Holmes advocated for the first time the metaphor of the marketplace of ideas as preferable to our proclivities to be intolerant. With open recognition of the troubling side of human behavior, he said:

"Persecution for the expression of opinions seems to me perfectly logical. If you have no doubt of your premises or your power and want a certain result with all your heart you naturally express your wishes in law and sweep away all opposition."

Holmes understood very clearly that free speech is counter-intuitive—an insight that applies to all learning, generally. It takes enormous concentration of effort and dedication to learn, to become educated, to achieve what you are being recognized for today. No one takes exams or writes term papers because that's their first choice about how they'd like to spend their time. We create contexts, the First Amendment and universities being two of the most important, in which we hope to overcome our impulses.

So, when we look at what is happening in today's political environment, we should not despair and wring our hands, as if we're confronting something wholly new and unprecedented. As bad as you might think things are right now, every generation has gone through versions of this—the intolerance around World War I I've just mentioned and the McCarthy era being two examples—and struggled to come through to the other side. Perhaps life online more greatly enables our worst instincts, but before amending our principles, I'd wait for greater proof of that view. This is just the most recent test, which we must work through, just as it is certain future generations sitting here will have theirs.

And this brings me to the third, and last, point. There is an available remedy, even if it is an uncertain cure. For most of the past century, the progress on openness has been bound to the belief that persecuting dangerous ideas comes at too great a cost and turns us into people we don't want to be; all views, therefore, must be given their chance, no matter what we think of them. To be sure, it is a risky enterprise. We choose to live in a wilderness of ideas where we have to fend for ourselves.

The remedy starts with engagement. You cannot stand back and then be shocked at the consequences. You have to expect and prepare for exactly what's happening now. Think of it this way: You've been drafted and there's no avoiding it. It does little good to stand on the sidelines and complain about the state of public debate. But it's also more than just joining the fray and advocating your viewpoint.

What's necessary—but very hard—is to make your own contribution to engaging in genuine public discourse in a way that reflects the deeper values of a tolerant and educated mind. Just as we now say that every nation has a responsibility to protect its citizens, the principle of free speech says you have a responsibility to participate, to protect this core value of our democratic society by exhibiting the qualities of mind and attitude that make the whole enterprise sustainable. This is how freedom of expression and robust debate survive and thrive over time, the only way really.

There is and will be a role for you. I can assure you of one true fact about your lives. There will come a time, probably several, when you will sense that around you the natural impulse to intolerance is rising and that you are in a situation to say or do something against it. It is a certainty that the pressure on you to succumb or go along will be nearly overwhelming. The "logical" nature of intolerance, as Holmes put it, makes it also insidious. It may be on a school board, a social organization, or an election—maybe too, you will run for President of the United States. Our hope is that you will draw strength from your wisdom and experiences gained here at Columbia and that you will stand for what we stand for.

And there is a role for Columbia. We can and should be more engaged than we are with the problems of the world, in the way that only one of the greatest universities in the world can. There is an urgency about the problems we are facing, as a nation and as a world, and there are not many who bring what we do to addressing them. Of course the heart of our enterprise is and must remain fundamental research and advancement of knowledge. But no university can survive, and no society can flourish, unless it aligns itself with the needs of the people. We are justifiably proud of the hundreds of engagements we have with the real world outside these walls. But we can and should do much more, and I hope in the years ahead you will take added pride in the things we have and will accomplish in this domain.

Here, then, is my argument: The rise of the illiberal democracy is just the latest phase of a permanent risk, borne of our natures and built into the premises of the principle of freedom of speech, the search for truth, and the quest for a good life. Better to take it as a given, prepare and be ready for it when it comes, and to deploy the only weapons we have: wisdom about human nature, our impulses and our ideals for ourselves, and the institutions we have structured in response to it. We must draw from within us, as hard as it may be to do so, the values that we strive to live by. This is and will forever remain a vital part of this great university's mission, and one I ask you to embrace as you leave this campus and go out into the world.

Congratulations to the Class of 2016.

CHAPTER 21

AFFIRMATIVE ACTION ISN'T
JUST A LEGAL ISSUE. IT'S ALSO
A HISTORICAL ONE.

New York Times, June 24, 2016

On June 23, 2016, the U.S. Supreme Court, for the second time in three years, upheld the University of Texas's use of affirmative action in admissions. However, the Court also warned that not every such policy in higher education might withstand the strict constitutional scrutiny that must be applied to the use of racial preferences.

The Supreme Court's decision this week in *Fisher v. University of Texas* is a profound relief, and a cause for celebration among those of us in higher education who have long insisted that affirmative action is vital to our schools' missions and to society as a whole.

The ruling means we can continue to assemble diverse student bodies and it has validated college administrators' judgment about the qualities needed to achieve educational goals. More important, the opinion greatly strengthens earlier precedent, set in *Grutter v. Bollinger* in 2003, that race-conscious admissions policies are constitutional.

Yet it's worth remembering the limits of today's affirmative action landscape, even after *Fisher.* The court's landmark 1978 decision in *Regents of the University of California v. Bakke* outlawed quotas but permitted the consideration of race to achieve a diverse student body; in doing so, it stifled deeper conversations in courtrooms and classrooms about why we need affirmative action and what it can achieve. And by severing the connection between affirmative action and our past, the court forfeited the opportunity to inform America's conversation about racial discrimination with the awareness that comes only from understanding history.

Justice Anthony M. Kennedy's majority opinion in *Fisher* slightly opens the door to a broader discussion. He acknowledged that the University of Texas' admissions program, which automatically admits a percentage of the top students at all public high school students in Texas, yields diversity primarily because of the stunning level of segregation in the Texas public school system.

There may be future Supreme Court challenges to affirmative action, as signaled by the passionate dissent Justice Samuel A. Alito Jr. read from the bench, and the strong opposition to affirmative action that remains. If so, the court should acknowledge in those cases the past and present realities of race in America.

The Supreme Court is at its best when it locates a specific controversy within a larger framework that explains our nation's fundamental values and ideals. This can be seen most powerfully by the Earl Warren Court's *Brown v. Board of Education* decision, which went beyond the rejection of "separate but equal" public schools and explained that the promise of equality requires a collective effort to achieve integration. Sadly, despite the fact that *Brown* is the foundation on which affirmative action is justified, a reference to the case is nowhere to be found in the *Fisher* opinion.

For now, universities must operate under the *Fisher* decision, which gives us greater stability. But it also reminds us that colleges have serious legal duties.

A university cannot justify its admissions policies with broad generalizations. Instead, administrators must articulate concrete reasons for pursuing diversity—for example, to prepare students for a diverse society or promote cross-racial understanding on campus. Colleges can establish panels to study whether and why those issues are important to fulfilling their educational goals, as Texas did.

Universities should assess whether these interests can be accomplished through race-neutral means. Schools could analyze what their student bodies would look like if they stopped considering race and instead pursued other initiatives, like increasing financial aid or focusing on socio-economic status. These analyses will position universities to better understand how race-neutral admissions practices would affect their student bodies and to determine whether the changes would be consistent with their mission.

Even if colleges conclude that race-consciousness is necessary at a given time, they cannot assume that it will always be so. They should periodically reassess whether their admissions plans remain legal and effective, and also re-examine every few years whether the conclusions of previous studies remain valid.

But the most important task for universities in the months and years ahead is one that we are uniquely well suited to perform: to help society at large—not only our own campus communities—better understand the painful and still-unresolved historical context within which the need for affirmative action exists. This context includes a public education system that remains nearly as segregated and unequal today as it was at the time of *Brown* more than six decades ago.

Just as universities are capable of seeing whether race-neutral alternatives to affirmative action are available, they can also provide a broader understanding for Thursday's ruling grounded in law, history and social science. We must shoulder both of these responsibilities.

CHAPTER 22

THE NO-CENSORSHIP
APPROACH TO LIFE

Chronicle of Higher Education, September 18, 2016

While debates over academic freedom and free speech on campus have been a constant in recent decades, the year 2016 saw rising concern and public conversation over the issue. Among the high-profile developments that spurred intensified public debate were a controversy at Yale University prompted by concerns over offensive Halloween costumes—which resulted in a popular dean's resignation—and a Gallup-Knight Foundation survey finding that, although students generally preferred that campuses be open environments that encourage a wide range of expression, an increasing percentage supported restrictions on certain types of speech, such as hate speech.[1]

Students at my institution, Columbia University, exist in a world where virtually every human thought ever conceived is open to study, examination, consideration, acceptance, rejection, debate, and analysis. To be sure, we have standards that guide us as we move through this vast wilderness of the human mind—we insist on notions like reason, fact, nonpartisanship—but nothing is out of bounds for intellectual inquiry.

Over the past couple of years, there have been a number of controversies on campuses across the country, including mine, which were all more or less about speech—the speech of fellow students, of residence-hall administrators, of faculty, of institutions through the naming of buildings and the display of pictures, and of outside people invited to the campus. The debate, in part, has been about what to do about speech that was considered offensive or dangerous. Sometimes there were calls for bans on speech and official punishments.

I do not want to discuss any of those specific issues; however, I do want to make two overarching points. The first is about proposals to stop speech from happening on campus, officially or through private acts of disruption. The rules of the road here are very clear. Even though private institutions like Columbia are not subject to the First Amendment since it covers only actions by the state, many of them, including Columbia, have voluntarily chosen to live by First Amendment principles.

The First Amendment as we know it today is not all that old—in a few years the nation will celebrate the 100th anniversary of the first Supreme Court decisions interpreting freedom of speech. Those came in 1919 in a series of cases under the Espionage Act of World War I, and in the process the court affirmed the jailing of the presidential candidate Eugene V. Debs for the crime of opposing the war and draft and for praising those who resisted.

Looking back, it was obviously not an auspicious beginning for the First Amendment jurisprudence we have come to embrace. For while court interpretations have ebbed and flowed in the scope of protection for speech since then, in the past half century we have all come to a pretty clear position that is unique among nations: With few exceptions, speech that is about or relevant to public issues and the search for truth, broadly interpreted, is fully protected against censorship, no matter how offensive or dangerous it might seem to the majority of the citizens of this country.

In this case, what's true for the country is also true for Columbia. We don't ban speech. We don't censor speech. But make no mistake: This is no simple, clear-cut, self-evident principle or policy; in fact, far from it.

You hear a lot of people these days talking as if this were all perfectly obvious and no reasonable person could believe otherwise. I have spent a good part of my life trying to understand why this approach is indeed the right and sound way to structure a society or a university. I can assure you, it is highly complicated. Nevertheless, it is our choice on my campus that students cannot expect the institution to intervene, to stop thoughts or viewpoints many of us may dislike, and deeply so. And we will not let others do what we cannot.

At the same time, we cannot just leave it there. Just because we cannot and will not stop or censor expression does not mean we will or should do nothing; that we are powerless. The burden we impose on ourselves by forgoing censorship is the responsibility to engage the debate. We can express counterviews, and give reasons why the contrary view was wrong, offensive, and dangerous. We can be upset and angry, organize an opposition, ignore or shun a speaker, or deploy humor to deflect injury. We can also listen, reflect, reconsider, and forgive. To say that we can't ban speech is, in a sense, easy. To say what follows next is very, very hard.

This brings me to that second essential point: How students today grapple with ideas, with thoughts and viewpoints in the myriad ways available to them, will determine who they are. Of course, they will never completely resolve this process; it is too complex for rules or clear guides. They will make many errors, and feel embarrassed looking back. Or they will feel proud and hope they can replicate what they did.

Does this open environment, created by the First Amendment for society— and, by extension, for our campuses—allow students to be confident in their beliefs, yet open to alternative perspectives? Courageous when confronting evil, or weak and fearful? Does it encourage them to change their minds when evidence and reason call for a change, instead of being stubborn and myopic about things they just don't like or can't refute?

I hope so. That's the best rationale we have for our no-censorship approach in life. We throw our graduates into the deep waters of that life, and we must make the most of every opportunity we have to prepare them to deal with the world they will confront. This won't always be easy—for us or for those students. We humans are not naturally disposed to be open-minded, to be tolerant, and willing to engage with thoughts that are foreign to us and contrary to our own beliefs and views.

Our natural instinct is to preserve our own ways of thinking, whatever they happen to be. Left to our own devices, we avoid discourse, we prefer to associate with those who reinforce our own ways of thinking, and we fear the uncertainty of not knowing what or how to believe.

But in the academic world, our basic intellectual inquiry emphasizes habits of mind that we think increase the odds that we will discover new ideas and truths. We stress being able to suspend our beliefs, to embrace self-doubt, to take joy in learning that we were wrong, to welcome knowing what is not true as another step toward knowing what is true, to be articulate about ideas, to relish complexity, and to use reason while knowing its limits.

To some extent, this commitment to constant self-reflection can make us seem ill-suited for the world outside, which too often elevates voices that are loudest and most sure of themselves. Yet our essential mission remains to invite students to join us in these special qualities of intellect that never stop questioning, whether it's society's conventional wisdom or their own beliefs. After all, it may be their only chance in life to see what's possible with such a truly open mind.

CHAPTER 23

OUR SPIRITUAL PLANK

Remarks at the Manhattanville Campus
Dedication Ceremony, October 24, 2016

In 2016, more than a dozen years after it was first proposed and planned, Columbia University dedicated its new seventeen-acre campus in Manhattanville, its most significant expansion in more than a century. Located slightly north of the historic, cloistered campus in Morningside Heights, the open and environmentally sustainable new campus was designed to welcome and benefit the local Harlem community while also providing academic space necessary for Columbia to remain among the world's great research universities. The first of these new spaces that would provide common ground for interdisciplinary research, teaching, and civic programming was the Jerome L. Greene Science Center, housing the Nobel Prize–winning researchers of the Zuckerman Mind Brain Behavior Institute.

On this morning, October 24, 2016, we assemble on this little square, at the feet of these two nearly finished and magnificent academic buildings, to mark the moment of inception of the new campus of Manhattanville—the most transformational expansion of Columbia University since the dedication of the Morningside Heights campus in 1896. In addition to these structures, housing the Zuckerman Mind Brain Behavior Institute and the Lenfest Center for the Arts, three historic buildings (Prentis, Studebaker, and Nash) are already homes to University programs and activities.

Within the next five years, three additional buildings (The Forum), and two buildings of the Business School (Henry R. Kravis Building and Ronald O. Perelman Center for Business Innovation) will rise from their foundations, which we can see right now from this spot. Two more, one focusing on world issues and the other on new areas of exciting discovery in engineering and data science, are in advanced stages of dreaming.

Altogether, within a mere six years, there will be some six thousand Columbia faculty, students, and staff inhabiting this now somewhat ghostly site, all busily going about their lives and taking for granted what it took so many some fourteen years to create—which is exactly as it should be. And there will be countless interactions with our neighbors in the surrounding communities, from educational offerings to health centers to artistic engagements and beyond. Thousands of new employment opportunities will become available. (Still more—now counting eleven—buildings over the remainder of the century will complete the campus.)

In an era when many people are raising concerns about cities becoming superficial playgrounds for the wealthy, or static museums of their former vital selves, preserved in amber where nothing new is imagined, or created, or made or built, Columbia University's presence here in Manhattanville, a project of such scale and location in the urban core—something utterly unique in the experience of modern American higher education—bespeaks an opposite reality—a continuity of "making things," from light manufacturing of the late nineteenth and early twentieth centuries to the acts of discovery, transmission, and implementation of knowledge so defining of this and future centuries. From one factory to a new kind of factory, as it were.

Columbia University has a long and highly distinguished history, with origins predating the formation of the very nation it now serves (and even the birth of its presently most famous graduate, Alexander Hamilton). Established in 1754 in Lower Manhattan, where the island is "washed by waves, and cooled by breezes, which a few hours previous were out of sight of land," as fellow Manhattanite Herman Melville wrote in *Moby Dick*, Columbia has forever fulfilled its elemental human need, as Melville further put it, to "get as nigh the water as . . . [one] possibly can without falling in." And, so, the University has built its ship along the water's edge, from Morningside Heights to Baker Field (in 1923) to our medical and health sciences campus in Washington Heights (in 1928) to the Lamont Doherty Earth Observatory in the 1940s. Now the addition of the Manhattanville campus, both physically and intellectually, must become our link—our spiritual plank—joining them all together into one seaworthy vessel.

I want to say only a few words about universities. Universities are dazzling institutions, the proof residing in their unique longevity and in their astounding production of new knowledge over time. They are also the strangest of institutions, a standing violation of every rule and rational expectation about how successful human organizations should be composed, which makes their success seem all the more brilliant and, in a way, dangerously satisfying. All that, however, does not mean we have arrived at a state of perfection in what we are or, even if we were able to become perfect at what we do, that we are all we might be. The prospects for advancement in human understanding are forever evolving, and so are the needs of humanity, which, in turn, must shape the nature and character of our mission to serve the public interest.

A truly great university, and Columbia is a truly great university, will continually ask itself whether it must change the ways in which it thinks and the ways in which it serves. It is my personal opinion that the intellectual frameworks we have inherited are not presently in proper alignment with the most important human issues and problems facing the world today and that, even if that is not true, the extraordinary needs of the world right now constitute an urgent and irresistible call for universities to become more directly involved than we have in many years with the implementation of the knowledge and values we so zealously foster and protect. Be that as it may, the period of the unfolding of this new campus in Manhattanville should be a time in which we demonstrate that courage and confidence in ourselves to re-evaluate what we take to be important and the roles we should assume in the world.

I have said enough. It is a truism of life that the more important the moment the fewer the words the better. Respectful silence, or at most murmurs or chants or, best of all, music, speak more to the magnitude of the occasion than our ordinary words and sentences ever can. So I only say this: For this noble institution, today is a time of high celebration and gratitude, of optimism and eagerness to be better than we have ever been.

Thank you.

CHAPTER 24

COMMENCEMENT ADDRESS

Columbia University, Low Plaza, May 17, 2017

On behalf of the Trustees and the faculty of Columbia University, it is my very great pleasure and honor to welcome all of you to this ceremony to celebrate the Class of 2017. It is our tradition to gather in this magnificent setting, surrounding *Alma Mater*, to affirm the knowledge acquired by our extraordinary students and to recognize their remarkable achievements. You represent 16 different schools, along with our affiliate institutions Teachers College and Barnard. All of you are now intellectually and loyally connected to those who have been here before you over the past 263 years and to those who will follow for centuries to come.

This day is all about the graduates and about what you've earned—earned through endless and mostly foggy hours of study; earned by overcoming again and again your natural inclination for procrastination, living by the principle of just-in-time, which means waiting until the last moment to study for exams and write papers (even though it's a well-known fact that the smarter you are the more you tend to procrastinate); earned through sacrifice of something we call sleep, not to mention nutrition and personal hygiene; and earned by persevering in those inevitable moments of self-doubt.

Now while this occasion is about you, there are a few people here today who have contributed mightily to your getting to this point in life and whom you'll never be able to thank enough. I can assure you that nothing focuses the mind like the successes and disappointments of one's own children. And, as much as we, your faculty, feel deep affection for you, nothing can compare to the pure adoration of your parents and families. Please, take this opportunity to thank them.

Because a graduation signifies such an important moment of achievement and transition in life, it leaves a deep impression on our minds. We also tend to remember vividly the events that were occurring in the world at the time. It is common to hear people say, "I graduated when such and such happened." Sometimes, what is recounted is fairly momentous; usually, less so. For those of us here today, I doubt that we will ever have trouble remembering what is happening in the world now, or the seriousness of the events coalescing in 2017.

Just how significant a turning point in world history this will be remains to be seen. But there appears little reason to doubt that this nation and much of the broader world is at an historic juncture. Some see ominous horizons, while others see reason for hope.

We read and hear daily (here and abroad) about the rise of populist movements, all rooted in nationalist impulses resistant to the continuation of globalization and multilateralism in its many forms—economic (e.g., trade pacts and treaties), political (e.g., the European Union), communications (e.g., the Internet), movements of people (e.g., refugees), and so on. Often this results in the embrace of authoritarian political figures. For many, this represents a foreboding reality. For others, it carries the promise of bringing discipline to growing disorder and awakening stagnant political and social systems desperately in need of fresh ways of thinking.

I believe passionately that we need new and better ways to address the myriad challenges facing our country and the world, but, for what it's worth, I share the first perspective—viewing these developments with profound concern.

Most of the debates taking place right now are about changes to particular policies: health care, tax reform, immigration, and national security. But, as is always true, the most important changes are and will be to the character of our deliberative process, the nature of the public forum, and our capacity for self-government. You don't need to be a free speech expert to know the following fundamental truth: In the end, we, as individuals or as a society or international community, are what we think, what we speak, and how we interact with one another. The outcomes of our public discourse, while important, follow rather than lead the life we live. So, it is right to ask, what is happening to our collective thinking and to the public forum in this new era?

My answer is that what is happening is not good, and it's actually very dangerous. There are many things I could focus on here, but one concern I would single out is how the new politics are characterizing and demonizing all things "foreign." There are a host of perfectly legitimate differences of opinion and responses when it comes to how to address major challenges like climate change, international trade, terrorism, the integrity of national elections, or privacy and hate speech in a digital age. The problem, however, is not with the fact that there are many hard questions or a vigorous debate about them, but with the emergence of, and stoking of, a state of anger and fear surrounding them. Genuine issues always undergird and help to mask the mental condition of fear, but, when it arises, it introduces a very threatening element into our debates and our world.

Now, I know it is too much to expect of political discourse that it mimic the measured, self-questioning, rational, footnoting standards of the academy; but there is a difference between robust political debate and political debate infected with fear or panic. The latter introduces a state of mind that is visceral and irrational. In the realm of fear, we move beyond the reach of reason and a sense of proportionality. When we fear, we lose the capacity to listen and can become insensitive and mean.

Our Constitution is well aware of this fact about the human mind and its negative political consequences. In the First Amendment jurisprudence established over the past century, we find many expressions of the problematic state of mind of fear. Among the most famous and potent is that of Justice Brandeis in *Whitney v. California* in 1927, one of the many cases involving aggravated fears of subversive threats from abroad. "It is the function of [free] speech," he said, "to free men from the bondage of irrational fears." "Men feared witches," Brandeis continued, "and burnt women."

Today, our "witches" are terrorists and Brandeis's metaphorical "women" include the refugees (mostly children) and displaced persons, immigrants, and foreigners, whose lives have been thrown into suspension and doubt by policies of exclusion. There are many reasons to oppose these policies, but one, in particular, strikes at the heart of our intellectual life and is best expressed by the mission of universities: Namely, that we should avoid, if at all possible, heedlessly erecting walls—intellectual walls—that will impair our ability to understand and engage our modern, inter-connected world. For the world today is imbued with profound issues and needs that, however much we might wish otherwise, are simply not going away—that no wall can block—and that deserve as much attention and thought as our collective minds can possibly muster. Columbia University, by our history, our location, and through our active and ongoing efforts, has embraced the responsibility to be an American university with an international scope—at home not just in a great, global city, but in the world.

We are properly proud of our international students and faculty, and of our research and educational work all over the globe. The free movement of people is vital to this intellectual work.

There are still greater dangers that will come with abandoning this path and with accommodating the policies and underlying attitudes, here and around the world, that would lead to a withdrawal from the global marketplace of ideas. It is a distressing fact of human experience that persecution of the "foreign" is part and parcel of rising intolerance at home. The same fears of the foreign that take hold of a population inevitably infect our internal interactions and institutions, yielding suppression of unpopular and dissenting voices, victimization of vulnerable groups, attacks on the media, and the rise of demagoguery, with its disdain for facts, reason, expertise and tolerance. The most infamous and shameful historical periods in which we departed from our core First Amendment principles of liberty of thought and expression always involved a combination of the two strains of intolerance—the foreign and the domestic.

This was true at the nation's inception with the revealingly named Alien and Sedition Act of 1798, continued on to the last century with the notorious Red Scare following the First World War, and persisted in the McCarthy era following the Second World War—both of which, interestingly, involved national paranoia and panic over efforts by the Russians to undermine American democracy.

All of this poses a very special obligation on those of us within universities. Not only must we make the case in every venue for the values that form the core of what we are and do, but we must also live up to our own principles of free inquiry and fearless engagement with all ideas. This is why recent incidents on a handful of college campuses disrupting and effectively censoring speakers is so alarming. Such acts not only betray a basic principle, but also inflame a rising prejudice against the academic community, and feed efforts to delegitimize our work, at the very moment when it's most needed. I do not for a second support the view that this generation has an unhealthy aversion to engaging differences of opinion. That is a modern trope of polarization, as is the portrayal of universities as hypocritical about academic freedom and political correctness. But now, in this environment especially, universities must be at the forefront of defending the rights of all students and faculty to listen to controversial voices, to engage disagreeable viewpoints, and to make every effort to demonstrate our commitment to the sort of fearless and spirited debate that we are simultaneously asking of the larger society. Anyone with a voice can shout over a speaker; but being able to listen to and then effectively rebut those with whom we disagree—particularly those who themselves peddle intolerance—is one of the greatest skills our education can bestow. And it is something our democracy desperately needs more of. That is why, I say to you now, if speakers who are being denied access to other campuses were to come here, I will personally volunteer to introduce them, and listen to them, however much I may disagree with them. But I will also never hesitate to make clear why I disagree with them.

This is a time, above all, for active engagement. That, of course, means you, when you leave here, and the rest of us, who stay to be with your successors. But I also believe that universities now need to rethink their role in society and consider new ways to apply the extraordinary knowledge and capacities we possess to activities that will improve the human condition and help to solve humanity's problems. Our special role as a university, of course, is to expand human knowledge and to educate the next generation. And to do that we must be careful not to take "political" sides. But, even with that injunction in mind, there is plenty of room for universities to be far more engaged than we have been. Many faculty members already find ways to do this on their own. But no university has adopted, as a central mission, the project of working closely with partners beyond the academy—in government, the private sector, and civil society—who have the power, influence, and relationships to transform the intellectual work of the university into the solutions so urgently needed in the larger world. As you know, Columbia is now planning to embark on that very mission through the new Columbia World Projects.

Whether it is through climate monitoring and seasonal forecasting aimed at mitigating the effects of climate change on public health, food security, and global migration; or by making the coming revolution in health care based on precision medicine's use of genetic sequencing available to the largest number of people—there are many areas where Columbia can be more actively involved in helping out with some of the world's greatest needs. I hope in years to come you will look back with pride on what Columbia has done, in traditional and in new ways, to help make your world, our world, better.

So I conclude where I began, by noting the pervasive sense that society is at an historic juncture. Each of us will have our own views about the proper resolution of the issues now dominating the public's attention and, even more significantly, about the populist tides we are witnessing.

This much, though, should be clear as you take stock of this auspicious moment in your own life: the way you think, and speak, and engage those who will be your partners in charting the future will count for everything. For our collective efforts to rehabilitate public discourse—a discourse that is being profoundly threatened by fear and intolerance—ultimately will have a tremendous impact in shaping the world we—and most importantly you—will live in. If you succeed in that project—in rejecting that fear, and engaging with the world with all its complexity, as you have done in your time here at Columbia—then the promising and essential work commencing here at your alma mater will, I am certain, have its intended effect. I wish you the greatest good luck as you take up this considerable challenge and begin the next part of your amazing life.

Congratulations, Class of 2017.

CHAPTER 25

CONVOCATION ADDRESS

Columbia College and the School of Engineering and
Applied Science, Low Plaza, August 27, 2017

---

*In 2017, President Bollinger welcomed the incoming freshman class during the first
year of the Trump presidency, which had elevated a range of concerns on university
campuses in an increasingly polarized American political environment. Especially high
on the list were sharp limitations on immigration, the empowerment of extremist
groups, and heightened racist and anti-Semitic rhetoric—vividly illustrated in violent demonstrations in Charlottesville, Virginia, just two weeks earlier.*

I t is a very great pleasure to welcome you, our newest students, to Columbia University in the City of New York. We cherish the enduring, life-long
relationship we now begin with you, at this critical time in your lives and
with this celebratory occasion.

We also feel a deep connection with your parents and families, for whom we
know this is a very poignant moment. We welcome everyone who is attending
this evening.

I regard it as a privilege to speak to entering students, which to my good fortune I have been doing for many years now. The transition from what your life
has been to what it will be from this moment on could not be more profound.
Not only will you be on your own and bear the primary responsibility for your
life from here on out, but, most importantly, you are about to become immersed
in a unique and probably never-to-be-repeated-in-your-lifetime intellectual
environment completely dedicated to advancing human knowledge and pursuing truth.

There really is nothing like a great university, and I strongly believe that among the great universities in the world there is nothing like Columbia University. Columbia is made up of an unmatched array of intellectual talent; it is more diverse in its composition, in every respect, and truly believing in the virtues of diversity; it is more international and global in its sensitivities and outlook; it has a unique curriculum, notably with the Core; and it resides in a national and global capital city and draws every day upon the riches of that special urbanity.

Moreover, I would also say this is the right moment to be at Columbia. The fundamentals of great scholarship and teaching are thriving, but there are also many enormously exciting initiatives underway and new experiments taking shape all the time. There's a new campus opening in West Harlem—the first at Columbia in over a century; with a master plan and the initial buildings designed by the architect Renzo Piano. While you are here the new campus will become populated with thousands of students, faculty and staff. We have an evolving net-work of Columbia Global Centers spread all across the world that are helping our faculty and students experience first-hand and to study the phenomena of globalization. We have new University initiatives in Data Science, Precision Med-icine, and Globalization, and last Spring we announced a major venture called Columbia World Projects, which is currently being designed to help make Columbia the home for bringing academic knowledge and capacities together with outside partners—from governments to institutions of civil society— to help solve significant world problems.

You will hear much about this in the coming weeks and months, including sev-eral opening projects. These are all just a few of the activities that may attract and engage your interest while you're here. I can assure you there is enough going on at Columbia to make you as breathless as the city does all on its own.

Which leads me to make a brief comment about you personally. It is easy, very easy, to feel utterly overwhelmed by all of this—Your studies, happenings at the University and the City. It is exhilarating, but it can also be stressful, highly stress-ful. Please know two things. First, we all feel the intensity of life here, more or less. You are not alone. And, second and most of all, we are all here to help. From friends to faculty to professional staff, we all have a role to play in helping one another work through issues, no matter how large or small, and to get the most out of the extraor-dinary experiences offered in this environment. So, let us help. Everyone is easily reachable, including me, so do reach out and I promise you we will respond.

Just a moment ago I spoke about the privilege of welcoming new students. It is a time to think about and speak to the combination of a student's new life in a university and its relation to the great issues of the day. There are, of course, always critically important issues on the horizon, and drawing attention to them can help one see one's education in a larger context. But, I have to say, this moment feels different, more portentous, more fraught with basic uncertainties about basic matters, than at any recent time I can remember. This is true both in the United States and across the world, as authoritarian regimes and attitudes are on the rise and democracies and multilateralism among nations appear to be in decline. All this seems to have come on suddenly, and our lack of preparation is revealed as we experience one shock after another.

I do not wish to be political or partisan here. The University, as such, must remain a neutral institution on matters of political debate. Generally speaking, we have no official position on trade, tax or health policies. But this does not mean the University has no stake in anything outside these gates or no legitimate interest in being a participant in the society beyond our research and teaching. This is a complex matter, to be sure, and beyond the scope of this talk. But I would say this: When the University is faced with a potential breakdown of the societal conditions that make possible what we do—for example, the loss of respect for facts, truth, and reason or the loss of respect for fundamental values such as freedom of speech and press and the rule of law, or the loss of respect for the rights of individuals and groups to be protected against invidious discrimination—then the University has both the right and the responsibility to speak out and even to act to bring about change.

The recent highly disturbing events in Charlottesville, Virginia, and at the University of Virginia, and the subsequent characterization of those events by the Administration, are among the most recent episodes indicating a breakdown. There is no question extremist groups in America and elsewhere are feeling empowered. And this has only added to that dangerous sense of empowerment. Many citizens and groups among us are experiencing a greater sense of vulnerability these days, because of verbal attacks, because of new policies such as those regarding immigration, and because of silences when hatred and prejudice manifests itself.

From the standpoint of freedom of speech, there is a kind of slow process of degradation happening. The First Amendment is relatively young, having only been formulated as we know it today over the last century. Beginning about

50 years ago, the Supreme Court in a series of decisions established a degree of protection for speech beyond any seen before or since in any society. So, with some conditions, speech of the Klan, neo-Nazis and White Supremacists among others is protected, even though their messages are evil. This posture is not self-evidently right (it is certainly contestable), but it is one born of painful experiences and over many decades, and one around which there has emerged a unique supportive consensus from both the liberal and conservative wings of American political and legal system.

There are many rationales supporting this approach; for me it's a remarkable effort by the nation to practice extraordinary tolerance in order to highlight and address a broad need across all social interactions to be more tolerant to differences than we are naturally inclined to be. But, whatever the rationale, the entire system we have built up over a century critically depends upon judges and leaders condemning the content of the speech at the same time we insist on "protecting" or "tolerating" it. Ambiguity about how the society "thinks" about these messages undermines what is supposed to be an act of tolerance, of magnanimity, not respect for the viewpoints proffered. Until now, such condemnation has always occurred. The point is that there are many ways in which this most recent episode in Charlottesville threatens core values and systems in the nation.

Now, the important question for us here tonight is what does this mean for you as you enter your studies at Columbia. And my answer to that question is that it makes you and your education here more important, more vital to the future of this country and the world, than I have felt in a long time. I hope and expect that you will very quickly discover that what you are learning here is not just some abstractions, or theories, or ideas about which great minds long ago have worked on and worked out and which you and we can take for granted and move on. These ideas, and more importantly the intellectual process and scholarly temperament by which you will grapple with these ideas, are absolutely and inherently very much alive and well, or not so well, today. In other words, what all this means is that your studies here and now are going to be as meaningful and as deadly serious as life ever gets.

Let me close with a word about freedom of speech on this campus. Over the past year especially, there have been many high-profile instances of speech being denied on college campuses, because it was deemed offensive, or because of feared disruptions and even potential violence, or because there was a wish to avoid controversy. Here at Columbia we are a private institution and therefore not covered by the constitutional right of free speech. The First Amendment only applies to "state" action, which includes state, but not private, universities. That being said, we—like most other colleges and universities—have voluntarily embraced the general framework of First Amendment jurisprudence for ourselves.

It is, of course, much more complicated than that statement might imply, but the essential elements are these: We, like the broader society, have a "public forum," in which students and faculty speak about public issues and often invite outside speakers in. Outside speakers have no "right," as it were, to use our campus absent an invitation, and I would not hesitate to deny an independent request to do so under various conditions. But, like the First Amendment itself, the scope of ideas that can be expressed here is very, very wide and encompasses many viewpoints and perspectives that certainly I, at least, regard as deeply offensive, dangerous and wrongheaded. Our choice has been and is to deal with that disagreement by means other than stopping the speech from occurring, which primarily means by accepting our responsibility to confront speech we dislike and to state our reasons for rejecting it. It is my—and our—job to see that this system is preserved and operates in the most productive way possible.

I have been thinking a great deal about you and what you might be thinking at this moment. I am confident in this University, just as I am in the nation and our institutions, that we will make it possible for you to start your lives on a secure foundation of the values and practices we both treasure and on which we have prospered. Certainly, we have much work to do, even if more than we might have thought. But it is a genuine pleasure to think of doing it with you.

Congratulations on making this transition in your lives and welcome to Columbia University.

CHAPTER 26

CAN THE FIRST AMENDMENT SAVE US?

Columbia Journalism Review, October 5, 2017

President Donald J. Trump regularly attacked the free press as "enemies of the people," alleging that the press spread "fake news," while he continued to disseminate false and misleading statements on a wide range of issues. President Bollinger's article led a special issue of the Columbia Journalism Review *addressing these threats to the foundations of public discourse and the associated challenges for mainstream political journalism to maintain its nonpartisan independence and credibility.*

"Persecution for the expression of opinions seems to me perfectly logical. If you have no doubt of your premises or your power, and want a certain result with all your heart, you naturally express your wishes in law, and sweep away all opposition." That was written nearly a century ago, in 1919, in a dissenting opinion by Supreme Court Justice Oliver Wendell Holmes, Jr. The case, *Abrams v. United States*, involved five Russian immigrants who had been prosecuted for their distribution of leaflets in New York City praising the Russian Revolution, criticizing President Woodrow Wilson's opposition to communism, and urging workers to launch a general strike in protest.

In an era of fevered intolerance of foreigners and immigrants (not unlike our own) and of fanatical wartime patriotism determined to crush any and all dissent, the defendants were convicted and sent away to prison for their crimes, all with the acquiescence of the United States Supreme Court. So, too, under the same statute, and with the Court's blessing, was the Socialist Party's candidate for president of the United States, Eugene Debs, for the crime of giving a public speech expressing admiration for draft resisters.

This was the opening moment of our modern interpretation of the language of the First Amendment that "Congress shall make no law . . . abridging the freedom of speech, or of the press," enshrined in the Constitution in 1791. Not until that time had the Supreme Court addressed the meaning of these words. From our perspective today, it was an inauspicious beginning.

But Holmes's vivid depiction, both of human nature and of the need to overcome one's impulses and instead put one's faith in the marketplace of ideas, ultimately carried the day. His themes were restated, amplified, and amended by other justices in subsequent periods of national stress and intolerance (notably the McCarthy era of the 1940s and '50s), until the Court in *New York Times Co. v. Sullivan* (1964) declared that the central purpose of the First Amendment was to ensure a political system in which discussion of public issues could be "uninhibited, robust, and wide-open." Over the next decade, the Court further entrenched this interpretation in a series of landmark decisions—from protecting the hateful and inflammatory speeches by participants in a Ku Klux Klan rally (*Brandenburg v. Ohio*, 1969), to denying the government's attempt to use "prior restraint" to prevent newspapers from publishing the classified information in the Pentagon Papers (*New York Times Co. v. United States*, 1971), to safeguarding offensive speech in public places, like that of the young man who walked through a Los Angeles courthouse wearing a jacket that said "Fuck the Draft" (*Cohen v. California*, 1971). Taken together, this jurisprudence pushed protections of speech and the press far beyond where any nation, then or now, has been willing to venture.

The impact of these unparalleled protections has not been limited to protecting individuals against prosecution by the state. From the seminal period following *Sullivan* to the present moment, these principles have shaped American norms and discourse in three critical ways.

For one, the First Amendment has become much more than a legal doctrine. It is a core part of the American identity. As much as it is about "rights"—the right of dissent, of sovereignty residing in the citizenry and not in the government, and so on—it is also about the character of the society. To listen to people speak of free speech and press is to hear about fortitude, bravery, magnanimity, self-doubt, and the capacity to reason and respond; to recognize the importance of compromise, and to learn to live with some degree of chaos, uncertainty, and discord; and to value creativity and change over always trying to preserve the status quo.

The second notable development has been that, over time, the interplay between this free speech ethos and the evolution of our constitutional jurisprudence has stretched our capacity for tolerance in both the public and private realms. Though the First Amendment applies only to state action, it has become a touchstone for broader society, influencing norms far beyond its legal reach. Private universities are among the many American institutions that have voluntarily embraced free-speech protections.

This broad reach is critically important, because the impulse toward intolerance that Holmes identified is not limited to censorship of speech. Rather, it is a problem that cuts across all public decision-making, where we are certain to encounter opinions we disagree with—sometimes fervently. That is the logic behind establishing such extraordinary protections under the First Amendment—it creates an exceptional sphere that stretches our capacity for tolerance beyond what feels normal. The goal is not merely to moderate our impulse to quash speech that we find objectionable, but to help us recognize how such intolerance permeates other spheres of human interaction, and to teach us to control it. Learning how to temper such impulses, Holmes understood, is critical to the success of our experiment in self-government.

The third notable fact of the last 50 years has been the coalescence of liberals and conservatives, on the courts and in the larger society, around this principle of freedom of speech and press. There are, of course, differences of opinion about some doctrines (the area of campaign finance regulation is the most obvious), but there is—or at least there has been—a remarkable bipartisan consensus in this one area of American public life.

Taking all of this together, one can see why the actions of President Trump represent such a major assault on—and an atavistic reversal of—the modern conception of freedom of speech and press in America. The ethos of tolerance has been replaced by one of intolerance. The press has found itself on the front lines of this assault. Beginning as a presidential candidate, and continuing through his Electoral College victory and inauguration, Donald Trump has systematically sought to undermine the news media's independence and credibility. The list is long, but his actions include: calling major news outlets "the enemy of the American people;" pointing to press pens at rallies and encouraging supporters to taunt and insult the journalists working inside them; disseminating images that depict violence against the media, such as a cartoon that showed a train labeled "Trump" running over a person whose head was covered with a CNN logo; threatening to change libel laws in order to sue news outlets whose coverage he viewed as unfair; smearing individual reporters with personal insults, as he did in a series of misogynistic tweets targeting an MSNBC anchor; and most recently, labeling journalists as "sick people" who are "trying to take away our history and our heritage."

Because the First Amendment is about character as much as restraints on state censorship, all of the Trump Administration's phony allegations about "fake news," the blatant disregard for facts, and the dissemination of false information provide an alarming abandonment of the foundations of public discourse.

This also explains why President Trump's response to the violence in Charlottesville—where marches by neo-Nazis, white supremacists, and other hate groups led to violent attacks, including a man who drove a car into a crowd of peaceful counter-protesters, killing an innocent woman and wounding many others—constitutes such a grave threat to the hard-earned, and ultimately fragile, ethos of tolerance. America's exceptionally strong protections of speech and the press can be sustained only if the public knows that officials—whether judges, mayors, police officers, or most of all presidents—condemn the hateful speech that is being protected.

Fortunately, when it has mattered most, our highest-ranking officials have been steadfast in performing this essential civic duty, demonstrating to the public that the remedy for bad speech is not censorship, but more and better speech. That is what Justice Holmes did in his opinion in the *Abrams* case, when—even as he defended the right of the defendants to publish pamphlets attacking the president and calling for a general strike—the justice made clear his disdain for the ideology of the authors, whom he called "poor and puny anonymities" driven by a "creed of ignorance and immaturity." And that is what generations of Supreme Court justices, presidents, and other prominent public officials have done since his time.

Until President Trump. His response to Charlottesville revealed the risk inherent when public officials equivocate in the face of such hateful speech. Their tolerance looks less like an act of magnanimity, and more like an act of tacit approval, giving a veneer of legitimacy to such bigotry. Even more dangerous is when public officials themselves take up the language of intolerance, as Trump did in his campaign rhetoric toward Mexicans and Muslims (among others). In the face of such negligence by officials, citizens may rightly begin to question whether the broad protections contained in the First Amendment could lead to discriminatory acts, policies, or even violence. And they may begin to call for the government to take a more hands-on role in censoring certain kinds of speech.

Unfortunately, all this is happening when there are two other trends in play. The first concerns the new structure of public discourse, in which research suggests the internet and its social media platforms are increasingly isolating individuals from ideas and opinions different from their own. To the extent that this is happening, there is now more fertile ground for intolerance to take hold. Conviction unchallenged increases belief and yields anger. This has been exacerbated by the fact that such platforms make it easier to disseminate hate anonymously, so that while officials can always condemn the hate speech itself, they cannot always condemn its source.

The second troubling development is the resurgence of autocrats throughout the world. The collapse of the Soviet Union, the great strides in development in regions of Asia and Africa, and the Arab Spring all brought hopes that fundamental freedoms would spread to populations previously under the thumb of repressive regimes. Yet for more than a decade, the trend lines have been moving in the wrong direction. According to Freedom House, 2016 marked the lowest point for democracy and global press freedom in 13 years. Journalists around the world are facing growing harassment and violence, with the Committee to Protect Journalists reporting that there are 259 journalists in jail worldwide, the largest number it has ever documented. Technologies designed to enable free expression and communication are being turned into tools of censorship and propaganda, not to mention domestic surveillance, as repressive governments learn from one another's worst practices.

In the context of this global crackdown, our ability to sustain the exceptionally robust freedoms that we have worked to build is more important than ever. Here, silence speaks volumes. When governments like ours say nothing about the attacks on media (and other serious human rights violations) in Turkey, or Russia, or Egypt, or elsewhere, authoritarian regimes everywhere take notice and are emboldened.

But above all else, the most distressing aspect of the recent period of aggression toward freedom of speech and press in this country is the willing rejection of Holmes's starting premise: that overcoming the natural and, in his terms, "logical" impulse to persecute others who disagree with or are different from us is the hallmark of a civilized society. When you relish intolerance, you are reversing course on one of the most profound tenets of modern thought. So that when a president stokes the fears and prejudices that exist beneath the surface, he models a different—and divisive—kind of behavior for citizens. In this way, just as our unparalleled protections of speech and the press have over decades laid the foundation for a broader ethos of tolerance, so can the lack of respect for these same rights quickly send us careening backward toward a pathos of intolerance that reaches far beyond speech, infecting all of our decision-making.

It makes little sense to argue whether the threats we feel today are greater or less than we have faced before. In truth, it is too early to say. Censorship and its attitudes have a long history in this country, as do intolerance and fear-mongering. From the infamous Alien and Sedition Acts of 1798, to the Red Scare following World War I, and on to the McCarthy era, episodes of fear and hatred, repression and evil deeds, gave way to the restoration of a belief in the power of reasoned debate. Perhaps we will travel that path once again.

CHAPTER 27

OPENING OF THE FORUM

Columbia University, Manhattanville Campus, September 26, 2018

In the fall of 2018, two years after Columbia dedicated its new Manhattanville campus, the University opened a third Renzo Piano–designed building: The Forum, a welcoming campus gateway at West 125th Street and Broadway. In providing a gathering place for conferences, lectures, performances, and cultural events, The Forum encapsulated the ambition to create new academic and civic spaces for a diversity of people and ideas, both locally and globally. The University Trustees voted to name The Forum in Bollinger's honor at the conclusion of his presidency in 2023.

Today we formally open The Forum, the third of the new buildings on the new Columbia campus in Manhattanville in West Harlem— the third child, so to speak, who is accompanied by the older family members of Prentis, Studebaker, and Nash. This comes some sixteen years into the making of our new Morningside Heights, whose own origins date back just over one hundred years to the beginning of the last century, and which was the Manhattanville of that time, following upon Columbia's earlier homes at midtown and then originally at the birthplace in Lower Manhattan. To describe this moment in this larger context is to acknowledge that we are only a part of a long trail of efforts to create and then to pass on to succeeding generations one of the greatest academic institutions in the world.

I have to say that this building, The Forum, is in many ways my favorite, and that is for several reasons. In my life, I have come to understand that to be the third among several siblings gives one some very special qualities, really quite lovable qualities. You have to struggle with and negotiate your way up and down the ladder of relationships, to fight for your rights, and to stand up for what you believe in. This confers on the child enormous capacities of empathy, unique abilities to cope with difficult and often self-centered older siblings and to nurture those below who are even more neglected, a determination to speak up for yourself, and many other irresistible charms. You might ask, "How do I know this, as a first-born child?" The answer is because I have spent pretty much my whole life in the company of a third born, namely my wonderful wife, Jean, who shares all of these qualities and many others with The Forum.

The Forum is also my favorite because it is three that begins to make a bigger whole, and, therefore, now, for the first time, we will have a true sense of a new campus.

The Forum is also my favorite because it stands for something I cherish and believe in. Its name, its identity, and its functions within the University—as the forum—all connote the mind at work, freedom of thought and speech, dialogue and debate, listening and speaking. And, importantly, a forum also indicates the taking of decisions, the making of choices, and the commitment to action. The idea of a forum, of course, is connected to an ancient idea of a sacred space where the realization of a collective existence—a community, in the true sense—is manifest. All of this also makes this space the perfect home for the new Columbia World Projects, which embodies this spirit and seeks to fill out a larger purpose of the University to engage with the world.

Finally, I love The Forum because it feels like a ship, and I have come in the second half of my life to belong to that community of people who love ships, which of course connects us to Renzo Piano and which, of course, is precisely what Renzo means for us to feel in this building. Honest to God, to be in the building is to feel as if it is moving. Renzo has said to me that the ship, meaning this building, is ready for navigation, and it is.

So here we are. The Forum, as our very special third born, as the part that now makes all of the other pieces greater than the sum, as a sacred space of thought and the exchange of ideas leading to action, and as a ship set to sail, it is ready to take us even further into the mysteries of life. It brings us visually, actually, and metaphorically closer to the water, to the ocean, which is the great symbol of the puzzle of existence. In this, we follow the train of humanity, as described by our fellow Manhattanite Herman Melville. Our goal, he famously wrote, is always to get closer and closer to the water, or "the watery part of the world," which represents the source of all these mysteries and puzzles. All of us, he declared, "cherish very nearly the same feelings towards the ocean...." Look at Manhattan, he said, and he might well have said Manhattanville, "Right and left, the streets take you waterward." Everyone heads towards it. "There is magic in it," he said. "Meditation and water are wedded forever." In water, we see the "image of the ungraspable phantom of life, and this is the key to it all."

So, with The Forum, this building, we lean further towards the water, and the key to it all.

Over the years and decades ahead, Manhattanville will have many days like this one, marks in the ongoing creation of a great university. From the declaration of the dream in 2002, to the finalizing of the rezoning process and agreements with our neighbors, to the opening of the Jerome L. Greene Science Center and the Zuckerman Mind Brain Behavior Institute where the study of mind anchors our self-reflection, to the opening of the Lenfest Center for the Arts and our creative and irrepressible School of the Arts as the gateway to the new campus, to this moment and beyond. Yet, certainly none will exceed in degree the depth of poignancy or importance of this little, new building, as it accelerates the noble lives of scholars, teachers, and students, and our relations with our neighbors.

Manhattanville, and The Forum, together with all of Columbia University, makes it possible for us to be part of something larger than ourselves, which is what we always say, in the end, we want.

CHAPTER 28

THE FREE SPEECH CENTURY: A RETROSPECTIVE AND A GUIDE, PART 1: ONE HUNDRED YEARS OF FREE SPEECH

Tanner Lecture I, Clare Hall, Cambridge University, November 5, 2018

The Tanner Lectures, founded in 1978 at Cambridge University's Clare Hall, were "established to reflect upon the scholarly and scientific learning relating to human values, the lectureships are international and intercultural, and transcend ethnic, national, religious, and ideological distinctions. Appointment as a Tanner lecturer is a recognition of uncommon capabilities and outstanding scholarly or leadership achievement in the field of human values."[1] President Bollinger delivered this Tanner Lecture in two parts, drawing on The Free Speech Century, *a book he coedited with longtime friend and University of Chicago Law School professor Geoffrey R. Stone.*

I

It is a deep, meaningful honor for me to deliver these Tanner Lectures, especially under the auspices of Clare Hall and of Cambridge University. It is unlikely anyone here today (except Jean) would know the layers of associations for me that make this particular moment much more significant than the usual lecture I might deliver. In 1983, Jean and I brought our two young children (ages 5 and 9) here to live and work at Clare Hall during a sabbatical from the University of Michigan

Law School. We discovered what so many others have also, this gem of an intellectual and personal home, set in this magnificent university and charming town, which altogether provides its visitors with a magical, out-of-time experience that stays with one for life. This special bond was made still more special when I was subsequently honored, in 1999, by Clare Hall as an Honorary Fellow.

It is also personally important to me that, when I was President of the University of Michigan, which is also one of the sites of the Tanner Lectures, I, too, oversaw the lectures, and Jean and I always enjoyed our annual meeting with the other presidents and spouses of host universities. In that moveable feast of companionship, we became good friends and admirers of Dame Gillian Beer and her late husband, John. So, even though I know firsthand from that experience just how difficult it can be to find Tanner lecturers, nevertheless to be asked actually to deliver one, and for it to be with Clare Hall and Cambridge University, makes me feel the pleasures that a former cast member of Saturday Night Live feels upon being asked to return as the host.

Finally, adding further to the layers of special meaning underlying this moment, is the subject of these lectures—namely, freedom of speech and press. If anything defines my life's scholarly work, it is this—trying always to understand this extraordinary human and social development, through the prism of the First Amendment to the United States Constitution. But it also defines my life in a deeper sense. My grandmother began working as the librarian in a small-town daily newspaper in the 1930s to support herself and my father (a young boy then) when her husband died prematurely. My father then followed her and began working at the same paper, first as a paper boy and from there working his way up the ladder. This was in Santa Rosa, California, and the paper was the *Press Democrat*, much later becoming for a while a property of the *New York Times*. I was born in Santa Rosa and spent many hours at the P.D. (as it was called), absorbing the distinctive smells and whirling activities of producing a daily newspaper. Later, when I was a teenager, my father became the editor and publisher of an even smaller small-town newspaper in Baker, Oregon. I worked there as the janitor and the developer of films (among other jobs), breathing, as can only happen in that coming-of-age period, the atmosphere of journalism and the press.

When I began my career as a young law professor (at age 27) at the University of Michigan, I turned almost instinctively to the First Amendment as my field of focus. Interestingly, in the strange ways of developing scholarly expertise, the year before, as a law clerk to Chief Justice Warren Burger, I had worked on one of the

First Amendment cases involving broadcast regulation. So, of course, I wrote my first article on what I saw as the puzzle of differential treatment under the First Amendment of newspapers and the new media of television and radio, the former protected against regulation and the latter subject to an approved regime of regulation.[2]

Following that I undertook a more ambitious goal of understanding the theoretical meanings of First Amendment jurisprudence, especially in the context of protecting extremist speech, which is what I pursued here in 1983 while at Clare Hall and which became a book, *The Tolerant Society*.[3] All my subsequent writings and scholarship, and the teaching I do every year, seem solidly rooted in and based on these glorious settings in which I was afforded the gift of pursuing my curiosity.

Throughout my career I have also been fortunate to have many other connections with the areas of freedom of speech and press. I have served on the Board of the Washington Post Company, including the time in which the newspaper was sold to Jeff Bezos. As President of Columbia, I am a voting member of the Board that selects the Pulitzer Prizes, a process I admire greatly. As an academic leader, in the odd way in which life works, I have had far more than my share of free speech controversies and issues. And I have been involved in more litigation about the First Amendment than I would care to recount, especially as a defendant.

All this brings me to the subject of my lectures this afternoon, and to another layer of meaning. These lectures happen to correspond almost perfectly with the publication of a book my good friend and long-time First Amendment colleague Geof Stone, of the University of Chicago Law School, and I have been working on for the past two years. It is titled *The Free Speech Century*, and is published by Oxford University Press, and I will draw on it for these lectures.[4] We invited 16 scholars and practitioners to reflect on the first one hundred years of First Amendment jurisprudence and to begin to grapple with some of the most significant questions we face now and will continue to face in this next century. Framed by a dialogue and epilogue between Geof and me, the essays offer reflections and critiques of the first one hundred years of cases, address some specific areas of controversy (e.g., campaign finance, campus speech, national security and publication of state secrets), assess the international implications of First Amendment jurisprudence, and try to come to terms with issues raised by the newest communications technology, namely the Internet and its various platforms and search engines.

Few people realize that all that we take today as constituting the rights of freedom of speech and press is only a century in the making. Not until 1919, in that period beset with fears and profound feelings of insecurity arising out of the First World War, the Communist Revolution in Russia, supposed international conspiracies to subvert democracies, labor movements, and immigration and foreigners, did the Supreme Court begin to decide what the fourteen words of the First Amendment—"Congress shall make no law . . . abridging the freedom of speech, or of the press"[5]—actually should mean in practice. From our perspective today, one has to say it began rather badly. While the great Justice Oliver Wendell Holmes, Jr., wrote for an unanimous Court in the opening three cases that speech could only be prohibited when the State could establish a "clear and present danger" of some evil within the legitimate powers of the government to do something about,[6] which seemed much more protective than the prevailing "bad tendency" test of the time,[7] the actual application of the new test to the cases before it was shockingly casual, when looked at with modern free speech sensibilities.

As Holmes said, famously, and of course correctly, free speech does not protect the person who yells fire falsely in a crowded theater[8]—that's not a very positive way to approach the task of trying to locate the outer boundaries of political discourse. The most egregious of the three decisions involved the prosecution of the leader of the Socialist Party of the time and its candidate for President of the United States, Eugene Debs. He delivered a speech in Ohio in which he praised individuals who had (illegally) resisted conscription. The government claimed this violated the Espionage Act of 1917, which made it a crime willfully to "obstruct the recruiting or enlistment service of the United States."[9] His conviction upheld by the Court, Debs was sentenced to ten years in prison, during which he received over one million votes in the presidential election of 1920. (It would be as if Hillary Clinton were jailed for her speeches.)

Within a matter of months, however, Holmes began to have second thoughts and to reverse his position. In a case involving five Russian immigrants who circulated a pamphlet in New York City calling on workers in ammunition factories to strike in solidarity with the Communist Revolution in Russia, Holmes dissented from the decision finding a "clear and present danger" and wrote these famous and eloquent words: "Persecution for the expression of opinions seems to me perfectly logical. If you have no doubt of your premises or your power and want a certain result with all your heart you naturally express your wishes in law and sweep away all opposition. To allow opposition by speech seems to indicate that you think the speech impotent, as when a man says that he has squared the circle, or that you do not care whole-heartedly for the result, or that you doubt either your power or your premises. But when men have realized that time has upset many fighting faiths, they may come to believe even more than they believe the very foundations of their own conduct that the ultimate good desired is better reached by free trade in ideas—that the best test of truth is the power of the thought to get itself accepted in the competition of the market, and that truth is the only ground upon which their wishes safely can be carried out. That at any rate is the theory of our Constitution. It is an experiment, as all life is an experiment."[10]

Within the decade, Justice Louis Brandeis had joined Holmes as one of the most eloquent free speech advocates, most notably in the 1927 case of *Whitney v. California*.[11] (Anita Whitney attended meetings of the Socialist Party and was part of the group that advocated a moderate, nonviolent platform, while a more radical wing advocated overthrow of the government through revolution.) Addressing the question of how to conceive of freedom of speech, Brandeis wrote in equally famous language about how "it is hazardous to discourage thought, hope and imagination; that fear breeds repression; that repression breeds hate; that hate menaces stable government; that the path of safety lies in the opportunity to discuss freely supposed grievances and proposed remedies; and that the fitting remedy for evil counsels is good ones."[12] He went on: "Fear of serious injury cannot alone justify suppression of free speech and assembly. Men feared witches and burnt women. It is the function of speech to free men from the bondage of irrational fears."[13] And: "Those who won our independence by revolution were not cowards. They did not fear political change. They did not exalt order at the cost of liberty. To courageous, self-reliant men, with confidence in the powers of free and fearless reasoning applied through the processes of popular government, no danger flowing from speech can be deemed clear and present, unless the incidence of the evil apprehended is so imminent that it may befall before there is opportunity for full discussion."[14]

These words and thoughts ultimately won the day, in the United States but also in many nations around the world, over the course of the 20th century. After another low point in repression and censorship in the 1950s, with the McCarthy era and the then-pervasive fear of a Russian threat to undermine American and Western democracies, where the Supreme Court again succumbed to national panic. In *Dennis v. United States*, a majority of the Court upheld the convictions of the leadership of the American Communist Party.[15]

The crowning achievement of the Holmes-Brandeis perspective occurred in the transformative environment of the Civil Rights and Anti-Vietnam War period of the 1960s and into the 70s. In this epic crucible of national transformation, the Supreme Court decided a series of cases that together compose the modern idea of freedom of speech and press. The decisions—led by *New York Times v. Sullivan* (protecting the *New York Times* against civil liability for running a civil rights advertisement that made false statements about the actions of the police in Montgomery, Alabama)[16] and supported by *Cohen v. California* (protecting an individual wearing a jacket in a public place with the words "Fuck the Draft" written across the back),[17] *Brandenburg v. Ohio* (protecting a meeting of the KKK),[18] Pentagon Papers (protecting the *New York Times* and the *Washington Post* in publishing stolen government classified documents),[19] *Red Lion Broadcasting v. FCC* (upholding regulations of broadcasting designed to expand viewpoints),[20] and *Miami Herald v. Tornillo* (rejecting regulations designed to expand viewpoints in the context of newspapers)[21] and many others —created the most elaborate and speech-protective jurisprudence of any nation in history, with, as I have indicated, profound influences around the world.

A centenary always seems like a natural time in which to step back and consider what has happened over that period and what it all means and should mean in the future. That is certainly true with free speech and press. We also live in a moment of enormous social and political change in the United States and across nations, which makes taking stock a necessity more than simply a convenient moment on the historical calendar. That is the genesis of *The Free Speech Century* and the topic of these lectures.

In this first lecture, I want to continue with the summary of the First Amendment experience and, more importantly, offer some observations on how to interpret and understand what has happened. Then, in the second lecture, I want to turn to the present and future and consider three of the most important questions of this present century: (1) Should the legacy of the last century be continued and what are its prospects given current political and global trends towards authoritarian regimes? (2) What should be the general approach to dealing with the rising importance of the Internet and its component elements, which are now widely perceived as increasingly dominant in shaping the public forum? (3) And, lastly, what are we to make of the fact that the modern world is increasingly interconnected and inter-dependent, yielding problems and issues that can only be resolved effectively through collective international action, with a new truly global communications technology to serve as a global public forum, but with vastly different competing conceptions of free speech and free press in contention? In other words, how should we think about free speech in a globalized world?

II

Understanding the last one hundred years of free speech and press in the United States is very much about understanding how we should deal with people who advocate illegal or bad acts, whether they be major, such as overthrowing the government, or more minor, such as taking over (occupying) public or private property. Context can shape everything, and this is the context that has shaped our thinking about the First Amendment. There have been many proposed tests for drawing that line. Besides "Clear and Present Danger," there is "Bad Tendency,"[22] "Express Incitement,"[23] "Abstract Ideas versus Steeling People to Action,"[24] "the Gravity of the Evil Discounted by its Improbability,"[25] and, finally, "Directed at Producing Imminent Lawless Action and Likely to Produce Such Action,"[26] this last formulation being the one we live under today. As I have indicated, the last one-hundred-year history is one of ebbing and flowing of protection, with the courts following the national mood. Since the 1960s, however, the scope of protection has generally been very strong.

From this, let me fill in the First Amendment map the Court has drawn up for our world of freedom of speech and press.

As the Court expanded the protection for speech advocating illegality, it also recognized a number of exceptions to freedom of speech and steadily narrowed them over time. And so we have, with laws banning obscenity, fighting words, libel, threats, invasions of privacy, and speech bringing about risks of violence and disruption caused by hostile audiences.[27] The jurisprudence now has many cases permitting and delimiting these exceptions.

Any notion of free speech must also figure out its horizontal dimensions, not only what words and language will be protected but also what nonverbal communications. Once you realize that all human behavior is or can be "communicative" or "expressive," you face the dilemma of how far to push the First Amendment interests analyzing government regulation of all conduct. This problem bedeviled the Court and analysts for decades, producing all kinds of analytically problematic solutions (e.g., the government cannot regulate "pure speech" but it can "action" or "conduct").[28] Eventually, the Court settled on an approach that focused on the government's motive behind the regulation: If the purpose is to stop messages or viewpoints, no matter what the conduct was, then the First Amendment would be fully deployed.[29] If, on the other hand, the government's motive or purpose has nothing to do with the "communicative impact" of the behavior, then the government will be afforded broad (though not unfettered) leeway to regulate.[30] In practical terms, this means that "free speech" encompasses far more than words or language, written or spoken, and, therefore, virtually all human behavior is at least in theory protected against state prohibition to the extent the state's motive is in prohibiting ideas "expressed" through that behavior. The implementation of this approach has required extensive intellectual refinements, adding to the intricacy of First Amendment jurisprudence.

Similarly, and also on the horizontal plane, the Court has faced the question whether to extend the reach of the First Amendment into realms of speech activity beyond the traditional political public forum—namely, those involving commerce and finance, labor and management, the workplace, the home and personal areas of life, and so on. In general, the decision has been to permit much greater discretion to regulate, while not withdrawing entirely and keeping a First Amendment foot in the door.[31]

There is also a vertical dimension in First Amendment analysis. How should we think about everything that might be "relevant" to "speech?" This can range from having a right of access to information under the control of the government, to a right of access to government-controlled spaces (e.g., public streets and parks) for speech purposes, to a right of access to a good education in order to be able to speak and discuss issues more intelligently. Here the Court has been less forceful in pressing free speech interests against other social interests. (Streets and parks must be available (the so-called Public Forum Doctrine),[32] but not many other venues; there are only limited rights of access (e.g., to judicial proceedings)[33], etc.)

There are three other dimensions of First Amendment jurisprudence worth special note.

The first is especially important. Once you have secured the scope of free speech and press against censorship, you then face the question whether you will leave things at that or whether you will permit (or even require) the government to intervene in the public forum, or the marketplace of ideas, to improve the quality of public discussion. There are many things that affect how freedom of speech and press actually function: the allocation and distribution of wealth through the economic system, the nature and distribution of educational opportunities, infamy or fame, discrimination against minorities and certain groups, and effective control over the institutions that disseminate information and opinion. This is a very rich and complex subject, but the key thing I want to note is that the experience of the last century includes a major public effort of this kind involving the public regulation of broadcast media. Beginning in 1927 and then 1934, at the origins of this new technology of communication, the Congress established a federal agency empowered to license and regulate the medium consistent with the most general of mission statements, according to the "public interest, convenience, and necessity."[34] Out of this system came many public regulations, most notably the so-called fairness doctrine, which required broadcasters to cover public issues and to do so fairly with respect to competing viewpoints. In 1969, over three decades from the inception of the regulatory regime, in *Red Lion Broadcasting v. FCC*, the Court unanimously upheld the fairness doctrine and the general system, saying that the public's right to be fully informed outweighed the interests of the privileged few who happened to control the outlets and that the government had a proper (perhaps even a constitutionally required) role in helping to secure the public's right to know.[35] In one of the more fascinating developments in the jurisprudence, some five years later, without ever mentioning its decision in *Red Lion*, the Court precluded any such public involvements with newspapers and print media (*Miami Herald v. Tornillo*, 1974).[36] The ostensible distinction between these two outcomes focused primarily on the physical limitations of the electromagnetic spectrum—the so-called scarcity rationale, which claimed that the extremely limited number of broadcasters physically possible due to the nature of the spectrum justified government intervention, which ignored, however, the fact that economic realities in the newspaper business produced an even more monopolistic outcome in cities across the nation.[37] (By the 1960s, over 90% of American cities had only one daily newspaper.) In my view, the "scarcity rationale" was a fiction that covered the desire to permit public intervention in a limited portion of the new highly monopolized mass media in order to ensure and enhance the quality of public discourse. While this system remains in place to this day, the rising political antipathy to any public regulation of any kind (beginning with the Reagan era) has reduced the significance and scope of broadcast regulation (e.g., the FCC eliminated the Fairness Doctrine in the late 1980s),[38] though has not by any means eliminated it.

A second area I should highlight is that raised by the Pentagon Papers case, which is illustrative of the willingness of the Court to check government power and to be highly inventive in doing so.[39] Every nation needs to figure out how to strike the balance between allowing the government to operate with appropriate secrecy and how to ensure that the citizens have the appropriate information they need about their government (which will always be too inclined to act in secret) to exercise their sovereign responsibilities. Pentagon Papers, and a few accompanying decisions, established a completely unique and, so far as one can judge such things, entirely successful solution to this problem. Like the dual system of the press/media created by *Red Lion* and *Miami Herald*, this was also one based on systemic and institutional judgments of a highly pragmatic variety, not one wedded to simple notions of logic and an insistence that everything alike must be treated alike, without opportunities for experimentation and for taking account of how people and institutions actually function in the real world. The question asked is, How will this system work in practice? not, What system is logical apart from practice? Without going into this in detail, the solution was this: The government will have full control over its information, with virtually no formal right of access in the press to this information. Leakers, if pursued and apprehended, which in practice rarely happened, may be subject to criminal penalties without any First Amendment protections.[40] The press, finally, even when it knows that it is receiving purloined information from leakers, will have virtually full protection to publish what it chooses.[41] (It is all even more interestingly ambiguous than this summary suggests, creating the subtle calculations each player has to make in this serious game of national secrecy chess.)[42] Up until recently, at least, it is fair to conclude that this method of balancing interests has worked, without unreasonable disclosures of classified information and with reasonable publication of classified information important for the public to know.

The third, and last, general observation I would like to make is really about the range of methods the Court has followed in inserting the First Amendment into areas of government regulation. Sometimes the Court has simply weighed in in a given area of controversy, in essence, to signal the presence of free speech interests. (The hostile audience cases are an example of this.)[43] But sometimes the complexities and doctrinal refinements resulting from the Court having taken extensive cases and issued a number of holdings are remarkable. This is notably true with respect to the areas of libel and campaign finance, which are labyrinthine in their doctrinal complexity. It is, in other words, worth bearing in mind how there are different strategies reflected in the jurisprudence.

III

To close this first lecture, I want to make a few final observations that will be important to the subjects of the next lecture.

It is a vital element of the history of freedom of speech and press in the United States that it has fallen to, or been taken up by, the judicial branch of government. Context is always important, and here the context includes the very special characteristics of the judiciary—lifetime tenure, decisions limited to cases and controversies, the self-restraint and self-education of stare decisis, or precedent, the mandatory norm of principled decision making supported by reason, and the necessity of explanation in detailed opinions, are all critically important. Of course, we know that standing somewhat apart from the political fray permits, at least in theory, a greater awareness of and resistance to the misleading passions of the moment. Given all these qualities and other virtues, it is easy to reach the conclusion that lodging the development of the rights of freedom of speech and press in the judicial branch gives you the greatest chance of having the kind of social and political life you seek, despite the risk that this will make other branches perhaps less attentive than they might otherwise be if they bore the primary responsibility for securing these rights. I share this conclusion, and it is clear to me that, if you seek the most effective law of freedom of speech and press, you should first seek an independent judiciary.

But I also think that we need periodically to look at what the judges have come up with and ask for more when we think that is needed. I feel that way about how we have defined and articulated the core purposes of the First Amendment. Holmes, as we have seen, began the whole venture by linking free speech to the search for truth. But it was Alexander Meiklejohn in the late 1940s who dismissed that relationship and argued instead for what he portrayed as a much more "practical" relationship between freedom of speech and the responsibilities of self-government.[44] This democracy rationale took solid control of the jurisprudence in the seminal decision in 1964 of *New York Times v. Sullivan* and has remained so ever since. For judges and justices who may always naturally feel a little tentative about introducing broad "values" into constitutional interpretation, saying that enforcing free speech against government regulation is simply fulfilling the more fundamental constitutional commitment to democratic self-government can be appealing. But it is far too limited. The role and meanings of the First Amendment are multi-faceted, and should be recognized as such. There is much more at stake and much more to protect.

In particular, while the political arena is critically important for free speech, so, too, is the system for the generation and preservation of truth and knowledge. This system, composed primarily of colleges and universities, but also of journalistic enterprises (which seek understanding far beyond the political sphere) and other institutions (e.g., museums), has yielded more benefits and contributions to modern life than any other, and its autonomy from the violations of improper government interventions is just as important as that of citizens engaged in the activity of self-government. Seeking truth is not some abstract idea, but rather one with highly practical operations and consequences. Nor is it just some individual interest. We have an elaborate system of institutions, with all the corresponding norms and cultures developed over time, specifically designed to perform this social need and public good. And even though there may not have been as many cases raising threats to this system, there have been some and there are likely to be more, and it is time to recognize this system as both fragile and in need of the shelter of the First Amendment. Meiklejohn, ironically because he was a lifelong academic, was too narrow in his conception of freedom of speech, and we should not let those notions delimit the scope of the First Amendment.

And, finally, another area where I believe we have allowed ourselves to be too one-dimensional in thinking about the significance of freedom of speech is with the protections afforded extremist speech. These cases have often arisen in the context of spiraling social fear and panic, leading to grave acts of injustice committed against and the scapegoating of people and groups who are often marginal individuals and relatively harmless dissenters. This is what both Holmes and Brandeis were trying to address. Holmes saw how "logical" it is for us to "persecute" people we believe wrong, especially in times of war and national stress. Brandeis' comment that "men feared witches and burnt women" graphically captures the breadth of this impulse to unjust intolerance. None of these feelings that lead us to persecute or to be excessively punitive towards others is limited just to speakers and speech. Women were burned because of irrational fears of what they might do—namely, casting spells, something that, if it actually existed, would have nothing to do with "free speech." But "men" feared bad behavior where there was none and committed crimes out of intolerant minds. It is that mind we are trying to change, at least when it rears its head in the zone of free speech.

And it is the very generality of our bad impulses that makes insisting that we refrain from giving into them in the realm of speech, perhaps exhibiting extraordinary self-restraint, all the more significant and powerful. The stopping of censorship in these cases, therefore, is more about our concerns about the reactions to speech than it is with our wanting to protect speech, as such. To say this is to speak about our character, our self-understanding, and not about protecting bad speech as some unfortunate by-product of our wish for "good" speech.

I have called this the tolerance theory of the First Amendment, and it is one of many facets of this amazing principle of freedom of speech and press that has taken on such extraordinary significance in the first century of its jurisprudential life.

In so many ways, through this process of creating an elaborate set of doctrines and reactions to the on-the-ground facts of multiple controversies, the value of freedom of speech and press has become more than a legal rule, more than even a constitutional law. It has become part of the very identity of what it means to be an American.

CHAPTER 29

THE FREE SPEECH CENTURY: A RETROSPECTIVE AND A GUIDE, PART 2: THE NEXT HUNDRED YEARS— A GLOBAL PUBLIC FORUM

Tanner Lecture II, Clare Hall, Cambridge University, November 6, 2018

I

In this lecture, I have three general areas I want to cover.

The first is to consider what needs to be done with First Amendment jurisprudence in light of contemporary conditions, to adapt it and make it better for the future. In this context, I also want to talk a bit about what I think is fairly obvious, namely the fact that we appear to have entered another period of grave intolerance and we need to consider the implications for freedom of speech and press.

The second area involves the newest technology of communication—namely, the Internet and its component elements. There is an enormous amount of attention now being devoted to the problems arising out of social media platforms, and I would like to offer some observations on how we might frame those debates.

The third area concerns the phenomenon of globalization and how we should be thinking about freedom of speech and press in this moment where the world as we know it is being transformed. Without question, the peoples of the world are becoming more inter-connected and more inter-dependent, which is the result of many powerful forces (economic, technological (especially with communications), as well as by the incredibly powerful drive of human curiosity and the impulse for improving one's life), all of which is easier to fulfill than ever before. Issues and problems generated by these forces (as well as those that arise out of actions of individual nations with consequences and effects on the global public commons) require some form of global collective action. Yet, as has been widely noted, the institutions, or the public goods, needed to cope with this seemingly irreversible process of integration and its attendant issues (irreversible, I would say, despite new attempts in the United States and, for a time preceding that, in some parts of the world, to impede or reverse its development) lag far behind. Nevertheless, despite the weakness of existing international institutions of governance, there are still ways in which global decisions are being taken, as has now been shown by the Paris agreement on climate change.

All of this means that we now have to conceive of something quite new, namely a global public forum in which issues can be addressed and knowledge pursued. Clearly, the most recent and manifest component of the new global public forum is the Internet. This new communications technology both contributes to the globalization phenomenon and provides the means of addressing its issues. But there is a lack of agreement in the world about what norms of free speech and press should apply to this medium, and that means that its usefulness as a public forum will be impaired, unless we take action, since now effectively censorship anywhere is censorship everywhere. (This is true both in the sense that, though I may live in a country that recognizes my right to say something, whatever I say there will instantly be published globally, and I may be "censored" or chilled from speaking by laws in other nations that forbid my speech; and in the further sense that censorship in other nations will stop speakers from speaking, speakers whom I may want to, and need to, hear.) In this century, sorting all this out will be a defining problem and central to the shape of our lives.

But establishing norms of openness is not the only thing to be done. The theme of knowledge production I have spoken about also has a critical role in a more inter-dependent world. The system of institutions devoted to the development of knowledge we have built up, mainly with universities, must also be preserved and protected as an international forum for the exchange of ideas.

II

As I look at the jurisprudence and experiences of the First Amendment over the past century, and think about what should be done now, there are several changes I would make. The most important, of course, as I suggested in the preceding talk, is to expand the vision underlying the First Amendment. But here are several more specific revisions:

From my perspective, it is a pity that the Court did not bring the same enthusiasm to the idea of a public and press right of access to information that it did to expanding the protection of expression against various forms of censorship. The key decisions (mostly in the 1970s) were narrowly decided (by a simple majority of justices), and they reflected almost a kind of weariness from the heady expansion of rights that occurred in the preceding decade. To be sure, conceiving of a robust right of access requires living with an incredible array of fact-specific situations, where the government needs for secrecy vary enormously in strength, as does the public interest in knowing what is going on. It is reasonable to fear a flood of cases. It also probably requires some differentiation between the rights of the "press" and of others, which makes many nervous and especially so now, when anyone, it seems, can claim to be a "journalist," which makes drawing that line more elusive than it was before. Still, in this one area, the United States has been far less venturesome than many other nations, where the idea of a right of access to information has flourished. At the very least, it would be good if the Court were to take some cases where the public's interest is strong and the government's interest weak and invoke the First Amendment. This would help to change the calculus more towards openness, which as a general proposition would be all for the good.

Then there is the horizontal dimension. Here the extension of First Amendment protection to extremist speech (e.g., advocacy of illegal acts, hate speech) continues to be very controversial.[1] (See, for example, Professor Catharine MacKinnon's essay in *The Free Speech Century*, "The First Amendment: An Equality Reading.") In my earlier remarks, I made what I believe is a stronger case for this interpretation of the First Amendment than the typical rationales offered, which tend to point to the problems of drawing lines between acceptable and unacceptable ideas and of needing to avoid creating opportunities for governments, judges, and juries simply to use any exception created in order to suppress unpopular speech. (I have never been persuaded by either of Mill's arguments in *On Liberty* that such speech should not be censored because it might be true or because even if not true we acquire a "livelier" sense of the truth by confronting falsehoods.")[2] In general, I see this as an admirable effort to come to terms with bad impulses revealed in the act of censorship (as I think people like Holmes and Brandeis saw), which is why we feel a sense of pride, not reluctant acquiescence, in extending protection this far.

But I also see this idea of extending our societal capacities for tolerance as ultimately dependent on the presence of distinctive social conditions that make that meaning possible. In other words, it has always struck me as important that, in every case where extremist speech is protected, the courts in their opinions have made it perfectly clear that the ideas being protected are bad, which is also always reinforced by similar pronouncements by other leaders in the society. This is one key reason why it was so shocking, and potentially consequential for freedom of speech, when President Trump said of the march in Charlottesville, Virginia, by the White Supremacists and neo-Nazis, that there were "very fine people" in those groups.[3] This remarkable statement sent shock waves through the society, bringing added denunciations of the speakers and of the President's comment. But the President's statement, along with many others like it, has put in doubt how the society is thinking about evil ideas, which then has potential consequences for what tolerance and protections will mean. The larger point here is that we have to see the application of free speech to bad and dangerous ideas as linked to the ways in which the private sphere is thinking and interacting with these ideas. This is why, for example, a neo-Nazi march in Skokie, Illinois, is a very different matter from one in Munich, Germany, where for obvious reasons the significance of protection is fundamentally different and why because of that Germany has chosen a different path. The scope of free speech, at least at the extremes, is dependent on how it will interact with what is condoned or condemned in the private sphere.

There are some areas of the jurisprudence that will require substantial revision in light of new conditions. Perhaps the most noteworthy is the Pentagon Papers case.[4] I have already described its unique and pragmatic resolution of an eternal and perplexing problem of government secrecy versus public knowledge. But there are now three changes in the world that make this arguably wise resolution problematic (each of which has to do with the developments I will focus on in a moment, namely new communications technologies and globalization).

These are: (1) the rise of new players who are likely to gain access to government secrets and who have little or no interest in drawing a responsible balance between the competing interests involved (e.g., Wikileaks and Julian Assange); (2) the ability of leakers to disseminate exponentially greater quantities of government secrets, which they cannot possibly vet in making a decision whether theft and publication will enhance the public good; and (3) the increase in the government's capacity to identify and then prosecute leakers (because of the ability to trace leaks through myriad forms of communications leaders now utilize, from texts and emails to phone calls and in-person conversations). The last change cuts in favor of expanding the right of access I mentioned a moment ago. The first two indicate that we can no longer count on the professional (and patriotic) judgments of the traditional press (e.g., Ben Bradlee and Katharine Graham of *The Washington Post* at the time of Pentagon Papers) to strike the right balance.[5] (In *The Free Speech Century*, Professor David Strauss discusses this new problem in his essay "Keeping Secrets.") For myself, I am in favor of preserving the Pentagon Papers regime, but on a sliding scale of First Amendment protections that would depend upon the editorial character and journalistic quality of the institutions in possession of the classified information. The obvious objection to this approach is that the courts should not be drawing distinctions between "responsible" and other publishers, but I see no practical alternative given (a) a need to counteract what will always be a problematic reality of excessive government secrecy and (b) no meaningful right of access doctrine at this point to combat that excessive secrecy.

Beyond all of these refinements, there is the big question that looms before us: Will the First Amendment stand up to the next wave of intolerance and oppression and what can and should be done to shore up its fortitude? I pointed out in the first lecture how the modern idea of freedom of speech and press was largely formed in the distinctive societal crucible of the 1960s. Since that time, there has not been a level of national fear that would generate the magnitude of intolerance seen in the eras of World War I and its aftermath and of McCarthyism in the late 1940s and 50s. That is, until now. The sudden rise of demagoguery, authoritarian-style leaders, and so-called populism in the United States and around the world forebodes a return to those earlier periods. The tactics of this strand of politics are well-trod: a call for a particular identity (e.g., religious, ethnic, racial, nationalistic); a claim that this identity is under threat, especially from "foreigners" and immigrants; fanciful ideas about possible policies and hyperbolic claims of achievements; disregard of the truth so that one can believe whatever one wishes; demonization of opponents; legitimization of private violence; and a bundle of other totalitarian strategies. In the United States, President Trump is deploying all of these methods. He has called for the jailing of his opponent (reminiscent of what happened to presidential candidate Eugene Debs); indicated he might not accept the election results if he lost; made false claims about the results of the popular vote in the election; asserted that media regularly and deliberately engage in purveying falsehoods and has repeatedly labeled them the "enemies of the people;" has himself, as counted by *The Washington Post*, engaged in over 5000 falsehoods and lies;[6] exaggerated his own accomplishments; demonized foreigners and immigrants; mocked and ridiculed opponents; approved of and incited violence against journalists; shown disregard for the rule of law; and endorsed, implicitly and even explicitly, violence towards certain groups. In a deep sense, the only thing that currently stands between full authoritarianism in the United States and where we are at the moment is the Rule of Law, which fortunately for now remains strong.

For the time being, at any rate, as Professor Tim Wu points out in his essay in *The Free Speech Century*, "Is the First Amendment Obsolete?," the ways in which censorship is now being manifested are taking nontraditional forms and not official assaults on freedom of speech and press.[7] As any sophisticated observer knows, unofficial and private intolerance can be just (or even more) censorial than the official varieties, so there is little comfort to be taken in where we stand at the present moment in time. If it were to change, however, and become official, how would the jurisprudence fare? I am not optimistic. It seems to me that, if we have learned anything in the last one hundred years, it is that in times of heightened insecurity and fear, which is especially true in times of war, the pervasive unwillingness to tolerate dissent, opposition, and nonconformity is an almost irresistible force for judges. Perhaps the fact that we have now lived long enough with the modern jurisprudence of free speech and press, and have often professed to be ashamed and embarrassed by the fever pitch of intolerance and its devastatingly unjust consequences in the two earlier low points in the evolution of the First Amendment, this will be enough to resist now or in the future. Some, like Professor Fred Schauer whose essay in *The Free Speech Century* entitled "Every Possible Use of Language?" argues that the extension of the First Amendment beyond the "core" of political expression (e.g., for commercial speech) jeopardizes its capacity to resist censorship in periods of crisis.[8]

But, besides the possibility that there may actually be strength in greater complexity, I worry that every new era of repression sees itself as unique in its own way and, therefore, unbound by prior teachings and lessons. (One thing that might be done, though, would be finally to overrule several of the Court decisions that defined the collapse of First Amendment resistance and that are widely understood to be implicitly discredited (e.g., *Debs*[9] and *Dennis*[10]). An editing, as it were, of the jurisprudence every one hundred years seems like a good principle).

Of course, speaking out is the thing to do to help reduce the slide into yet another deep pit of censorship. I believe there is an important role for universities to play in this process. The academic mission is compromised by becoming political, but the qualities of mind that characterize that mission cannot survive a world or a nation that loses respect for truth, in a profound sense, and that falls so far below the norms of civil public discourse as to be dysfunctional. This becomes an existential and not a political issue for the university.

Small things might also be done to help. I would just note the recent establishment at Columbia of the Knight First Amendment Institute, which we launched with a $50M endowment and the mission of advancing research, teaching, public education, and—more to the point—litigation on freedom of speech and press. This is the result of a collaboration between Alberto Ibargüen, president of the Knight Foundation, and me to lodge in a relatively secure and independent institution (namely, a university) an organization that will be engaged in helping secure the First Amendment of the last century in as meaningful a role in the society in this next century (and beyond). For the past century, a benefit of what was effectively a monopoly status for much of the press, which combined both wealth and a strong journalistic ethos, was that there would always be an advocate with the desire and the financial endurance to see through to the end any challenge to government abuse of power. In today's world, however, because of the effects of the Internet, the wealth of the traditional media has been depleted, and the new media (e.g., social media platforms), while they have abundant wealth, lack the ethos. Our hope is that the Knight Institute will be there to fill the gap. It is now up and running, with one notable success in obtaining a judicial injunction against President Trump for excluding people from his Twitter account on the basis of the content of their comments.[11] A District Court held that this violates the Public Forum Doctrine. (The government has appealed the decision.)

III

I now want to turn to the very complex and controversial subject of the Internet, the potential for public interventions or regulations, and the First Amendment.

I would start by observing that there has been an extraordinary change in the general view of the Internet and its consequences for the public forum. At the beginning, it was hailed as the ideal form of what freedom of speech and press were intended to create. It would equalize opportunities to participate in the forum, allow instant communication and universal access to all knowledge, and provide the first ever truly global communications system. That it would undermine the financial model of the traditional press was regarded as a boon for freedom of the press, not a threat. Today, in contrast, it is difficult to find anyone willing to extoll its virtues. Instead, there are regular cries about the destruction of the public mind: citizens can choose to avoid public issues altogether and do as a matter of practice. When citizens do choose to confront public issues, they tend to be highly selective in what they encounter, which means they succumb to the natural human wish to be around only opinions that reaffirm their own, a practice which over time tends to make a person more intolerant towards and angry about opposing views. Meanwhile, we now are keenly aware that the global characteristics of the Internet (about which I will speak more in a moment) make Americans more vulnerable to propaganda, manipulation, and falsehoods propagated by foreign governments and malicious actors. Exhibit one of this risk materializing is the consensus view of the United States intelligence agencies that the Russian government took the extraordinary step of actively trying to influence the 2016 presidential election and to discredit the democracy. Finally, there is (1) a deep concern that the monopolistic status of social media and their remarkable user base gives these for-profit companies undue control over the distribution of information and ideas, however much they profess to be "neutral" in exercising this power; and (2) an equal concern that the business model of these companies relies on their being able to control massive amounts of personal data.

One of the things that is most striking is how few actual, concrete proposals there are right now for dealing with many of these issues. In *The Free Speech Century*, we have three essays that together reveal just how vexing these problems are and how novel. (Professor Emily Bell, "The Unintentional Press: How Technology Companies Fail as Publishers." Monika Bickert, the Head of Policy Management at

Facebook, "Defining the Boundaries of Free Speech on Social Media." And Professor Tim Wu, noted earlier.)[12] (I am putting aside for the moment the issues around privacy of information, which I think are proving more amenable to a regulatory regime.)

The outline of a policy response to these problems will focus largely, I anticipate, on warnings and notations about information being inaccurate or misleading. Banning foreign government involvement in elections will no doubt continue (although even this can become complicated very quickly), and certainly there will need to be a new framework developed in international law for illegal intrusions, and highly aggressive efforts to influence public opinion, that will draw red lines and indicate appropriate national responses, just like the world has over centuries developed with respect to traditional violations of sovereignty, such as with physical invasions of territory. But providing more information about speakers and their messages when they have been designated as false and propagandistic will be the heart of the first round of remedies for the present concerns about manipulation of public opinion.

Given all this, here is how I would think about where we stand.

In one sense, I am not at all troubled by thinking about creating some kind of public regulatory oversight for the development of these technology companies. The fact that it is too early in our experience with this new communications technology to weigh its potential benefits and harms to our public thought process, and to devise specific public interventions to enhance the first and limit the second, does not seem to me automatically to foreclose government, or public, involvement. We have been through this before. In fact, this is more or less exactly the situation we found ourselves in with broadcasting beginning in the first half of the last century, with similar concerns, as I indicated in the first lecture. The response at the time and carried through to this day was to create a government agency with a very general mandate to figure out regulations that would serve the "public interest, convenience, and necessity." (Censorship, as such, was explicitly prohibited.)[13] And the Federal Communications Commission did so with regulations such as the Fairness Doctrine, requiring broadcasters to cover public issues and to do so fairly in representing different viewpoints on those issues. That system, as I have noted, was upheld by the Supreme Court. I know that the conventional view on this is to see the broadcast model as a unique and inappropriate precedent for this application, but I do not share that view. So, from my interpretation of the First Amendment, there is a model readily available in the existing First Amendment jurisprudence. The government, under continuous oversight by the courts, might be a partner with private industry in the evolution of this new technology of communications.

Still, with all that said, I would not be inclined to pursue this course at the moment. I think it is still too early, and we would benefit from thinking through other alternative approaches to dealing with the problems we are beginning to perceive. Here it is important to recall the lesson I take from First Amendment experience that we always tend to overrate the risks with new communications technologies. That also happened centuries ago with the printing press, and it happened in the last century with some regulations of broadcasting and films.

I say this only as a preliminary caution, and cognizant that current events are fueling a competing view that the need for government intervention or other regulatory oversight is not premature, but urgent, and perhaps already late. At a minimum, we must entertain the possibility that we could be in the midst of an aberrant advance in communications technology that breaks the historical mold with respect to our ability to count on a benign result. The digital revolution and social media have affected personal introspection, the experience of childhood, availability of solitude, sexual habits, expectations of privacy, public discourse, and democratic governance—not to mention communal recognition of the truth—in the space of little more than a decade. They also have demonstrated a capacity to magnify our worst human tendencies, a view espoused not two weeks ago by Apple CEO Tim Cook in an important speech he delivered in Brussels, where he sounded an alarm about "rogue actors and even governments [who] have taken advantage of user trust to deepen divisions, incite violence and even undermine our shared sense of what is true and what is false."[14] Perhaps the current round of society-shaping technological advances is the one that will finally overmatch our ability to bend the technology to our will because its prevailing impact is corrosive of the very qualities and characteristics that society has fallen back upon to manage previous advances.

The presence of these competing views is, if nothing else, proof of the benefit to be gained from: (1) watching how the tech companies respond to the criticisms about their platform; (2) watching how citizens themselves respond to the proliferation of bad speech; and (3) conducting deeper research and analysis of what we are actually facing. (It can be helpful to step back and take a comprehensive perspective on what we have created. Remember, for example, that, when the

Court declared that all streets and parks had to be open to speech without regard to viewpoint, that also enabled the Klan and neo-Nazis to push their messages more effectively than before.)

It seems to me there are also many things we could institute or enhance that would be beneficial in themselves and also respond to problems we perceive now. For example, in my view one of the greatest risks we are encountering today is the financial undermining of the traditional press. We need different ways of getting and receiving ideas and information, and we need—as I have suggested several times already—institutions, which are more than the sum of individual actors. The print and broadcast media are among the institutions we need to fortify. While I know in the current state of American politics this is an idea unlikely to succeed, I would greatly increase public support for our public broadcasting system, and even provide such funding for the press generally. With any public funding mechanism, there are always risks of providing leverage for censorship, but there are well-known ways to minimize that risk and bring it to an acceptable level, in my view.

Finally, I would also hope that universities and colleges would be prepared to become greater participants in the public forum. About two-thirds of high school graduates go onto some form of higher education. That number could be much higher with more public funding. How we educate and train each new generation, in light of the changing nature of the public forum, will be important. In many ways, it is by far our most important "social" and "political" "platform." Meanwhile, we need more and better journalism schools and, in public education, a curriculum that, from an early age, develops in every rising generation a new form of digital literacy, which prepares our citizens to be more intelligent and wise consumers of news in an increasingly complex online environment. And we would all benefit—universities as well as the public—if universities became more engaged with practical issues facing the society and the world.

(To this end, we have launched at Columbia an important initiative called Columbia World Projects, which commits the university to work with outside partners in solving significant societal problems, in limited time periods.) And, finally, I would say all this provides yet another reason why it would be good for the Court to articulate how the system of knowledge preservation and development, which I set forth in the first lecture, also is part of the "central meaning of the First Amendment." We should be focused on the broad ways in which we advance knowledge and art, which have value independent of our political culture yet are also intimately connected to it—undergird it, in fact. Looking at all this as a whole also makes us more aware of the potential for a positive role of the state, since the system of knowledge is significantly suffused with and sustained by public funding (e.g., the National Institutes of Health, the National Science Foundation, and the National Endowments for the Arts and Humanities).

We are early in the development of these new media and still very much finding our way. The technology companies themselves have evolved out of a vision of simply providing a means, a platform, for people to communicate, along the lines of a public utility. The legal upshot of this vision is reflected in the early law absolving them of any liability for harmful and illegal speech distributed on their platforms. (i.e., Section 230 of the Communications Decency Act of 1996).[15] The more they have been transformed into a major, perhaps even dominant, public forum in the society (and the world), the more they have come under enormous pressure to limit speech. From a free speech perspective, this is both good and bad. The more dominant and monopolistic their control of public thought and discussion becomes, the more their restrictions on speech effectively become the equivalent of government censorship. On the other hand, the First Amendment is often absolutely dependent on the private sphere being more restrictive than the constitution permits. (This is one of the lessons of extremist speech.) All this produces a kind of paradox. The government is increasingly wary of the power of these companies, and we now see it using soft power (e.g., congressional hearings at which tech executives are brought in to testify) as a kind of tacit regulation. The tech companies are clearly very worried about an onset of regulation and negative public reactions and are increasing efforts to control speech content on their platforms. But the more they do that the more they are putting in jeopardy their initial vision of neutrality and the legal benefits of protection against liability. Fundamentally, we are on a course where these technology companies are moving inexorably to becoming curators, editors, of information, knowledge, and opinion, however much they resist going there. The fact is that algorithms are a form of human editing, but they are very limited as editors; and, in the end, algorithms will not be able to do all we will expect of these institutions.

IV

I would now like to turn to the enormously complex and important issues surrounding the development of a system of freedom of speech and press in a new globalized world. Of course, this is a hugely difficult matter, not least because the views about this vary so greatly around the world and because we have no simple way of resolving those differences of perspective. But the fact of increasing interdependency driven largely by markets and economic activity (e.g., trade, foreign direct investment), the new global communications technologies, and the movements of peoples (whether caused by human curiosity, ambition for a better life, or physical and political need), is very, very real. And so is the fact there are major problems that have to be dealt with because of these phenomena, problems that require collective action of some form because they cannot be solved otherwise (the consequences of global warming being the primary example here). That we are in a period of rising hostility towards "globalization," which not coincidentally is often being expressed and manifest in social and political movements that are also threatening to freedom of speech and press, does not, I think, mean these forces of globalization will be reversed completely. On the contrary, it seems to me, this is more proof about the overwhelming power and strength of the process of integration. As with the Internet, the swing in attitudes about globalization—from Panglossian idealism a little more than a decade ago to outright denunciation and pessimism now—from Davos to Detroit, as one might describe it—has been dramatic. Meanwhile, as the foundations of the world continue to shift towards inter-dependency, the need for attending to the system of freedom of expression to support it will continue to grow in importance.

I see the general problem as having two dimensions. One is that every individual nation will have to decide for itself how it will arrange for its citizens to relate to the rest of the world, both in speaking to the world and in hearing from it. My immediate interest is with how to shape our thinking about the First Amendment in the United States in this regard.

The other dimension is how we will evolve a "global" set of norms about freedom of expression. In an important sense, there will be a dialogue among nations, explicitly or implicitly, as each one separately grapples with its own solutions and approaches. In a deeper sense, there will be a serious question over how much individual nations will be prepared to give up, or adjust, their own sovereignty over the realm of "speech" to a more international or multinational system. We are building on an existing foundation, created in that seminal period following the Second World War, when most of the current international system was created. Article 19 of the 1947 Universal Declaration of Human Rights[16] provides a vigorous international version of the First Amendment to the U.S. Constitution, declaring: "Everyone has the right to freedom of opinion and expression; this right includes freedom to hold opinions without interference and to seek, receive and impart information and ideas through any media and regardless of frontiers." This is now widely accepted as constituting international law, and it has been embedded further in the International Covenant on Civil and Political Rights (1966)[17] and in various regional charters around the world (e.g., American Convention on Human Rights (1969)).[18]

So much always depends upon our basic understanding about what we are trying to do, and here again we see the need for a shift in our basic mentality. When the Universal Declaration of Human Rights was drafted and signed onto, the world was trying to recover from two devastating world wars and to reduce the ways this might be repeated. The idea of "human rights" was thought about in that context. Governments that denied basic human rights to their citizens were believed to be more inclined to be aggressive towards other nations and thus to ignite yet another conflagration. Respect for human rights, and free speech and press most especially, was thought to be important to preserving peace through halting the tendencies of totalitarian regimes.

This logic still has relevance today, but there is a new reality that brings into focus a new rationale. That new reality is made up of the forces of globalization and its resulting issues, and the new rationale for freedom of speech and press is the need for the capacity to solve these issues and to advance knowledge so that the world can be a good place to live. It is critically important that we envision the international norm of freedom of expression with this new purpose in mind.

A

Let me turn to an examination of how the United States should think about the First Amendment in light of the modern world of globalization. Here, too, we need to begin to develop a new mind-set, built on an awareness of how the United States cannot continue to think of itself, in this area of free speech and press, as existing in isolation, in a bubble separated from the necessity of developing global knowledge and public opinion. That does not necessarily mean that Justices should somehow become "liberal internationalists," or think of themselves as acting on behalf of world citizens. One can accept and embrace the realities of a global system of expression for addressing global problems and still think about it solely from the standpoint of what the First Amendment must guarantee in order for American citizens to be able to participate effectively in that system.

What is actually involved here is really just an extension of what we went through in the last century, represented most significantly by what the Court did in *New York Times v. Sullivan*,[19] which imposed strong limits on what individual states could do—and had been doing since the birth of the country—in the way of protecting individual reputations at the expense of open and free discussion of public officials and public figures. As the nation became more inter-connected—with a national as opposed to a local economy, with an expanding national consciousness about issues like segregation and discrimination, the environment, and war, and with a new inherently national communications technology (again) both contributing to this new national reality and enabling national decision making about these issues—it had to develop national standards for free speech and press. The spirit of that necessity pervades *New York Times v. Sullivan*. Now this same process is happening on a worldwide scale, and we will need in this century to devise ways of coming to terms with this change, which, of course, will be far more difficult since there is not a "Supreme Court" to appeal to for enforceable international law.

With this in mind, you can quickly see that there are a host of very specific and concrete areas and problems that will have to be addressed over time. Here are some of them:

With the reality now that virtually anything said on the Internet will be instantaneously transmitted around the world, we will have to decide to what degree will we weigh in limiting free speech within the United States the effects the speech will have outside of the country. This could be either in inciting violence or in causing violent reactions because of its perceived offensiveness. A prime illustration of this problem was, in 2012, the publication on YouTube of a purported trailer for a privately produced "film" about the Prophet Muhammad, which led to riots in the Middle East.[20] How should the classic "hostile audience" doctrine developed in the domestic context be applied here?

United States citizens might wish to participate in helping foreign actors in their political activities. To what extent should the principles developed for protection of domestic political activities apply abroad? In *Humanitarian Law Project v. Holder*,[21] a U.S. activist group sought to provide legal assistance to the Turkish PPK, which in federal law is designated a foreign terrorist organization and thus is prohibited from receiving any "material support." The Supreme Court, expressing deference to Congress and the executive branches over matters involving foreign policy, held that a different, and minimal, standard of protection should be applied in such cases.[22] Whatever one thinks about the particular circumstances in this case, the lowered First Amendment protections for speech activity outside the United States seem badly out-of-step with the need for a global public forum. This will have to be reviewed and the gap closed.

The corollary problem is this: To what extent can foreign actors—governments, organizations, and individuals—be prohibited and prevented from participating in the U.S. public forum? In the United States now, of course, there is heightened concern about Russian government "meddling" in the 2016 U.S. election. This involved hacking into the Democratic National Committee computers, stealing emails, and publishing those emails (through Wikileaks); using fake accounts to distribute false information and inflammatory opinions; and hacking into the voting systems in several states. The U.S. intelligence community has warned that these actions have taken the general spying regime to a completely new level, perhaps even threatening American democracy. Currently, foreign states are forbidden from using money to influence our elections,[23] and anyone who represents a foreign government in the U.S. political system must register with the federal government.[24] Of course, hacking computers is illegal.[25] But what "speech" by foreign governments and actors should be prohibited as well?

A related problem is when cable operators, which are generally regulated because of their natural monopoly status, refuse to allow foreign state broadcasters (such as Al Jazeera or RT) to distribute their content to cable customers. Should this be allowed and the public deprived of access to foreign media, because those media are regarded as offensive, or propagandistic, or mouthpieces of bad state actors?

A major point of contention for this new global system is the border. Traditionally, as with foreign policy, the courts have been extremely deferential to the government in deciding how to go about admitting and denying entrance to foreigners and treatment of U.S. citizens. The recent so-called travel ban of the Trump Administration is an example. The purported rationale was national security, but it was challenged on the ground that it represented invidious religious discrimination (against Muslims).[26] Academic institutions filed amicus briefs providing the courts with information about the importance of free movement of students and scholars to research and education, but they stopped short of claiming the ban violated the First Amendment.[27] (Another example would be a policy, reportedly under consideration by the Administration, to deny visas to Chinese nationals to study and work at universities in the United States, as a way of protecting U.S. intellectual and research property from being stolen or taken.)[28] If we envision the First Amendment as protecting the system of knowledge production I recommended earlier, a key component of which is the exchange of ideas through interactions with scholars and students internationally, should a strong First Amendment interest be weighed in the balance here?

There are many more examples of border decisions that evoke these large questions: visas denied to foreign citizens on the basis of viewpoints, special visas required of foreign media to operate within the United States, and restrictions on U.S. citizens leaving and coming back to the country based on their beliefs and expressive activities. Recently, the government is reportedly considering giving customs officials the power to require any prospective entrant to disclose all of their Internet identities, addresses, and handles.[29] In this heretofore largely First Amendment-free zone, what should be the role of the First Amendment?

Still another illustration is whether U.S. courts will or should enforce judgments against U.S. citizens obtained in foreign courts involving restrictions on speech that would not be permitted under First Amendment law. This is especially problematic in the area of defamation actions secured in foreign courts. This will test and require amendment of the custom of reciprocity in the recognition of foreign judgments.

I do not have the time here to resolve each of these problems. But I would suggest several recommendations for how we (the Court) should approach solving them. Here, as always, everything should start with an open recognition of what we are trying to do and why.

The key is to acknowledge that we now have an interest under the First Amendment in building a framework of general principles and specific doctrines that will enable U.S. citizens to participate in the global public forum, and to receive and hear voices from around the world. This also applies to the system of preserving and growing knowledge.

This means, of necessity, that we must at the very least reduce the deference paid to government actions in the foreign policy and foreign affairs arena and in immigration and customs.

While there is a long tradition in comparative law of taking note of legal doctrines and decisions in other countries, today's world requires that our courts at the very least be conscious of how their decisions will be received abroad and realize that we have an interest in other nations becoming more protective of speech and press and, therefore, in understanding what we are trying to do and why. We need to think about how we speak to them, as well as ourselves. (See, e.g., Professor Sarah Cleveland's essay "Hate Speech at Home and Abroad" in *The Free Speech Century*.)[30]

In that process of persuasion, we should recognize and openly address the facts of our own history and how it is marred by bad decisions, too. We did not come to where we are either quickly or in a straight line. We have a century of experience, and it is important to draw on it in all its parts, good and bad.

In this realm, enlarging the vision of the First Amendment from serving democracy to the development of knowledge and the myriad benefits of that will be better received in a world in which other forms of government prevail. The idea of freedom of speech serving the Madisonian conception of citizen sovereignty is necessarily limited on the global stage. The advancement of knowledge is far more compatible with a reality of multiple systems of government.

B

Lastly, let me turn to the massive problem of developing global norms on freedom of speech and press around the world. This can occur at two levels: Just as with changes within the United States, it can be within each nation. But it can also be at the regional or global level, where national sovereignty is sacrificed in return for a system deemed to advance the public good, and where in fact we already have a foundation of articulated principles and a variety of international and UN institutions that engage in reporting on, investigating violations of, and issuing reports on freedom of speech and press in countries. There are many matters we could inquire into. I could speak about strengthening these international institutions and their capacities to issue and enforce judgments (much of the movement in the last century has been at the regional level, in Europe, Latin America, and now Africa); or about using other areas of international agreements and institutional mechanisms to enforce free speech and press standards (of particular interest to me has been the potential of international trade law, and the WTO and of Foreign Direct Investment treaties, to press for greater free speech and press rights; or about preserving the complex governance structure of the Internet so that this critical communications system is not balkanized; or about how to expand the use of laws in nations with strong free speech and press cultures to do things like restrict visas or freeze financial assets of leaders of countries that violate freedom of speech and press norms (as happens in the United States); or about how these nations could put more pressure on other violating countries (e.g., the recent Khashoggi case); or about exploring the periods in every civilization when there was respect for tolerance and openness of expression and the development of knowledge, so that every nation can find for itself a model to build on for today, rather than creating the false sense that these freedoms and values are really just American or Western notions. These are all interesting and crucial subjects, but I would like to focus for just a moment on what seem to me to be two very important factors in the development of free speech norms in the coming century. One is an overarching observation; the other is more tactical about building out a legal system.

The first has to do with China. We all know that China is well on its way to becoming a global superpower and, because of that, what it becomes will have a profound influence on our world in this century. But China's evolution into a world superpower is more than an economic and political reality. China is also creating a bundle of values that will affect the rest of the world, or at least contend for influence.

It is important that we understand, in this regard, that among those values, is a view of freedom of expression and knowledge that is strikingly at odds with that of the First Amendment and with Western Enlightenment and liberal values. This has to be taken very seriously. In fact, it may be said there are now two conflicting philosophies about free speech and press emergent in the world today, each contending for influence and ultimate dominance. Any serious discussion about the future of freedom of expression in the world in this century must start with this contest of perspectives. (In *The Free Speech Century*, Professor Tom Ginsburg discusses this in "Freedom of Expression from Abroad: The State of Play.")[31]

Until recently, the general view among sophisticated observers of China has been that either of two possibilities would unfold. One view was that once a threshold of modern development of the economy and social system had been reached (e.g., when the vast migration from rural to urban areas had taken place, the economy had shifted from an export-driven system to an internal, consumer-driven system, and the average standard of life had improved significantly), the country would of necessity and choice become more open in terms of free expression—a fact the government would have to accept. This would follow the course of history of other developed nations and would be consistent with the rising expectations of its increasingly educated, affluent, and travelled population, as well meeting the needs of an economy more and more dependent on knowledge and creativity. The other view was darker, though equally favorable toward an evolution of greater openness: namely, that modern China had been created out of an inherent contradiction (an open market economy and a closed authoritarian political regime) that would at some point inevitably implode, or come into conflict. And, when that happened, this latter view held, the forces of openness would likely emerge victorious.

Today neither of these theories seems any longer descriptive of reality, nor of the path China is likely to take. As China has become more and more successful economically, it has also become more and more confident in its overall system, which includes rising levels of repression of dissent and general censorship. In fact, in China today there is now a much more direct and open challenge to the view about free speech and press that has defined the United States. That challenge argues that the U.S. political and social system will itself implode because of the extreme positions we have taken under the First Amendment. By the new Chinese view, protecting extremist speech, allowing radical dissent to flourish, denying protections to the government against attacks and falsehoods, and so on, all have contributed to a steady decline in social and political cohesion and the necessary trust in the government and the state. For this view, the election of Donald Trump is proof of theory.

How should we think about this challenge? One can start by understanding whether what we are facing today in the United States, and in other democracies that are turning illiberal, is a sign of the failure of the free speech experiment or a downward cycle that is inevitable, given our understanding of human nature, and one we know we must continually work against and offer alternatives to, by creating strong and enduring institutions built on the idea of open and free inquiry. Not surprisingly, I believe the latter. But we cannot prove these ideas, except through the quality of life we witness over the long term. We can, however, make our case more effectively than we have.

Looked at with the perspective of one hundred years of First Amendment jurisprudence, what we see today in the U.S. is, in a profound sense, not surprising at all, nor proof of a failure of the interpretations we have given to the First Amendment. Every society will face these political and intellectual recessions periodically. The success of the nation over time will be in its acquired capacity to recognize the sources and to minimize the effects of these regressions.

For us to do that and to play a more effective role on the world stage and advocate for a robust principle of freedom of speech and press, however, we have to change ourselves, beginning with how we organize our knowledge and expertise. I know this from my own work in the First Amendment. As I have indicated, I came of age, as a scholar, in the period of this last century in which the tectonic plates of free speech came together to form a single national system of principles and doctrines defining freedom of speech and press. My scholarly expertise encompassed that range. But in the new globalized and inter-connected world, I know too little about the developments across the world, outside the United States. In my field of law, I took the United States and the rest of the world was assigned to those who did international law and international human rights. Given current realities, of the world we are heading into, that separation of knowledge will not work. We all need to know more than our fields have led us to know.

In the last decade, I have tried to change this, for myself and for my field. At Columbia, I established a project on Global Freedom of Expression. One of its functions is to do something quite simple, namely, collect in one place, on a website, all of the decisions about freedom of speech and press in nations around the world.[32] We also give special prominence to those decisions that refer to international norms. The idea is that over time (a long time, to be sure) we will create more of a sense of community—of common law—around these issues than exists today, since courts and commentators can easily look in one place and see what is happening there, comparisons can be made, and materials can be assembled for courses to educate the next generations of students. As a result, their knowledge will not be so limited as mine, and they will be much better prepared to apply that knowledge, both in their professional lives and in the way they exercise their rights and duties as citizens.

This is basically what many law professors did in the United States in the last century in various areas of common law (contracts, torts, etc.), when for the first time they collected decisions in individual states and then wrote treatises about the emerging "common law" they were helping to create from scratch. By bringing together these formerly separate and discrete cases, they created something new—a "common" and shared effort and a zeitgeist for seeing everything as a whole rather than as discrete parts.

In this next century, seeing the development of freedom of speech and press around the world as a whole is the vision we must seek. Then in such a world we would all know about recent cases such as *Okuta v. Kenya* (2017)[33], in which the High Court of Kenya held that criminal defamation laws were unconstitutional; or *Primedia Broadcasting v. Speaker of the National Assembly* (2016)[34], in which the Supreme Court of Appeal of South Africa struck down Parliament's rules prohibiting live broadcasting of incidents of disorder in Parliamentary sessions; or *Alestra v. Mexican Industry of Musical Property*,[35] in which the Mexican Supreme Court struck down a government agency's suspension of public access to a particular website; or the NorthKoreaTech.org case in which a South Korean Court of Appeals held that a website could be blocked only in exceptional circumstances, that blocking of the named website by the South Korean intelligence services unduly limited the Korean public's right to know, and that foreign website operators (NorthKoreaTech.org was operated from the UK) have standing in South Korea by extension of the right to freedom of expression of Koreans;[36] or the decision of the Kerala High Court in India to dismiss a petition claiming that a magazine cover depicting a woman breastfeeding her child was obscene and a violation of laws that protect women and children;[37] or the case of Tufik Softić, in which the Constitutional Court of Montenegro, for the first time in Montenegro, recognized that states have positive obligations to protect journalists from attacks and threats on their life;[38] or the very recent decision of the Supreme Court of Brazil to protect the rights of university students and faculty to express political views (saying, memorably, that "The only force that must enter universities is the force of ideas");[39] and many, many other judicial decisions that extend and apply the globally emerging principles of freedom of speech and freedom of the press.

The first one hundred years of free speech in the United States is instructive as an experiment in the evolution of "human values," the broad subject of the Tanner Lectures project. At this point, it is a jurisprudential beehive of cases, opinions, and doctrines that bring a kind of order to a realm of human activity and its relationship with the State. Given its starting premises about human nature and government, what it has aimed for is nothing short of wondrous. It asks of us something deeply counter-intuitive, against the grain of our inclinations, all in the name of sheltering our quest for knowledge and of realizing our democratic choice for self-government. It has itself not always succeeded by its own terms, and now it is being tested again by new threats arising from the natural "logic," as Holmes described it, of "persecution," by a transformative new technology of communications, by global power struggles, and a shrinking world that needs all the discussion and understanding it can muster. There is nothing simple about any of this, and it has been one of my purposes in these lectures to highlight some of the key complexities. At the same time, our ignorance about critical elements of what needs to be done now will make things harder than they should be to sort out. The hope is that, after a century of free speech, we will be able to learn from our experiences and do even better in this next century.

CHAPTER 30

HOW THE U.S. COULD PROSECUTE JAMAL KHASHOGGI'S KILLERS

Washington Post, March 31, 2019

On October 2, 2018, the Saudi Arabian journalist and Washington Post *columnist Jamal Khashoggi was lured to the Saudi consulate in Istanbul, Turkey, ostensibly to complete paperwork needed for his upcoming marriage. He was brutally murdered there by agents of the Saudi government. The Columbia Global Freedom of Expression director Agnès Callamard, serving as United Nations Special Rapporteur on Extrajudicial, Summary, or Arbitrary Executions, led one of the subsequent independent investigations of the assassinations. President Bollinger offered this novel legal approach to the case.*

The First Amendment permits any individual in the United States to criticize political leaders, in public, without fear of retribution from the state. Journalists, whose job may entail investigating public officials, are afforded additional protections. But what happens when a U.S.-based journalist's work offends a foreign leader, who then turns vindictive? Should the journalist not expect the same protections?

The question is not an academic one: This is the case of Jamal Khashoggi, the U.S.-based Saudi Arabian dissident, author and contributing columnist for *The Post*, who was unsparing in his criticism of the Saudi regime. Six months ago, on Oct. 2, he was tortured and murdered at the Saudi Consulate in Istanbul and, according to U.S. intelligence authorities, at the apparent direction of Saudi Crown Prince Mohammed bin Salman. The Saudi government, after weeks of denials amid intense international criticism, eventually conceded that Khashoggi had been murdered at the consulate, supposedly by rogue Saudi operators. The regime promised their prosecution—and then, nothing.

In an ideal world, international conventions could be used to try the suspects in an international criminal court. But Saudi Arabia does not recognize the international criminal courts and has not signed on to relevant conventions.

There is another solution.

The deadly assault on Khashoggi—a legal resident of the United States, with children who are U.S. citizens—was also a brazen and an egregious assault against American values and against the First Amendment rights he exercised in this country. Federal prosecutors thus have an obligation to investigate and potentially bring a criminal case against Khashoggi's killers. It would be somewhat novel to prosecute the murder of a noncitizen abroad, committed by noncitizens—and there would be legal hurdles to overcome—but there are reasonable legal bases for a U.S. federal investigation and prosecution.

Principles of international law caution against one country asserting jurisdiction to prosecute crimes committed in other countries, but U.S. courts and international law recognize that extraterritorial jurisdiction—regarding crimes occurring outside the United States—can be warranted in certain circumstances.

Extraterritorial jurisdiction may be appropriate, for instance, where a crime offends the vital interests of the prosecuting state. The murder of a prominent journalist writing for a U.S. newspaper is a prime example of the sort of "censorship abroad" that, in today's increasingly and inherently globalized discourse, undermines freedom of speech and the press here in the United States. Courts have also found extraterritorial jurisdiction for an offense that occurs in one country where the effect is felt in another (one example being shooting someone on the other side of an international border). And extraterritorial jurisdiction is considered appropriate for crimes such as piracy, terrorism and torture that are universally condemned by the international community—which the Saudis' offense unquestionably was.

Consider the case for a torture prosecution. The relevant federal statute criminalizes any act committed by a person acting "under color of law"—the legal term for when someone has the appearance of legal authority, even if they don't have it—intended to inflict severe physical or mental pain or suffering. And the statute applies only to "acts of torture committed outside the United States." Torture inside a foreign consulate is certainly sufficient basis for the FBI to investigate.

International law recognizes that torture is so heinous a crime that countries have the responsibility to prosecute torturers within their borders, even if the crime is committed elsewhere. Whether a perpetrator of torture arrives in the United States voluntarily or involuntarily is immaterial; it only matters that he is "found" here. If U.S. authorities can arrange to capture the Saudi suspects and transfer them to the United States, they can be prosecuted for torture. This is not far-fetched; the United States has done it before.

A second potential prosecutorial path would be a federal civil rights case, based on a statute protecting individuals' exercise of their constitutional rights. If two or more people conspire to "injure, oppress, threaten, or intimidate" any inhabitant of the United States in the free exercise of constitutionally protected rights—and if death results—the perpetrators could face life in prison or be sentenced to death.

Certain questions about the statute's applicability in the Khashoggi case would need to be resolved, including whether the victim must be in the United States at the time of the offense if the victim is a noncitizen, but the statute's legislative history strongly suggests that it would apply. Jurisdiction would be appropriate because of the vital U.S. interests implicated, and because the oppression of Khashoggi's constitutional rights is felt in the United States, where he practiced his journalism.

The case for U.S. jurisdiction would be bolstered if prosecutors could show that aspects of the crime took place in the United States—for instance, if the Saudis communicated with Khashoggi in the United States when luring him to their consulate in Istanbul. Aggressive prosecutors can even utilize incidental contacts such as wire transfers through U.S. banks to build a jurisdictional case for conspiracy. Federal prosecutors have undertaken investigations based on far less evidence than the Khashoggi case presents.

So far, the United States has been largely negligent in responding to Khashoggi's murder. That the perpetrators of this grotesque crime must be punished is obvious, but so is the United States' obligation to defend the exercise of constitutional rights—especially freedom of speech and press. Both goals could be achieved by the practical and direct application of existing U.S. law. Anyone on U.S. soil, whether a high-profile journalist or an ordinary citizen who criticizes the powerful, needs to know that the government has the First Amendment's back.

CHAPTER 31

COMMENCEMENT ADDRESS

Columbia University, Low Plaza, May 22, 2019

O
n behalf of our proud Trustees, our esteemed faculty, our distinguished alumni, our devoted families, and our unparalleled friends gathered here, and across the globe virtually, I welcome you to this very special moment in time. Today, we continue a 265-year-old tradition that binds us with a sense of pride, of hope, and of deep and never-ending curiosity. We initiate those who are committed to a world of openness and debate, who have learned the power of discovering the unknown, and who have accepted the great responsibility that comes with acquiring knowledge, into a community steadfastly poised to shape our world for the better. At the end of our time together today, joining a legacy of those who have come before them, we will have a new class of alumni representing sixteen distinct schools, along with our affiliate institutions of Teachers College and Barnard College. The potential for tomorrow is palpable.

And, as we explore the profound meaning of this moment, there is one special part of our community that deserves unique recognition. Graduates, as much as we, your faculty, feel deep, deep affection for you, nothing can compare to the pure, unqualified adoration of your parents and families. Though you will never, never be able to express fully the infinite gratitude I know you feel, please take this opportunity to thank them.

In my remarks today, I have three parts. I want to talk about the idea of the academy, about the enemies of the search for truth, and about what we are to do.

THE IDEA OF THE ACADEMY

In awarding you the degrees in your respective fields, we recognize your academic accomplishments and now acknowledge your expertise in some area of study. But you are now also an expert of higher education in America, simply by virtue of your presence and deep engagement with this little world over the past several years.

This means two things.

First, whether you are happy or sad about leaving us behind, whether you will return for yet another round of being a student, or you are intent on rejoining us at some point in a professorial capacity and becoming a permanent member of this community, I can assure you that this is true: What you have just experienced will stay with you for the rest of your lives and in all likelihood it will take on greater and greater meaning with the passage of time.

The second point is that I want to ask you this morning to take stock of what is now your deep and experiential knowledge about the nature and role of universities—like Columbia—and with that knowledge then to reflect on the state of modern societies and the threats that we are now facing to the deepest values that undergird these institutions—to reflect on what is at stake in our own country and for the people of the world. We need to raise our voices at a time such as this.

The idea of the academy, as something separate and discrete, removed from ordinary daily life, is as old as human civilization. The desire to step back from the fray, to grasp what is happening at this moment in history, to find a meaning to it all, and to figure out what is a good life, is forever with us.

Who hasn't, at one point or another, wanted to emulate Michel de Montaigne? If only we could retire from public life, take up residence in a tower on a beautiful estate, and write essays connecting the wisdom of the ancients with contemporary human existence—and in that self-reflective pose discover our true purpose and meaning. This is a secret dream that we all harbor.

As always, Shakespeare was familiar with this dream, and he used it to give us many notable characters whose pursuit of this ideal often ended in trouble.

There's Prospero in "The Tempest." While the Duke of Milan, he wishes only to be "transported, and rapt in secret studies," and he feels that his "library was dukedom large enough." This, however, creates the opportunity for his evil brother to stage a coup, landing Prospero on a remote island where, to be sure, his dark arts mastered in "secret studies" come in handy, as may yours.

Or there's Ferdinand, King of Navarre, in "Love's Labour's Lost," who enthusiastically enlists his three subordinates to join him as "brave conquerors" who will foreswear the baser impulses of love, food, and sleep in order to study and learn—only to be confounded in his dedication when he finds himself falling in love.

I suspect that many of you during your time here have lived closer to the experience of Ferdinand than to Prospero.

The advent of the modern American university, which largely happened over the course of the last century, has been the institutionalization of that human dream. And this little physical space in which we gather together this morning is, in many respects, the near perfect fulfillment of that human vision. I know of no other that can match it.

The columns, pillars, pediments, domes, classical inscriptions, ascending steps, granite and limestone and marble and brick facades, which surround us, convey the message that this is its own universe. A place governed by a strictly observed code of academic inquiry, an insistence on open dialogue informed by an all-pervading skepticism, and respect for the legacy of human achievement. Created about a century ago, the Morningside Heights campus represents the ideal of an ordered, classical, and even inward-looking world. To walk onto this campus is to feel one's IQ go up by 10 points.

Part of the genius of this system of universities involves adding you into the mix. It is the combination of brilliant scholars who dedicate their lives to exploring what we know, might know, and must know about all things in the universe, who work daily at the edge of accumulated human knowledge, sheltered by the principle of academic freedom, guided by the norms of a scholarly temperament, working within the decentralized governance structure of the university, together with the most brilliant and curious youth brought in from all over the world, to whom we teach everything we know so that they can go on with their lives and know even more—it is all this that creates the utterly unique context of the modern research university and that unites the exhilarating intertwined ambitions of scholarship and teaching.

The structure and functioning of these institutions are unique; no other organization has ever been designed in these ways, nor would it seem to anyone sensible to do so.

From the outside, it all looks ungovernable.

From the inside, and I can singularly attest to this, it IS ungovernable.

And, yet, it works, and fabulously so.

Over the course of the 20th and now 21st centuries virtually every new discovery of significance emanated from academic research institutions, which now number in the hundreds.

My friend and our distinguished alumnus Warren Buffett likes to say that the American system operates with a "secret sauce" that has brought this nation to the pinnacle of human success in maximizing the welfare of its people. And that secret sauce begins with the knowledge created right here.

Over time, our great research universities drive human progress, they lay the foundation of life as it can be, more than capitalism or government policy. In life, personal and social, ideas are everything, or almost everything, and universities are all about ideas.

So, it works. That is, it works provided certain conditions outside the academy are maintained. Universities are not invulnerable to the actions beyond their borders. And they depend for their vitality on a societal respect for and commitment to what we do.

ENEMIES OF THE SEARCH FOR TRUTH

What is important to realize is that the ideals that define the academy and guide the activity pursued herein, just like the primary freedoms by which we live in a democratic society, do not come easily. They are, in fact, often counter-intuitive. The embrace of freedom necessarily means you must accept a certain degree of uncomfortable disorder and even seeming chaos, and this sometimes unnerves the best of us.

There are many wise people who have commented on this fact of life. My favorite is the great Justice Oliver Wendell Holmes, Jr., who in setting forth the first articulation of the modern First Amendment jurisprudence, noted that the choice of openness required for the search for truth runs against human instinct. He bluntly explained how the impulse to persecute those we disagree with is, actually, "perfectly logical," given the natural wish to believe what we want to believe.

But Holmes understood—as we should by now, as well—that a tolerant society is necessary for the purposes of seeking the truth, that this is produced through an act of collective commitment to live according to its values, and that this requires constant vigilance and persistent re-assertion of those values. Yet, we often lapse.

Unsurprisingly, then, history provides countless illustrations of these ideals colliding with people and governments who felt threatened by the currents of thought of their time and who chose to be hostile to imagination and enamored of their own power and beliefs.

At the end of the First World War, Western civilization had lost its way and political and economic divisions were unraveling the status quo. Fears of Russia and the spread of communism and socialism, along with growing unrest among labor, gave rise to fear and panic among those who wished to preserve the world as it was.

All these forces of instability, in turn, escalated into repression, censorship, and the scapegoating of marginal populations of radicals, dissenters, nonconformists, foreigners, and immigrants. The leader of the American Socialist Party and candidate for President, Eugene V. Debs, was imprisoned for delivering a speech in which he praised draft resisters.

Today, a century later, a new threat to our core values has emerged, around the world and in this country. The rise of authoritarianism—often in the guise of democratically elected despots—has become the defining feature of modern life. The tactics, unfortunately, are age-old and time-tested. There must be an in-group, conceived around religious, ethnic, racial, or nationalistic lines. And an out-group, typically foreigners, immigrants, elites, or an opposing party.

Passions are stoked, and the assault on truth begins—the necessary predicate for discrediting your opposition and for creating supporters. It usually starts with attacks on the press and journalists, and then it moves to universities and students and professors, since truth is the real enemy, and whoever pursues it must be declared the enemy. Evidence of nation after nation making this distressing turn is now all around us.

We must be careful not to underestimate the negative consequences to our own values caused by this pervasive foreign censorship and suppression. Given the ever-increasing integration of peoples of the world through the powerful forces of economic activity, communications, and movements across borders, we depend on professors, students, and ideas flowing freely through our community of institutions. We may, therefore, sometimes look at these acts of intolerance abroad as matters of mere foreign consequence, but they almost always have much more direct immediate consequences for our own values.

The most recent case that vividly makes this point is the hideous torture and murder of Jamal Khashoggi, a Saudi national and unsparing critic of that regime. A violation of international law and human rights? Yes, it certainly appears so. But it was potentially a violation of American law and the interests protected by those laws. For Khashoggi was a columnist for the *Washington Post* and a legal resident of the United States, with two children (of his four) who are U.S. citizens. As such, he was protected by the First Amendment for the things he said and for which he was killed. This is a crime under American laws against torture and violations of civil rights, for which there is extraterritorial jurisdiction to pursue prosecutions. So, it is deplorable that no action has been taken, in this country, to bring his killers to justice and to vindicate U.S. interests—a precedent that should concern us all.

Of course, there is no shortage of attacks on the truth and on truth-seekers right here, at home. The undermining of honest discourse has occurred, so far, not through official acts of censorship but through more indirect—if not very subtle—means of suppression: The free press is labeled the "enemy of the people." The irrefutable science underlying our understanding of climate change is portrayed as a fabrication propagated for a political agenda. And universities are increasingly cast as incubators of intolerance and enemies of free expression—a sensationalist charge disproved by the consistent presence on university campuses, including Columbia, of controversial speakers from both the Left and the Right.

Some might argue that all these verbal attacks on the press and universities, as well as all the other daily falsehoods that accompany them, are harmless—only a superficial attack without lasting consequence. For us, however, in a university, where truth is everything, we cannot accept that characterization. It cuts to our core.

WHAT ARE WE TO DO?

So, what are we to do?

Fortunately, there is experience to guide us in our response, and nowhere is that experience more resonant than at Columbia.

Precisely 100 years ago, in 1919, during the chaotic and repressive post-World-War-I era I referenced earlier, a moment of civic peril laid bare a fight between Imagination and Ignorance. The fight was fierce and provoked two distinct responses, each of them worthy of special note, celebration, and emulation today.

First, the United States Supreme Court took three cases—including that involving presidential hopeful Eugene V. Debs—and began interpreting the words "Congress shall make no law abridging the freedom of speech or of the press."

It took the Court and the nation another fifty years to get it right, with special help of the civil rights and the women's movements, but when we finally did, and when it all came together, the United States had created the greatest shield for freedom of thought and of expression of any nation in history. The search for truth became its core, animating idea, and American universities flourished over time to institutionalize and idealize that way of life.

Also, in 1919, at the more local level, on this campus, a new, year-long required course for Columbia freshmen was launched called Contemporary Civilization. Though, today, we know CC as the genesis of the famed Core Curriculum, then it was nothing more than a bold experiment in higher education. The objective, reflected in the course name, was to apply learning and reason derived from classic texts to the problems facing society in the aftermath of a cataclysmic war. The idea was to double-down on the academic mission, and it has made a difference, as generation after generation has attested to its value in creating an open mind and intellect.

Both of these century-old, intellectual innovations arose from the same sensibility. Both assumed that the best side of human nature includes the desire to learn and to live by the truth, and to acquire and create knowledge. And, while our natural negative instincts—activated by our fears, greed, and lust for power—sometimes divert us from that quest, a life worth living will only follow from a determined effort to engage with ideas at the most profound levels. Even those ideas we dislike and firmly believe to be in error.

This time—your time—presents a conundrum. This is, above all, a moment when we must reassert our commitment to open inquiry, to reason, and to the sanctity of knowledge and understanding. As was the case a century ago, these pursuits are increasingly out-of-step with the currents of the broader world, making it all the more essential that we express our devotion to that endeavor. We must not apologize for this, but relish and champion it and find our own new contributions to this end.

Yet, at the same time, our world demands that we, as a university, be more permeable to—more blended with—life beyond the academy. The most striking physical manifestation of Columbia's modern engagement with the larger world will be our new Manhattanville campus, which is intentionally designed to be open and welcoming to the world. Indeed, all of us feel the moral imperative to be working on solutions to global problems that frequently appear to be beyond the grasp of sovereign governments and our mostly diminished international organizations.

Moreover, to spend any time here at Columbia is to be confronted with your sense of duty and purpose—along with your well-earned belief in your own ability to make a difference.

This push and pull—of "truth seeking" and "meaningful action"—is a tension endemic to higher education today and to the lives you will live. The twin goals of "serv[ing] society and the world," while protecting our "distinctive intellectual outlook," is something we always have felt, but its centrality to our enterprise has only intensified over time.

Happily, as we confront this dual agenda, there is this heartening and indisputable reality: No group of graduates could be better equipped to navigate this precarious path than you.

After all, when you chose to attend Columbia at the beginning of a journey that finds one of its conclusions today, you elected to become part of a University that for 265 years has been distinctively defined by its commitment to addressing the "insistent problems of the present."

One of the legacies of receiving a world-class education is the sobering awareness of the inadequacy of our own knowledge. Some years ago, one of the people I admire and respect most, our Manhattanville architect, Renzo Piano, had just turned 70, and I asked him what it felt like. He said that, as much as he had thought about and prepared for that moment, it still came to him as a shock. (Now, I can attest to that feeling of shock.) But, more than anything, he said, it made him feel that our proper life-span should be 210 years: 70 to learn, 70 to do, and 70 to teach the next generation.

This lovely description captures an elementary fact of life: A good life always has the feeling that we are learning more and more as we go and that we could do even better if we just learned a bit more.

I hope that you are fortunate enough to carry that spirit of life with you, and we must hope together that it continues to define this nation and the world in the century ahead.

On behalf of Columbia University, I extend to all our graduates, the Centennial Class of 2019, our warmest congratulations.

CHAPTER 32

CONVOCATION ADDRESS

Columbia College and the School of Engineering and
Applied Science, Low Plaza, August 25, 2019

N o occasion in the academic calendar is more meaningful, or filled
with happiness, than Convocation—the formal welcome we extend
to you, the newest members of our community. The beginning
of the academic year is always a time characterized by hope and excitement
about the possibilities ahead. But what makes it truly special is the renewal of
our purpose by your presence. I mean this, and, on behalf of the entire faculty
and the institution as a whole, I want to convey to you our enormous pleasure at
your joining us. I also want to say, to the parents and families attending this evening's ceremony, that we appreciate the complex feelings you are experiencing
at this moment. Pride, joy, apprehension and anxiety, relief—these emotions are
heightened at this time, and, if we're successful at this Convocation, they will be
made even more intense. Thank you all for becoming part of this very, very great
institution that we all love and cherish.

I want, in the few moments I have with you tonight, to talk about the fundamentals of Columbia University and of universities generally—what we are about,
what we do, what we are committed to and believe in—and to contrast that with
distressing trends in the world beyond these academic gates. I want to try to speak
to you in the moment—your moment, really, for this will be a significant part of
the reality in which you will be in college, which is always part of what makes the
whole thing such a distinctive life experience. I seek here to offer some context
for what will follow after this Convocation, as you settle into the experience of
being a student at Columbia.

What is a university? This, of course, is a profound question, beyond the range of a small Convocation talk to answer. But, for our purposes now, here is what I would say. Universities are all about knowledge, about discovering truth, about unraveling the mysteries of life and the natural world we inhabit, about grasping and holding in one's mind the complexities of existence. A university is not about making money or profits, or exercising power, or creating policies, or worshiping a deity, or being in a club, or having a good time, or building a relationship. These ambitions are often—usually—fine in themselves, and universities are not entirely removed from them, but they do not constitute the essence of a university. Our essence is in the sense of wonder, curiosity, and the steadfast pursuit of understanding things better than we know now. There is always a forward momentum to universities. We most certainly have enormous respect for the past, and we are full-fledged members of that little troupe of explorers who have populated humankind over the millennia, but we are always in the moment and moving forward with the strong currents of curiosity.

So, this is what we are at base. But there are three important additional points to be made here. One is to recognize that this spirit of inquiry is not the result of some independent right or privilege we happen to possess. While we are a "private" university, we are still a publicly chartered institution, which gives rise to profound responsibilities to our societies and to the world. In that sense, there is very little difference between "public" and "private" universities in America, and altogether the spirit of serving the public good by advancing knowledge over time has resulted in the greatest system of higher education and research universities in the world, with incalculable benefits to humanity. I assure you, we are all fully conscious of our public mission.

The second point to be made here is the pursuit of truth in universities takes place within a framework of norms and principles that are rigorously enforced and zealously guarded. In universities, you must adhere to facts, commit your ideas to logic and reason, give appropriate acknowledgement to the ideas and contributions of others, recognize counter-arguments and perspectives, demonstrate open-mindedness and a capacity for self-criticism, and conduct yourself with civility and respect for others—especially those with whom you disagree. We know we are extreme in these conditions—any act of brazen falsification or falsehoods or of taking the ideas of others as your own suffers the academic capital punishment of banishment from the scholarly profession. To be a scholar you must situate yourself in these norms.

And now the third point about universities—which may seem inconsistent with what I have just said about the norms of a scholarly temperament, but is not, in fact. Universities are also living communities, civic communities, and, as such, we have in addition to research and teaching what in essence amounts to a public forum, where faculty and students can discuss and debate the issues of the day. In this realm, we abide by the constitutional principle of freedom of speech—and that means that virtually anything can be said about any public issue (with some exceptions I won't go into here). No one outside this University has a right to come onto the campus and speak, but, as part of their free speech rights, faculty and students may invite outside speakers from time to time. And in this limited public forum, within the University, we have chosen to follow the nation and to protect all viewpoints on public issues, no matter how offensive or dangerous they may be. This is, to be sure, a reasonably debatable choice, but it is our choice and therefore a reality of life that we must all learn to live by—one in which there will be "uninhibited, robust, and wide-open" debate, where we must rely on our own voices to reject ideas we deplore rather than shrink from that world into censorship. Challenge that reality if you wish, but do not expect the institution to protect you from it while it stands. Columbia, in particular, has a long and proud tradition of protecting and engaging with difficult speech.

So, this is what a university is. It may sound banal, but it is accurate nonetheless. It is by design, by principle, different from the outside world, to some extent— not separate from it, but different.

There are, of course, and it's worthy to note, criticisms of our institutions. Universities, it is sometimes said, are too ideological, too left-leaning, lazy, out of touch with the real problems of society, too rich, too expensive, too suppressive of free speech, and so on. I have written and spoken about each of these critiques on many occasions. I cannot say more about them today. But I do want to acknowledge them, and I do want to say that we are ourselves highly self-critical and always trying to be better at what we do. We understand that we need to take a more global perspective on the world, for example, from the standpoint of our scholarship and teaching. We now have nine Columbia Global Centers spread around the world ready to assist our faculty and students in that effort. We understand that universities should be more active and systematic in making research and knowledge generated here available to those who can use it to benefit humanity. A new initiative called Columbia World Projects is experimenting with how to accomplish this goal, and we will this year be looking deeper into the institution to see what can be done more broadly. We sometimes call this the fourth purpose of a university, how to bring academic knowledge to work in the world, in addition to our mission of research, education, and public service. We will this year also focus specifically on what more we can do to mobilize the resources of the University to focus on consequences of climate change. So, there are criticisms—some are fair, some not—and, in the spirit of academic inquiry, we are always open to criticisms and intent on improving.

Now, I want to shift from the university to the world beyond the university, briefly. I want to take note of a very dangerous phenomenon that has arisen here and across the world in the last several years. The problem we have today is that there are trends in the outside world, especially the political world, that increasingly reject the fundamental principles on which the very special qualities of universities have been established. It is a hard fact of contemporary life that there is a declining respect for truth, reason, knowledge, civility and decency, and human rights. Universities must refrain from taking sides on political issues, so I am not here speaking about the fierce debates now occurring on trade policies, immigration, or abortion, and so on. What I am speaking about is the lessening regard for what we broadly call the search for, and respect for, truth and for the intellectual framework and character needed for that search to fruitfully happen. When anything can be said and believed, the conditions of democracy are lost, and when democracy is lost, a university cannot survive. It has no meaning. We, of course, are not there yet, but the trend is there, and it is the defining fact of our—most importantly, your—time—so much so that I think it cannot go unmentioned even on an occasion as celebratory as this.

All this said, this is not by any means a time for despair. I think this is demonstrated for us by three interconnected events that occurred in times of similar stresses 100 years ago exactly. The descent into chaos and destruction that was World War I, the ideological conflicts around the political systems that created such upheavals in nations, and the intolerance and injustices inflicted on dissenters, minorities, immigrants, and vulnerable populations defined the era in which people who still believed in the validity of Enlightenment values stepped in to repair the breaches. They are role models for us today. Of immediate interest to you is the creation of the Core Curriculum, as mentioned, the singular and defining feature of a Columbia education. Whatever one believes should be included or excluded from the Core, which is, very properly, an ever-ongoing debate, the very idea of a core, of being immersed in a body of knowledge and thought, of being exposed to the works of many of the greatest minds engaged in the quest for truth, not in some pre-digested form delivered through the medium of the lecture, but to be lived with and to be debated and discussed with your peers, the efforts to probe the most profound questions of life—this was a reaffirmation, a doubling down, of the values of knowledge, at a moment when the world seemed to be coming apart at the seams.

Similarly, in 1919, this was precisely the moment when the United States Supreme Court began its modern interpretation of the principles of freedom of speech and press, which over the course of the last century that followed has made this country the most protective of thought and speech and press in history. This, too, was premised on the same idea that truth is the goal of life and society, and that demands an intellectual character composed of extraordinary tolerance and a capacity for self-doubt. This was, as it were, the First Amendment's Core Curriculum for America.

And, finally, in a more generalized sense, approximately one hundred years ago was the beginning of the modern research university and all the values I summarized at the outset. And today, Columbia, stands at the very top of those institutions.

Then, as now, out of the potential unraveling of the values of knowledge, reason, and truth, people and institutions stepped forward to renew the values.

I say all of this for several reasons. It is always valuable to restate the philosophical underpinnings of what one is doing. So, as you begin here, that's good for you to know. But it is especially valuable and important today because of contrary trends that threaten to undermine those bedrock principles. And, finally, it is good in these moments to appreciate the elements of our daily lives that reflect the efforts of those who came before us to sustain and build up that foundation, to realize that the foundation is fragile but enduring, and to never take what we have for granted. Every time you enter a Core Curriculum class, or any class, or feel the exhilaration of learning and thinking something new, or engage in the campus debates on the pressing issues of our time, I hope a part of your mind will remind you of these deeper principles at work and of where they came from.

Good luck and welcome to Columbia.

CHAPTER 33

THE FUTURE OF THE UNIVERSITY

Keynote Address at the European Strategy and Policy Analysis
System Conference, Brussels, October 19, 2019

---

*After developing an informal agreement for the leaders of the European Parliament
to visit Columbia University annually for a day-long discussion about their Future
Trends reports (organized by Columbia World Projects), President Bollinger was
invited to Brussels to provide a keynote address discussing the nature of universities,
modern critiques, changes in American higher education, and opportunities for
partnership.*

I t is a very great honor for me to be invited to speak with you today. My
subject is universities, American universities specifically, and I want in my
remarks to comment on three things: First, I want to say something about
the nature, or character, of these unusual and very special institutions and about
the sources of their success. Second, I want to say something about the criticisms
and critiques one hears today about universities. And, third, I will comment
on how American universities are changing, in major ways, and will continue to
change in the coming decade. At the end, I may add a few comments on how the
Trump presidency is affecting our system of universities.

My purpose is to offer a small contribution to the discussion you are having
now about the challenges that lie ahead for Europe, as reflected in your,
"Global Trends to 2030" report. Specifically, I want to explain how changes
that are taking root in American higher education mean that the world I come
from should be an increasingly valuable partner and resource, as you pursue
the difficult but essential work of thinking seriously and critically about the
future.

I

First, then, let me turn to the nature and success of American universities. In the United States, there are some 60 major research universities. Most of them are "state" or "public" institutions, rather than "private." The principal distinction between the two is no longer in their basic character or values, as it once was, but rather primarily in their respective sources of funding. While both "public" and "private" universities have access to large revenue streams from the federal government—mostly having to do with biomedical and scientific research—only "public" universities receive annual financial support from their respective state legislatures. Over the last century, this blended system of major research institutions—both "public" and "private" in official form—along with a myriad of colleges and other non-research universities, has become widely recognized as the premier system of higher education in the world.

These institutions are, indisputably, the primary source of discoveries that have fueled virtually every meaningful advance in modern life and have brought us to where we are today. From groundbreaking medical breakthroughs to agricultural innovations credited with saving billions of people worldwide from starvation, to the Internet, to artificial intelligence: this and so much more are the result of university-based research.

We need, therefore, to start by recognizing the astounding successes and achievements of the modern system of research universities. At the same time, these successes highlight a striking—and even strange—fact, namely that these institutions are organized in what can only be fairly described as the most bizarre ways. No expert in organizational structure would ever come up with the academic institutions we have developed, nor predict that they would be as successful as they have been and are. Essentially, the idea of a university is to hire quite young, and therefore naturally unproven, people who have succeeded brilliantly in their studies, give them a period of 5 to 7 years to see what they can do in the way of original work, and then, if approved, offer them a lifetime appointment as a professor, with more or less full control over the course of their research and thinking. To a professor the concept of a "boss" is utterly foreign. One might reasonably think that this would be a recipe for mediocrity and laziness, producing precious little advances in the search for truth. But, in fact, it seems to activate a sense of dedication and determination in virtually everyone. The atmosphere of a university is vibrant, purposeful, and constantly creative—generating invaluable results, all of which are easily witnessed in modern daily life and traceable to the labs and libraries that constitute the independent academy.

There are, to be sure, many strongly voiced criticisms of universities, which I raise in part because they have some truth, but mostly to say they are not fully true and they detract our attention from this remarkable story of success. We are said to be inefficient and too costly, leaving students who are not from affluent families with life-disabling debt, at a time of historic inequality. We hear over and over again about the $1.5 trillion in outstanding liabilities resulting from student loans—coupled with dire predictions that this system will implode in just the way the subprime mortgage market did in 2007–2008. We are described as having our heads in the sand, not seeing the impact of digital technology on producing equally effective but far cheaper education, just as newspaper editors whose former business model is now crumbling beneath them could not imagine a world in which people would not go to their front porch every morning to pick up their daily newspaper. This new reality, it is said, will inexorably lead to the certain upending of our business model as education—like news—moves onto the Internet. We are criticized for being too left leaning politically, too politically correct in our thinking, and too coddling of the new younger generation that seeks "safe spaces" where they will never have to confront an opinion they don't like.

These are, of course, serious and complex issues, but here are my very quick responses: Yes, it is true that, over the past decades, tuition has risen considerably more than the Consumer Price Index. Two points: First, before addressing whether the comparison is apt, I must point out that at a private university, such as Columbia, undergraduate financial aid is such that the admissions process is truly "need blind," and, so, if your family has an income of $60,000 or less, you essentially come for free. Our public universities, however, face a different set of financial constraints, namely the precipitous and deeply regrettable decline that has occurred in the funding provided by state legislatures, something I witnessed firsthand as president of the University of Michigan. For these institutions, who generally do not have the endowments or streams of private donations, that lack of state legislative commitment and support has been the primary driver of the increased expenses they must shoulder, which has translated into higher tuition rates. There is a problem of inequality resulting in differential access to higher education. But we, like all institutions, go out of our way to find students of need. The real problem is the inequality of access to good education at the K-12 level, which bars talent from emerging.

Now, second, on the matter of the university costs and tuition outpacing the CPI, this is an issue that begs the following question: Should we understand rising costs for housing and food (which is basically what is measured by the CPI) in the same way that we evaluate increases in the cost of neuroscience research that may one day cure Alzheimer's disease, to pick just one example? I believe that it is, indeed, wrong to equate the two. For in a world where the frontiers of knowledge and the number of subjects warranting sustained exploration are rapidly expanding, it would be self-defeating to impose an ordinary inflationary gauge on the resources society devotes to academic research.

As far as charges of coddling students who are not prepared or willing to embrace the challenges that come with freedom of speech, I have written and spoken about these issues. In essence, I think these critiques are overdone, and out of proportion to and not reflective of reality. It is possible, as always, to cite notorious examples of controversial speakers being protested and disrupted, invitations and honors revoked under pressure, and other instances of closed-mindedness and intolerance. And critics of higher education, often with a larger political agenda of undermining the credibility of our institutions, will never hesitate to do so. But one has to keep everything in perspective and recognize that countless controversial speakers visit our campuses every day, all without incident. And, while it is only my experience, perhaps, I do not believe that classrooms across our universities are being used to advance political ideologies and viewpoints. The Scholarly Temperament, as I call it, just like the Judicial Temperament, in which partisan politics are kept at bay, is as strong today as I have ever seen it.

Finally, as to the notion that universities will face the same fate at the hands of the Internet as printed newspapers, this is a hard, and dangerous call, but I do not believe there will be a parallel experience here. The personal relationship of teacher and student cannot be replicated on the Internet, nor most important of all, can the culture of open intellectual inquiry be reproduced elsewhere, and the value to students of attending our schools will, in my view, continue to be prized. We will, of course, see.

II

Having now made reference to the modern research university's contributions to society, and also acknowledged several critiques of the current system of higher education as it exists today in the U.S., I would like to turn to where we are headed.

The laudable—and ambitious—project described by your Global Trends report is to gain the foresight needed for successfully guiding the efforts of the European Parliament and the EU's other governing bodies over the next decade. The report begins with a series of provocative questions: "What are the dynamics we are missing? Are there ways to think differently about the forecasts we are [quote] 'certain' about? . . . What different futures can we imagine within the framework of what we know—and do not know?" The report is replete with prompts for readers to "learn more" by examining information contained therein, while also acknowledging that there are many deficits in our knowledge. Throughout its pages, it identifies a series of foundational questions to be answered.

The nature of this project—examining and understanding the large forces defining the next decade—really requires sustained intellectual exploration and credible research. Accordingly, I would assert, the objective established by the report is unlikely to be achieved unless it is paired with a deliberate and intentional effort to enlist the intellectual resources available for, and devoted to, creating new knowledge. These intellectual resources, of course, reside primarily in the academic community's research universities.

I would also suggest that we would be foolish to ignore ascendant forces in the political arena that actively and sometimes aggressively reject reasoned and evidence-based discourse because it leads to inconvenient truths. These actors resist the very approach to democratic governance you have described—and manifested—in your report. But this is yet another reason to engage the engine of productive knowledge (i.e., research universities) on which society's foresight is based.

Now, against this backdrop, I want to discuss two related, yet distinct changes that are occurring in American universities. I believe each is relevant to your objectives.

The first concerns how universities are becoming more global in their intellectual orientation and in their physical presence around the world.

And the second has to do with the modern research university's escalating engagement with practical affairs and public issues and the increasing concern for the impact of scholarly research beyond the academic gates.

These are matters of great significance to Columbia University, which is, I like to believe, assuming the lead on these transformations. But in this discussion I am emphasizing broader trends across American research universities.

As I said, we are in the midst of a highly complex transformation that involves globalization and the modern research university. But the essential change is that universities are assigning much more significance to the accelerating inter- dependence of nations and peoples in framing the important questions and puzzles to be addressed through scholarly inquiry.

To understand this shift in orientation I need to provide a brief recap of how we arrived here. After the Second World War, and for the next two decades, the broad intellectual framework for universities included developing expertise about the world. But it was done in a very particular way. Regional institutes were estab- lished, and we saw a proliferation of courses and scholarly research devoted to international human rights, war and peace studies, and international institutions. Students from across the world were invited to our campuses, and our students studied abroad. This was a very successful transition to a new world order. There were domestic concerns and international concerns.

But, during the 1980s and 90s, the coherence between academic pursuits and world affairs began to break down. Many disciplines and fields—among them political science, economics, literature, law, and so on—became focused upon abstract and theoretical issues detached from practical consequence in the out- side world. At the same time, the world itself was undergoing a dramatic trans- formation, spurred by three historic forces: the opening of markets and trade; a global communications revolution delivered by the Internet; and a profound increase in the movements of people around the globe. This re-ordering of world affairs raised questions and presented new challenges that were captured neither by the prevailing post-World War II academic framework, nor the intellectual fashions of the time. The result was the creation of a university culture out-of- alignment with the world beyond its borders. The expertise on regions and nations of the world was affected by this, sometimes withering and often isolated.

American universities began to wake up to this new reality and the need for more direct engagement about a decade ago, and thus far, three strategies have been deployed in response.

The first has been significantly to increase institutional practices already in place: more international students, more faculty exchanges, and expanded study abroad opportunities for students. The second response has been to establish branch campuses (with separate faculties and student bodies) around the world. Perhaps the most notable example of this has been the Dubai International Academic City—more commonly known as "Education City" in Dubai—which was launched in May 2006 and is home now to more than 12,000 students who study in 13 international institutes of higher education sponsored by many American universities. Other examples are NYU's branch campuses in Abu Dhabi and Shanghai, and Yale's in Singapore.

Neither of these approaches—exchange programs and branch campuses—seem to me in the end, however, to come to terms with the underlying issue of the need for bringing our scholarship and education in better alignment with the world as it is. Their purpose is to facilitate being abroad; being abroad and studying the new inter-dependent world are not the same thing, and these strategies end up having too little effect on transforming the intellectual orientation of the home institution, which, as I've said, I believe is the heart of the problem of modern intellectual life.

For this and other reasons, I have favored establishing so-called "global centers" around the world. Columbia now has nine, with another on the way. These small, flexible, presences allow faculty and students be out in the world, teaching and conducting research while being physically stationed abroad, with the expectation that they will soon return home to inform the thinking on our New York campuses. Other universities are moving in this direction.

The upshot of all of these efforts, however, and what I can predict for the future, is a greatly increased presence of American research universities across the world. This will be a major transformation.

That leads to the second change underway, which is a growing willingness on the part of universities more consciously and more explicitly to bring academic research and scholarly capacities to bear on practical problems facing humanity.

At Columbia, two years ago, we established an entity called Columbia World Projects with this specific goal in mind. To understand the significance of this development from the vantage point of a university president, you must consider this tension intrinsic to all major research universities: On the one hand, to do what we are expected to do, universities must remain somewhat removed from the world of everyday affairs. On the other, there must be some degree of alignment between what the world takes as important, and what we, as scholars, take as important. The two ways of being must be simultaneously present for our institutions to succeed.

There are parts of a research university that easily navigate this tension and do so in straightforward fashion because of their particular mission. For example, like most universities, Columbia has an academic medical center that is both a leader in medical and bio-medical research and also a major health center providing the highest level of clinical care to patients.

Yet, no university has assembled and expanded the discrete efforts populating our institutions so that they can be understood as constituting a distinct and central purpose of the university. We must encourage these efforts, give them proper academic recognition, provide them with support and assistance, and, perhaps most importantly, describe them as essential to the university's larger mission. The ultimate aim, however, is for the university, as an entity, to take on projects that position the university as an actor taking some responsibility for participating—through academic work and with outside partners—in solving human problems. I call this the Fourth Purpose of the university—in addition to scholarship, teaching, and public service (which is a form of citizen volunteer work).

In our modern world, where nations are frequently overmatched by societal problems extending beyond their borders, and international institutions often struggle to cope with the issues they must confront, it is critically important that other parts of civil society step forward to help by working in partnership to achieve solutions. If this assessment is correct, then what is unfolding at Columbia will continue to expand and will become a trend across major research universities. In my view, this is both a responsibility of our institutions and a much-needed corrective.

Climate change is, of course, the quintessential global problem, one that is solvable only by collective, global action, and one that accordingly calls on all of us to participate in developing a response. While coming to terms with this reality places an immense strain on our academic institutions, it is also galvanizing, for there is an enormous demand for basic intellectual thinking and research, which we need to supply more of. So, too, is the need for action, which we should be ready and willing to assist in. Thus, right now, Columbia is taking upon itself this very challenge and considering seriously the creation of the first School of Climate Change in America, which would be closely linked to the spirit of Columbia World Projects.

When you take all of these observations together, the upshot is that we can expect the extraordinarily successful system of the American research university to continue thriving, to become more and more academically focused on very real and practical problems of the modern, global world, and to become more engaged with outside partners in helping to solve those problems. These are trends I believe we should all welcome and applaud.

III

I feel I cannot end without adding a comment about the phenomenon of the rise of so-called "populist" and "nationalist" politics across the world and in the United States—and the lamentable rise of authoritarian-style leaders—and the consequences thus far for our universities.

The tactics of these movements are familiar to every person here. They typically begin with a call for a particular religious, ethnic, racial or national identity; followed by claims that this identity is under threat; then comes the proposal of dubious public policy solutions and hyperbolic claims of accomplishment; all of this built on the foundation of a relentless disregard for the truth and assertions that the media are deliberately spreading falsehoods, so that followers may believe what they choose. Along the way, opponents are demonized, particularly "foreigners" and immigrants, and the evil and potent political empowerment of private intolerance is effectively deployed.

The manifestations of this dispiriting historical moment are discussed endlessly—even obsessively—around the globe, and certainly here in Brussels. We cannot look the other way or ignore this political and social phenomenon. Clearly, you have confronted this frightening politics in your 2030 report.

What, though, has been the impact on major research universities and higher education in the United States? So far, at least, I think the actual impact, broadly viewed, on the pursuit of knowledge, and on our daily research, scholarship, and teaching, has been minor—at least compared to other "dark moments" in American history—such as the McCarthy period of the 1950s. Federal funding of research has continued to grow; there have been relatively few attempts at overt censorship; and campuses remain vital and vibrant.

Still, there are two areas of concern.

First, there have been significant disruptions in the flow of international students, beginning with the travel ban targeting Muslim-majority countries just weeks after Donald Trump took office and expanding to other countries since, with fewer student visas being offered by the State Department. The impact on many of our students, and their feeling of vulnerability, has been acute. This anxiety was recently exacerbated when the FBI—under the auspices of helping the government thwart the illegal transfer of intellectual property to foreign rivals— asked college and university administrators to develop new protocols for monitoring foreign-born students and visiting scholars, particularly if they are ethnically Chinese. In an op-ed in the *Washington Post*, I publicly challenged these efforts by the federal government as ill-advised and contrary to the spirit of open inquiry that has been the keystone to the great success of discovery of new knowledge.

The second, and more insidious assault on the university is the persistent undermining of respect for truth and facts, and the creation of a culture of hatred and prejudice that now infects the private sphere in America. This systematic, coordinated campaign to erode public trust in our institutions comes at immeasurable cost, especially for journalism and the press, which are always, from my perspective, the first layer of society that feels the brunt of intolerance just before universities do. As journalism goes, so in the end goes the scholar, in my experience.

I would like to close, however, on a note of optimism, which I am able to offer because of the history of my field (i.e., freedom of speech and press and the U.S. Constitution) and my home of Columbia University. I do not believe this is a time for despair. Precisely one hundred years ago, in the United States (and here in Europe) our societies were subject to extraordinary stresses that also put at risk truth and reason, civility and decency, human rights and compassion. And those who believed in Enlightenment values stepped in to repair the breaches. That's when the U.S. Supreme Court first began its now century-long journey to establish protections for freedom of thought and expression never before seen in the history of the world. And that's when Columbia University joined many other institutions and individuals in celebrating the best of human nature by doubling down on academic virtues and creating a new, year-long required course called Contemporary Civilization, part of what's now known as our Core Curriculum— with the objective of applying the learning derived from classic texts to the problems facing society in the aftermath of a cataclysmic war. These two great achievements in advancing the search for truth were born in dark and troublesome days. We can do the same.

The work you are doing here to think deeply and seriously about overcoming the formidable problems we face, and to build a stronger future, is part of that continuum. Thank you for inviting me to join you in this endeavor.

CHAPTER 34

STATEMENT TO THE UNIVERSITY SENATE PLENARY REGARDING THE BOYCOTT, DIVESTMENT, AND SANCTIONS (BDS) MOVEMENT

Columbia University, Low Library, March 6, 2020

In 2020, during a period of rising anti-Semitism around the nation and the world, many university campuses continued to debate proposals for "BDS"—institutional Boycott, Divestment, and economic Sanctions against Israel. President Bollinger had spoken out repeatedly against BDS and academic boycotts, including his 2007 statement in opposition to the British Academic Union's proposed boycott of Israeli scholars and schools—a statement that was ultimately signed by approximately three hundred other college and university presidents. A growing number of Jewish students at Columbia expressed the view that the campus environment around this debate was increasingly suffused with anti-Semitism. President Bollinger spoke to those concerns at the University Senate prior to an undergraduate student council vote on BDS.

I want to speak about a difficult matter—about a concern I have regarding the risk of a rising anti-Semitism on our campus. Any bigotry and prejudice towards groups is intolerable, especially (for all the obvious reasons) within a university, and we should be quick to condemn its presence in any form and in any context. In my life, I have tried to do so, whether it be racism, sexism, homophobia, anti-Arab, anti-Muslim, anti-Asian, or any other kinds of bigotry. Over the past year, I have increasingly become concerned about anti-Semitism, and I feel it is important for me to say something now.

There is an upcoming vote among undergraduate students on a proposal to recommend that the University divest from companies doing business with Israel that profit from the treatment of Palestinians in the West Bank and Gaza. There is no question that this is a highly contentious issue, both the underlying issues of Israel and the Palestinians and the idea of divestment as a means of protest about Israel's policies.

I do not support the proposal for divestment. That is for two reasons. One is the longstanding understanding that the University should not change its investment policies on the basis of a political position unless there is a broad consensus within the institution that to do so is morally and ethically compelled. This is a necessary though not sufficient condition. I do not believe that consensus exists with respect to this proposal.

But I disagree on the merits, too. I believe this imposes a standard on this particular political issue that is not right when one considers similar issues in other countries and in other contexts around the world. To my mind this is unwise, analytically flawed, and violates a sense of fairness and proportionality. I well understand that some others whom I respect hold different views, but, if I am called upon to take a position, this is the one I have come to over many years of thought.

My concern today, however, is not just with this proposal, but with the broader atmosphere in which this and other related issues are being debated. Feelings are charged. Divestment is a piece of a larger and controversial BDS movement. That movement is itself but a variant on a vast and ever-present debate about Israel, the West Bank, Gaza, the Middle East, the region, and from there outwards to the rest of the world. Critical matters are at stake, to be sure, but what must be avoided at all costs, and what I fear is happening today, is a process of mentality that goes from hard-fought debates about very real and vital issues to hostility and even hatred towards all members of groups of people simply by virtue of a religious, racial, national, or ethnic relationship. This must not happen.

No single issue is an island. When a swastika appears on our campus, it is not just an isolated event. When there is a rising anti-Semitism in the country and around the world, every single instance of it in any context is more alarming than it might otherwise be.

I plead with everyone on our campus to be careful and vigilant against legitimate debate turning into anger, then to hatred and demonization, and invidious discrimination.

I can say that Jewish students are feeling this, and it's wrong. I feel it, and it's wrong. We all feel it, and it's wrong.

These are delicate matters to talk about. Atmosphere is elusive. It is easy to dismiss feelings of insecurity and affront as being too sensitive. Many groups suffer forms of discrimination and prejudice that are unacceptable, and to single out any one for concern is to risk being accused of neglecting the others unmentioned.

Furthermore, there are often, as here, excessive claims of hostility that one does not want to legitimate by referring to lesser but still very real problems. With respect to anti-Semitism, there are now claims by outsiders that Columbia is an "anti-Semitic" university with systemic bigotry. This is, of course, preposterous. No Jewish student, faculty member, or staff I know believes that this is the case; nor do I. But the absurdity of the claim does not and should not stop me or us from speaking out against instances and episodes of anti-Semitism that do exist.

I view it as my responsibility to say when I see something that should concern us. I do so now, and ask that we all work to ensure that the debates we have about debatable matters be done in good faith and with a sense of shared humanity and respect.

CHAPTER 35

ANNOUNCING THE COLUMBIA CLIMATE SCHOOL

Columbia University, July 10, 2020

For many decades, Columbia University established itself as a pioneer in the study of geosciences and our changing climate, from the founding of the Lamont-Doherty Earth Observatory in the late 1940s to a longstanding affiliation with NASA's Goddard Institute for Space Studies and the establishment of the interdisciplinary Earth Institute in 1995. (Columbia professor Wallace Broeker first coined the term global warming *in the 1970s.) Having developed the core theme of a university's "Fourth Purpose" in applying its research and teaching to practical solutions addressing society's myriad challenges, President Bollinger established the Columbia Climate School, the institution's first new degree-granting school in a quarter of a century.*

Dear fellow members of the Columbia community:

Anyone who has spent a long career in academia knows firsthand that fields, disciplines, and subjects evolve and change, as new opportunities for knowledge are revealed, as new people come into the academy, and as new generations of students enter the scene. Today, I am writing to share a profoundly important new chapter for Columbia University, in a field that deserves the scholarly brilliance and creativity that only we as a University can deploy.

At their core, all universities are public institutions, in the sense that we are created by public favor to enhance human understanding, educate our youth, and convert knowledge into public good. The genius underlying all of this is rooted in strong scholarly values that are reinforced daily, within the uniquely dynamic intellectual communities that universities represent. As scholars, we are inherently independent-minded, reflective, and committed to sustained and deep inquiry no matter the time frame.

But our legitimacy and, frankly, our intellectual energy derive from being more or less aligned with the world's problems and needs. We are not free to ignore the issues of our age and pursue whatever we want. We are ultimately responsible to our societies and the world. To that end, we must answer the call to serve. And when necessary, we must evolve and change.

At the beginning of the last academic year, I appointed a Task Force, led by Earth Institute Director Alex Halliday, to explore what more the University should be doing with respect to climate change. The fundamental question was, and is, whether the scale of our efforts (within our University and universities generally) in this area of massive human concern is sufficient to meet the existential dimensions of the problem. In other words, as I wrote then, "Are we marshaling our academic resources in ways that are proportionate to the magnitude and gravity of the challenges civilization will face?"

In addition, concretely, would our efforts be significantly enhanced by the creation of a school devoted to these matters? The answer of the Task Force to that question was yes, as is mine, and as was the unanimous vote of the University Trustees at our recent June meeting. It is my honor, therefore, to announce that Columbia is establishing the Columbia Climate School, the first new school in 25 years at the University, and an institution that I have every expectation will be the most important climate school in the United States.

The creation of a new school is an exceedingly rare and significant event at this or any university. The ability to hire faculty, to create a student body and grant degrees, and to nurture a strong community of intellectual collegiality inhering in the pursuit of a particular knowledge base is especially empowering in the academic universe. How this new School will evolve remains to be determined. However, we are hardly starting from scratch. Columbia is already at the forefront of academic discovery and involvement in the issues of climate and society.

The School, at least at the outset, will be somewhat unconventional in its structure, building capacity from a hub of existing, world-class research centers and programs, including the Earth Institute and its many centers: the Lamont-Doherty Earth Observatory (LDEO), the International Research Institute for Climate and Society (IRI), the Center for Climate Systems Research (CCSR), Center for International Earth Science Information Network (CIESIN), and more. Additionally, even at the present moment, virtually every school and many departments within the Unviersity, from the arts and humanities to medicine and engineering, already support work in the field of climate. The new Columbia Climate School will be able to draw upon and reciprocate support for those efforts. It will, therefore, work in partnership with the deans and faculties of other schools throughout the institution. It is also notable that the School will be able to utilize the capacities we have created to be truly global in character and focus, especially with the vibrant Columbia Global Centers, and to bridge the world of scholarly endeavor with that of action and implementation, especially with the burgeoning Columbia World Projects and the other components of what we are calling the University's Fourth Purpose—our mission of being more present at the intersection of knowledge and change.

Inevitably, given the breadth of the phenomena, impacts, and human experiences associated with climate change, the School will figure out areas of special concentration. There already is a rich roster of strategic capabilities, with fields of expertise for which Columbia is currently recognized as the world leader (e.g., climate modeling and forecasting), and others that we will seek to develop further (e.g., food security). We recognize, of course, that climate change is not simply a physical problem but rather one raising a host of societal issues, most notably those encompassed by the principles of social justice. The School will open our eyes to the fact that the accelerating damage caused by climate change is likely disproportionately to affect vulnerable populations in regions at heightened risk of diminishing benefits of health and life.

With the Columbia Climate School, we are moving to take on in a scholarly way—as only a great university can—an area of tremendous public attention and increasing concern, as enduring as anything else we might conceive of. Like the problem itself, this effort may seem daunting, but it is most certainly a moment for institutional pride.

CHAPTER 36

COMMENCEMENT ADDRESS

Columbia University, online, April 30, 2021

Like many peer institutions during the COVID-19 pandemic, Columbia opted for a remote "virtual commencement" held entirely online in the spring of both 2020 and 2021.

We come together today, virtually, of course, to recognize your extraordinary achievement—graduation from a college or school of Columbia University and membership in the Class of 2021—an achievement made all the more worthy of admiration and celebration by these extraordinary times. Commencement is always an amalgam of the familiar and the singular. There is ceremony and ritual repeated year after year, connecting us to generations of Columbians stretching long into the past. But it also brings us to a higher elevation than ordinary life and allows us to see better into the future. Poised at this moment, however, this rite of passage contains the thousands of unique and personal stories of determination and exploration, of growth and self-discovery, of knowledge and expertise—your stories, in other words.

On behalf of the entire University, I offer our warmest congratulations. If we were assembling in-person, this would be the moment when I would offer the graduates the opportunity to thank their parents, families, spouses, and loved ones, since no one arrives at this moment without their backing. Assembling virtually, we have the possible advantage of being able to do this not by distant applause but by actual hugs. I, therefore, give you this moment to be together.

I

Let me begin by saying something about the times we are in.

Who among us does not feel unmoored? The flow of events, their scale and strangeness and sheer volume, posing one or another personal and societal challenge of obvious urgency, is overwhelming, and that is an understatement. It has been a searing experience for us all to be alive at this time, an incomprehensible mix of momentous change, wearing monotony, unfamiliar hardships, and, at times, inescapable sadness. Just focusing the mind becomes a challenge.

And yet nothing can be more important right now than developing the power of intellect, which is the reason we came together here, at Columbia, as members of this unique community, for this period of time. Never has society more desperately needed to reap the benefits of science, newly discovered knowledge, and the pursuit of truth. How otherwise can we possibly pretend to be sufficiently equipped to comprehend and to come to terms with the world to which we now bear witness? Just think about it:

A pandemic that has spared no one.
A crisis of democracy that is testing the viability of civic society.
A racial reckoning that we must confront with the full force of our
    collective consciousness.
The impact of potentially catastrophic changes in our climate, already felt
    incessantly.
And perhaps most sobering of all, the collapse of norms in intellectual and
    public life— the very mechanisms that we as a society rely upon to solve
    problems and drive progress.

In all my life, I have never seen anything like our current difficulties. I graduated from college in 1968, and Jean and I came to Columbia in that year. We all know the turbulence of that period—the political movements, the disruptions, the instabilities, and the dangers to the country. Everyone understood we were in the midst of a once-in-a-century upheaval—the type of turmoil that is often essential for real change to happen.

But this is of a different order. So much of what we take for granted as basic conditions of life have been upturned. My own field of free speech is a prime example.

A central premise of free speech, ever since the Enlightenment, has been that wide-open, public debate may produce bad and harmful speech, including falsehoods, lies, deceits, and bigotry, but that the best and most effective remedy for this is to trust in good speech to answer and triumph. But now technology, especially in the form of social media, has called into question that optimism. Concerns over the exponential increase in bad speech and in the ways people communicate cast a shadow of doubt over a premise that has guided us for over two hundred years.

So, this has been our, your, new reality. Any one of these crises would have been plenty to deal with. All of them intersecting and occurring at once has displaced the world as we know it.

And, so, I begin by acknowledging what you have lived through as a student at Columbia.

II

Now, while it is important to understand and recognize how difficult this period of time has been for you, it is also the right moment to express our gratitude for universities, to Columbia, in particular, and to the remarkable people who comprise our community and who make such important contributions to helping the world overcome just the sort of challenges we face today.

I like to say, and do so frequently, that no rational process would lead to the design of a modern university. If that wasn't clear enough 14 months ago, today it borders on a cliché. As organizations, universities are as complex a structure as it gets.

And, yet, they have survived and thrived over the decades and centuries.

As if by some magical force, universities nurture and take advantage of the human desire to know, to understand, and to share and make good that knowledge. Every day our lives are sustained and undergirded by discoveries from the academy. Consider the past year. Vaccines followed experiments unlocking the basic elements of life. Guides for surviving a pandemic followed a century of study and preparations by public health experts. Treatments for viruses and other diseases were invented in academic medical centers and shared with the world. All the while, we have watched with enormous admiration and respect as, month after exhausting month, Columbia's nurses, doctors, healthcare, and social workers persevere, selflessly devoting themselves to caring for the sick and those in need.

They have waged a titanic effort to save lives and to support the most vulnerable among us, and they have earned our everlasting gratitude.

There are still other areas of challenge where universities demonstrate their uncommon worth. For example: The realities of climate change have been documented by earth scientists (beginning, I have to say, at Columbia University and our Lamont-Doherty Earth Observatory), and responses have been imagined by social scientists and scholarly engineers. The conditions of democracy, including the principles of equality and freedom of speech and press, have been elucidated by legal scholars, political scientists, and journalism professors. And, most importantly, the faculty in the humanities and the arts have helped us know who we are, how to live, and what to live for, especially when times are hard.

Universities have stood as beacons of respect for truth, of reason and civility in the pursuit of truth, and of the idea that a good life can only rest on a foundation of these principles.

Let us, therefore, take this moment to celebrate Columbia and all of our colleagues in universities all across the world.

III

Now, I want to say a few words about you—about being a student and graduating at this particular moment. There is no getting around the fact that this has been an astoundingly difficult period in which to be a student, and you have suffered. Yet, it is also true that you have endured and responded to these challenges. Much of life is anticipating and preparing for adversity. Often we have only a vague sense of what it might be like. To have struggled through, and ultimately overcome adversity on this scale is, in a way, an educational miracle. Extremes in life are no longer abstractions to you. You have met them, learned about life, and succeeded where you could.

As students, you know that we learn both by study and by experience. In both, we learn best in cases of extremes. What we study is most often fashioned in the context of extremes. Shakespeare's plays (one example of many I could give) are not about usual times; they are about crises. And so it is across the intellectual spectrum, whether in the study of disease or of legal cases. In extremes, human nature and life are fully revealed, everything is more vivid and clear. Little is left to the imagination because what we need to know is right there before us to grasp, to absorb, and to comprehend.

In law, there is a famous saying that "hard cases make bad law." With law, as with life, we seek stability, and, when things are hard, they are complex and difficult to resolve in our minds. Hence, law from hard cases is inherently unstable. But life is different. We need and want to understand everything in its full complexity. That is the central and defining ambition of a university: to be able to hold everything, even ideas that are contradictory, in your mind simultaneously. When you are learning in times of extremes, that is what you get. So, hard cases may make bad law, but hard times make sharp minds.

All your life you will draw upon and learn from the experiences you have just had. The period of time around 1968 was revolutionary in many respects, like today. I cannot tell you how many times I have said, "I graduated from college and came to Columbia in 1968," and that statement reflects my sense of having been part of meaningful and historic experiences. I am sure you will do the same, saying, "I graduated from Columbia in 2021," and, you, and everyone else, will know what that means. It is profound.

It will, to be sure, take time for the meaning and significance of this experience to reveal itself. Give it time, be patient, and let the power of reflection and enlightenment take hold.

We as an institution must do the same. Just as the Columbia Class of 2021 will become a singular identity for all of you, you as a class will leave your unique mark on us, as well. With the power of reflection and enlightenment, Columbia and all of us attached to it will adapt, evolve, and grow. And your place in our history will forever be sacrosanct.

Thank you and congratulations to you, the Class of 2021.

CHAPTER 37

COMMENCEMENT ADDRESS

Columbia University, Low Plaza, May 18, 2022

On behalf of our Trustees, our faculty, our distinguished alumni, our families, and our many friends of Columbia University, it is my very, very great pleasure to welcome all of you gathered here today—and, notably, for the first IN PERSON commencement in three years. I am also delighted to welcome the tens of thousands of you who are joining us virtually, a way of being together we have come to know so intimately. We are all here to continue our 268-year tradition of celebrating the significant achievements of our graduates, representing seventeen schools, along with our affiliate institutions of Teachers College and Barnard.

So, I cannot imagine beginning my remarks to you in any other way than by acknowledging the extraordinary context, really the historical context, in which you have been students at Columbia and in which you have arrived at this remarkable milestone in your lives. This is always a magnificent ceremony—striking in this grand academic setting, in the parade of colors and in the joyful faces.

Satisfying the requirements for a Columbia degree is never easy; the demands are as rigorous as any in the world. So, you should, indeed, be very proud. We, certainly, are of you. But, as much as we, your faculty, admire you and are proud of what you have achieved, nothing can compare to the pride of your family and friends who have supported you all along the way. Please take this opportunity to thank them.

Under ordinary conditions, we justifiably celebrate the sheer labor and talents that have brought you to this point. But your Columbia journey has been nothing like any I have ever witnessed. I can barely begin to touch the surface of the times: A once-in-a-century pandemic; life-jarring climate-induced catastrophes jolting us into a state-of-emergency mindset; a world flirting dangerously with authoritarianism, repressing human rights and yielding naked aggression to a degree not seen since the era leading up to the Second World War; violent acts of racism that add still another horrible chapter in the struggles of Black Americans to overcome invidious discrimination, made worse by a refusal of many citizens even to acknowledge the historical and ongoing truths of this injustice; and of other innocent groups, suffering other injustices. Together these forces seem biblical, in scope and in gravity. As I recite these multiple and intersecting plagues of our time, I know each one of us is privately taking stock of how these events—singly or altogether—have affected our own lives and the lives of those close to us. Collectively, we can be certain that many among us have suffered deeply; and not one of us has been untouched. To all of you, therefore, in recognition of the many challenges you have had to endure and overcome, we say with more conviction and more respect than ever before, Congratulations to the Class of 2022.

My remarks to you this morning are about matters that are dear to my heart (and I hope dear to yours, as well)—as they involve free speech, deep knowledge and expertise, universities and their role in making a good society and the responsibilities we all bear, especially in these momentous times, to think clearly and to think well, no matter what we are doing. It is common for me on these occasions to speak about the glorious principles of freedom of expression and its offspring of academic freedom. But on this day what concerns me is a different problem—not of censorship, but instead of an over-abundance, an excess, an abuse of freely expressed but deeply misguided speech that threatens a moral, ethical, just, wise, and sane world. I'm concerned about the increasingly pervasive misuse of free speech.

Let me start with what is clear and critically important to recognize—namely, that the modern phenomenon of systematic campaigns of disinformation is spawning and amplifying the very crises I noted at the outset. Denials of the effectiveness of vaccines, of climate science, of election integrity, of the past and ongoing effects of discrimination—these and so many other malicious efforts at misinformation are polluting our collective mind. We are all very much aware that the great advancement of our age, the Internet, is being used to augment the malign effectiveness of these campaigns, and probably to a degree never encountered before in human societies. Just a few decades ago a crackpot theory or idea had a lot of hard work ahead in order to break into the general population where it could use anger and paranoia to take root. Now it happens in seconds. We have, it seems, entered what we might call the Age of Disinformation.

This is no small matter. From a First Amendment standpoint, I can tell you that this poses urgent questions. Over the course of the last century, and especially in the last half century, we have created the most speech-protective society in the world—indeed, in human history. At its core, there is a simple premise: Bad speech, including falsehoods and lies, is better remedied by opportunities for more speech rather than by government intervention. This means we live in a wilderness of human thoughts and ideas, with the hope that we might become more intellectually self-reliant and capable of tolerance.

We know by nature we are not perfect. We know there is a natural human impulse to latch onto beliefs, to group with others who believe similarly and will provide mutual reinforcement of our rightness, which then manifests itself in a concerted drive to convert or stop those who disagree, thus producing a cycle of escalating intolerance. We are not born believing in the First Amendment. Indeed, openness of mind is counter-intuitive; it must be learned both in principle and in lived experience, and our worst impulses that we constantly have to live with mean it will always be in jeopardy. Which is why we had to create a hard-to-change constitutional freedom and then take it to an extreme, as a lesson in life in tolerance. But the profound question before us today is: Does this basic premise, does all of this still hold true?

Like any fundamental principle, however, the First Amendment is far more complex than this little précis presents, and we have allowed it to adjust to new circumstances in the past. It is worth noting that the last new technology of communication—namely, broadcast media—was regulated in the public interest precisely in order to deal with many of the very same dangers we now see with social media and related platforms on the Internet. This stands as a potential model for us now. And that is where the debate is taking place.

But let's return to understanding the problems we are facing and the gravity of the threats. There is more than simply the circulation of particular falsehoods. Deliberate disinformation and propaganda also, and more importantly, undermine the very idea of deep knowledge and expertise itself. Disinformation is now powering a particularly pungent form of populism in which experts are discredited, even ridiculed, and an arrogance of feeling one can believe whatever one wants to believe is settling in and becoming normal. This attitude is in direct conflict with universities, because we are society's primary institutions for preserving and advancing what humanity has struggled to learn over the millennia. Over the past several years, our own faculty have been targets of this abuse.

But the dangers are even worse: Attacking expertise is a common tool of fascism and authoritarian regimes. When we discredit a particular piece of knowledge, we make it harder to think well. We undermine the essential task of a self-determining society to draw on the vast body of information and thought painfully developed over centuries and held safely within our academic institutions and across our cultural institutions and professions. Falsehoods today are increasingly accompanied by a rejection of a necessary humility about the limits of our knowledge and of a basic trust in others who have devoted their lives and careers to understand a deeply important subject.

So, the stakes are, indeed, very high, and we, universities, along with the democracy as a whole, are vulnerable to these campaigns and new conditions. The issue is then what comes next. Let us assume that the First Amendment will be rethought. It is time to ask: How can we think about all of this outside the First Amendment?

There is, of course, much to say about this, but I have two key points: One is not to let free speech stand in the way of condemning disinformation and doing all we can to stop it; the other is to think of universities as the models for society and how to think.

It is increasingly dangerous to assume, as many long have, that the strong protections afforded falsehoods under the First Amendment necessarily implies that it is wrong to do what we can to stop falsehoods and disinformation generally. Is "free speech" an "absolute," as some would have it, and should we, accordingly, refrain from doing anything to stop bad speech in ways beyond official censorship? My answer to that is: Not for a second should we think that way. That way lies madness and the loss of a well-educated society.

"Good thinking" is a critical goal of any individual or society. The rejection of "bad thinking"—however difficult it is to define precisely—is a necessary condition of that.

Indeed, this is what we call education—the development of the human capacity to think well—with reason from knowledge, and with respect for facts and a reasonable openness to relevant ideas and opinions. This is not easy, to be sure, which is why we devote so many years to arrive at where you are now.

In fact, the very human impulses noted at the outset that lead us to improperly censor others also lead us to think badly by not rejecting what we should. Not to put too fine a point on it, but, if a student receives an F for a lazy paper filled with falsehoods, it will not do the student any good to proclaim that the paper should not be penalized because it was an exercise in freedom of speech. "Free speech" is not an end in itself but a thumb on the scale in a particular direction. It would make no sense to order our lives entirely in that direction. Keep it always in mind, of course, but do not allow it to take precedence over other principles we value—in the case of the failing paper, the importance of sharp thinking and quality writing.

This brings me, lastly, to the importance of institutions in society—institutions such as universities, the press, and other civic institutions. We need to recognize that these institutions are designed to help organize our discussions, not just about politics but, really, about everything. Those of us here today have been incredibly fortunate to be part of this great university. Whenever I let my mind try to take in the full breadth of what happens here—in laboratories, in clinics, in libraries, in studies, in classrooms, and work all over the planet—I am exhilarated. But I am also filled with humility because I know so little of all that is known here, and at similar institutions. To come to a university such as Columbia is to learn to be humble; to realize how little you know and always will.

I love being president (I recommend the job highly!), not least because I get to know just a little bit more of that amazing whole. In this time of our many trials and crises, as we reap the benefits of universities, we need to do all we can to protect them. They are not perfect, for sure. I feel strongly, for example, that we need to make the boundaries between us and the rest of the world more permeable and more connected in the betterment of human society and the world. This mission, which I call the Fourth Purpose of the University—in addition to teaching and research and service—might help people more broadly feel more respectful of what we have to offer.

But another reason I love being president of Columbia is the opportunity to be in your midst. As students in our classrooms and laboratories, you are what makes academic life worth living. We may be daunted by this troubled moment in history, but I am most certainly convinced, to the core of my being, that every one of you in your own way will help to solve these problems and to heal the world. You have demonstrated that human capacity to think well, and I know you will deploy it in meaningful and inspiring ways. Most of all, you will have the proper degree of humility that a truly great education instills.

On this day, we celebrate you, all that you have accomplished, and the institution that nurtures us, especially in this new historical era we have entered.

Congratulations to you, Class of 2022.

CHAPTER 38

CONVOCATION ADDRESS

Columbia College and the School of Engineering and
Applied Science, Low Plaza, August 28, 2022

Having announced his intention to retire at the end of the 2022–2023 academic year,
this was President Bollinger's last convocation ceremony welcoming new undergrad-
uate students in Columbia College and the School of Engineering and Applied
Science—and their families—to Columbia.

I t is a very great pleasure and honor, on behalf of Columbia University,
joining our outstanding deans Josef Sorett, Amy Hungerford, and Shih-Fu
Chang, to welcome you as among our newest students and members of our
academic community. We know this is a profound step in your lives, one naturally filled with extraordinary excitement, anticipation, and even some anxiety
and apprehension. We also wish to extend an equally warm welcome to your
parents, families, and friends, whom we know share in all of these feelings, and
more, some perhaps you will never know. We are grateful to them for entrusting
us with your development as a person and as a scholar, and we will do all we can
to fulfill those hopes and expectations.

This is a day of enormous consequence for you and, as Amy said, of some consequence for me. This will be my last Convocation address to entering students.
At the end of this year, I will return to the faculty and continue teaching and
writing full time. Other than my family, nothing has given me more pleasure and
satisfaction in life than serving for two decades as president of this magnificent
institution. During that time the University has changed significantly, as universities are inclined to do, and, in one respect, relevant to today, I would like to

note it has changed a lot. When I began, this ceremony of greeting new students was held only in Levien Gym with a few desultory speeches and no family and friends welcome. That seemed out-of-character for a great institution, and we immediately initiated this more appropriate and expansive gathering to better mark the moment, and it is now a hallowed and treasured tradition. I, therefore, take very special pleasure in seeing all of you here this evening.

Yes, Columbia has changed, but it is also important to say that its central mission of being utterly and completely dedicated to the life of the mind, at the very highest levels, to the discovery and advancement of knowledge, and to the transmission of that intellectual process to each succeeding generation (and now to you)—that central mission is the same, and every single day we are eager to get to work—and, now, you will, too.

I have noted that this is my last Convocation not to draw attention to myself but because I want to say to you this evening something that is distilled from my long experience. I have lived my entire adult life within universities, beginning as an assistant professor of law at the age of 27, and the life of the mind has been my life's work. In that time, I have learned an enormous amount, of course, and I would like to share a few of the things I think might be helpful for you to consider as you start your journey.

I have seven severely condensed thoughts to convey, but before doing that I want to emphasize just how unique a great university like Columbia is in human affairs. We are all about knowledge—how to grasp it, work with it in our minds, add new dimensions others have thus far missed or overlooked, and communicate all of that to the world. (I believe universities are and should be more engaged with the outside world in making things happen for the better, what I refer to as the Fourth Purpose of universities, but that's for another day.) What we do is hardly a small mission. Nearly everything we take for granted as making up the elements of modern life, including warnings and understandings about climate change, has roots in our academic research (I mention climate change not only because it is of central importance to humanity but also because it was first noted here at Columbia and serves as a prime illustration of my point about the role of universities, and the special role of Columbia). In this community so dedicated to knowledge, we are constantly judging—indeed, grading—ourselves. Peer review is a serious enterprise on which the integrity of the whole thing depends. Therefore, you must be prepared to enter the life of the mind with eyes open and a readiness to be evaluated every day.

With that, here are my recommendations for your journey.

First, you can make yourself smarter if you work at it. This may be my most important message of all. In all likelihood, each of you will experience, more intensely than you ever have before, NOT understanding something that others seem to get effortlessly. You may lose track of the discussion, listen to a lecture without following the argument, read a book and feel lost; look at a painting and see nothing special only to find later how others see layers and layers of meaning. And you may get grades below your expectations for yourself. The critical point is that you never feel any of this is due to an unchangeable part of your intellect. If I have learned one thing in life, it is that over time (perhaps over a lifetime) you can change your capacities of your mind for the better. You just have to believe that and to work at it. Sometimes it's due to terminology or concepts you are unfamiliar with (not many people naturally speak in terms of "opportunity costs," or "Due Process"); sometimes it's because our minds somehow throw us off (like when our natural sense of direction is confounded); sometimes it's because we lack the knowledge base needed to enter the conversation (great literature is often opaque to the uninitiated); and sometimes it's because we just don't follow the way in which the discussion is happening (e.g., using words rather than images). Whatever the reason, trust me, you can get better—indeed, much better—at thinking, but you must not accept where you are as a given and you must study yourself and practice doing better. You can catch up, you can build and improve your intellectual capacities; you can make yourself smarter. (Many years ago, I asked a Nobel Prize physicist whether I could ever really understand quantum mechanics. He thought for a bit and then said, no, he didn't think it was possible. It's possible he made some assessment of my intellect and concluded that I, specifically, could not understand it. But I prefer to interpret his comment as being that I needed to have a much deeper background in knowledge before I had a chance of really understanding. That's, of course, true of a lot of knowledge, and it doesn't stop me from trying to do better with the knowledge I have, even though I know I'll never have as a profound an understanding as others. I recommend you follow the same course.)

Second, you must constantly be alert to your bad intellectual impulses. This idea is related to the first. Thinking well is not easy; indeed, it's not entirely natural. You have to work at that, and against your instincts. This is a basic premise in my field of freedom of speech—namely, that censorship is more normal or natural than open-mindedness or tolerance. Forming beliefs and rejecting differing beliefs is what our minds do if not checked. Unfortunately, we are living in a period when this is even more prevalent than usual. In the university, we are all about seeing complexity, exploring different ways of seeing things, holding multiple perspectives and possibilities in one's mind simultaneously so we can examine them carefully, being skeptical, and acknowledging we may be in error. So, if your natural impulse is to simplify everything and to resist complexity, then you will continually struggle. Beware of your bad impulses.

Third, I really encourage you to think big, even unrealistically big. Set big goals for yourself. Let yourself have high aspirations, both for knowledge and for doing things. Let yourself have your own big dreams. (This is one natural impulse I would not discourage.) It adds meaning to our lives, a sense of purpose, and for the most part is relatively harmless (depending, of course, on the substance of the dreams!). Most importantly, as Samuel Johnson said, big dreams are often a necessary element to achieving anything in life, for, "There would . . . be few enterprises of great labour or hazard undertaken, if we had not the power of magnifying the advantages which we persuade ourselves to expect from them."

Fourth, you need to develop the capacity to be enthralled—enchanted—by greatness. This is a complicated one, but the essence of the thought is that we need to develop a genuine respect for great works and accomplishments across the span of humanity (including an appreciation of expertise, something painfully lacking in today's political culture). How to do that is not as straightforward as one might think, but I have always found it beautifully captured in this quote from Virginia Woolf in her diaries. She writes of her astonishment at Shakespeare's genius when she turns to him, while writing herself: "I read Shakespeare *directly* [after] I have finished writing. When my mind is agape and red-hot. Then it is astonishing. I never yet knew how amazing his stretch and speed and word coining power is, until I felt it utterly outpace and outrace my own, seeming to start equal and then I see him draw ahead and do things I could not in my wildest tumult and utmost press of mind imagine." This is, indeed, amazing to read a great writer appreciating an even greater writer. But the principal point is that we all need to find ways to have greatness become evident. Greatness does not yield itself easily.

Fifth, I urge you to make close friends along this journey of life beginning now. Here I do not mean the personal friendships that are often and quite rightly thought of as being forged in your college years. I mean the great minds and works you will encounter in your studies. Select a few, those who appeal to something inside you, and live with them; make them part of your daily life; read a page, or a paragraph (or look at an image or hear the sounds or see the actions), and let your mind probe deeper and deeper into their meanings and hear your own thoughts in response. Great human achievements warrant a lifetime of attention. I urge you to begin to gather your closest friends among them. Remember again, it's a lifetime journey you are embarking on today, and you can decide whom your companions will be. I have mine; I hope you will have yours.

Sixth, please do not think that smartness is everything in life. This needs to be said because the intellect is such an overwhelming interest and focus of the university that it becomes necessary sometimes to acknowledge openly that we over-emphasize one important dimension of life. Nowhere else in the world will you find anything close to us in ascribing the highest value to the intellect and its powers. We're good with that and we hope you are, too. But not for a second should you, or do we, think that encompasses all that is important for a good life. Being a good person, as simple and as complicated as that little statement is, is certainly equally high on our list of human qualities. We try to be that here, as well, but we also know, and you need to bear in mind always, that we are not doing everything here. I would only add that being a good person starts with how we treat each other in our little community, and, as Edmund Burke observed, it radiates out from there to humanity broadly.

Seventh, and last, I urge you to enjoy this period of life you are entering because, in all likelihood, it will never be like this again. This unconditional embrace of the life of the mind we nurture here is unique. Nowhere else in the world will you encounter this way of being, certainly to this degree. It is in details that larger world views are often revealed. And for us that detail is the footnote. Everything that is possible to know and understand is our ambition, reason is our method and our guide, and adding just a bit more is our goal. Every step is documented and attributed, and the footnote serves as the foundation. So, whenever you see a footnote, think of the academic culture behind it. And, so, to recognize the uniqueness of our mission is also to realize that once you leave it, as most of you will at some point, life outside will, naturally, have different priorities, and those priorities will make this life difficult, if not impossible, to recapture. So, I urge you not to take it for granted and to enjoy it thoroughly while you're here.

So, these are my few recommendations to bring along with you on your journey. Of course, you will encounter many people offering many recommendations for you to follow, especially now at the beginning. I say, take them all to heart!

It's a natural impulse (again, a harmless one) for people to offer suggestions to those who are just starting out on some venture, and I'm sure you are being patient and tolerant of that inclination. Perhaps, while I have presented my own recommendations, you have been thinking: After all that time, is this all he has to offer? I wholeheartedly agree with that puzzlement. I can only say in my defense that I am still working on being smarter, I have not arrived at full command of my bad impulses, I am working with a set of completely unrealistic goals, I am painfully aware of how short I come up against the great minds we study here, including all of my closest friends. But remember, intelligence isn't everything, and, most of all, I want to say how much I and we look forward to being with you in the next four years in what promises to be an intellectual adventure of a lifetime.

Congratulations on joining us at Columbia University in the City of New York.

CHAPTER 39

WELCOME REMARKS

Resilience in Journalism and Free Speech in the Age of
Social Media Symposium, Tow Center for Digital Media,
Columbia Journalism School, April 18, 2023

---

*From the outset of his tenure in 2002, President Bollinger focused on a range of new
interdisciplinary initiatives on free speech and free press in the digital age. Several of
these centers and institutes were based at Columbia Journalism School, including
the Tow Center for Digital Journalism and, in partnership with Stanford Engineering, the Brown Institute for Media Innovation. Others, like Columbia Global Freedom of Expression and the Knight First Amendment Institute, also took practical
action, including high-profile litigation and public advocacy supporting free speech
and free press amid relentless change in the increasingly online public square.*

Thank you, Jelani Cobb, our great dean following two great deans,
Nick [Lemann] and Steve [Coll]. It's just fantastic to have great journalists who are also great academics and charismatic leaders. I want
to recognize [founding Tow Center director] Emily Bell, our Nobel laureate guest
Maria Ressa, all the participants who have come here for this, with support of the
Tow Foundation. And, of course, Len Tow himself, who's been a dear, dear friend.
And I've had so many conversations with Len over time in which we've talked
about how universities can change and do good. He's argued rightly, I think, that
we no longer teach geography, and we should! He's also an advocate and patron
of theater, and it's just wonderful to be with him today. And, to say thank you.

I was very fortunate to have spent my professional life studying, speaking
about, and acting on the principles of freedom of speech and press, and on

journalism. When I sat in my office for the first time as an Assistant Professor of Law in 1973 and wondered what, if anything, I knew about such that I might write about it, I turned naturally to the First Amendment. I had grown up in the context of a small town newspaper where my father was the editor and publisher. In high school, I was the janitor, melted the lead pigs for the linotypes and developed the films. I felt I knew something instinctively about journalism and the press. At that time, the First Amendment was not really a field, although it was becoming such after the seminal Supreme Court decisions of that era—*New York Times v. Sullivan, Brandenburg v. Ohio, Cohen v. California*, and of course, *Pentagon Papers*.

I was also lucky because it turns out that free speech and free press never go out of date, but keep providing new and fresh problems to be solved. Columbia seems to be an excellent progenitor of throwing up free speech problems and they sit at the core of democratic societies. By that time, the general theoretical framework for the First Amendment had been laid down. Given a commitment to self-government by citizens exercising their responsibilities to create laws and public policies and to elect those who would represent them, we should maintain their freedom to talk as they will and we should not allow dangerous or offensive speech to be a reason for allowing the government to intervene.

Speech as a discrete and somewhat arbitrarily selected category of human behavior would be carved out and shielded from public regulation. Indeed, to a degree, certainly this was true in the United States, never before tried by any society in human history. It was said to be an experiment and a relatively new one because the first Supreme Court cases interpreting the First Amendment didn't happen until 1919. This view of free speech continues to be the dominant, very simple but profoundly important theory to this day. But what also interested me in the 1970s was a separate line of First Amendment thinking that was represented in the decisions involving the new technology of communication of the 20th century, namely broadcasting, radio, and TV.

The year before I started as an Assistant Professor while clerking on the Supreme Court, I was responsible for a case involving claims by the Democratic National Committee and an anti-Vietnam War group to have a First Amendment right to purchase advertising on radio and television stations, which the majority of the Court rejected. But no one thought the claim was absurd given the constitutional appropriateness of public regulation more generally, which had been upheld just a few years before. In that broadcasting universe, the "monopolistic powers" of the new media with incredible national reach and a new capacity to affect minds was deemed the greatest threat to the interests of the public. And the role and responsibility of the government was to establish public policies to counter and to moderate those threats, not by censorship, but by requiring openness, fairness, and equality in public discussion of public issues. These different conceptions of freedom of speech and press lived in different worlds, neither referring to the other. I thought the proposed distinctions between print and broadcast media did not justify the differential treatment and said so, but I did think having two systems was nevertheless rational and good from a First Amendment and policy standpoint.

Over the decades, the print model of the First Amendment has achieved greater and greater status in most people's minds. But, the broadcast model has still remained alive, even if not so well. The century's new technology of communication—the Internet and social media—has arrived, and now we face a similar set of choices at every level of law and policy. Many believe, and I include myself among them, that the values at stake are even more serious, even more grave than ever before.

Geof Stone and I have now collaborated on multiple projects involving major issues of the Constitution, especially the First Amendment. We have just completed a book on the arguments for affirmative action as Jelani noted. And next fall, we will publish a volume of essays on the constitutional journey from *Roe v. Wade* to *Dobbs v. Jackson's Women's Health Organization*. We plan then to turn our attention to the 50th year anniversary of *Buckley v. Valeo* [NB: the landmark 1976 decision that upheld statutory limits on political campaign donations, but struck down limits on campaign *spending* as a violation of the First Amendment]. We have published volumes on the First Amendment at the 100th anniversary of the first Supreme Court cases, and on the *Pentagon Papers* 50 years later. But, I would say that the volume on the regulation of media, social media, and the First Amendment, the subject of this conference, is the most vexing of all that we have done.

Our feeling was that this new technology and all its positive and negative attributes needs the same attention that we directed at broadcast media and press in the last century. We wrote what we thought, gathered 18 experts in law and others from other fields, and then assembled a commission to reflect on all this and make recommendations. The views range from arguing that 'we have all seen this before and nothing new needs to be done' to 'we have seen this before and everything needs to be rethought.'

In so many ways and over time I have wondered about the complex evolution of the world from 1973 and before to the present. The power of speech has never in human affairs been greater. But the risks of propaganda, disinformation, and intolerance have never been greater or so apparent either. Nor have the risks of government involvement in speech in modern history ever been so apparent.

I watched my father once or twice steel himself against physical threats for publishing the truth. But today, that problem of private censorship and intimidation is far more frequent and serious than ever before. And just as a matter of economics and the press, we know, sadly, that the little newspaper he ran and that I worked at as the janitor would not be viable today.

With all this in mind, let me close with this basic truth. There is certainly no better place to think about all these profound problems of our age than here at Columbia. That truth begins with the existence of our great School of Journalism, the only one in the Ivy League, where gifted and engaged faculty, centers, and institutes, like Emily's, along with talented and eager students, take up these and other issues. But then we have scholars also throughout the University—in Law and Engineering and Arts & Sciences, and beyond. And now we have the Knight First Amendment Institute and the Columbia Global Freedom of Expression Initiative to help with both thinking and action.

I want to thank everyone here, especially Jelani [Cobb], Emily [Bell], and Len [Tow] for taking on these immensely complex and important issues.

CHAPTER 40

FAREWELL DINNER REMARKS

Columbia University, Manhattanville Campus, April 28, 2023

These more personal remarks were delivered at a celebratory dinner in President Bollinger's honor on Columbia's new Manhattanville Campus, attended by a wide range of faculty, deans, trustees, and friends of the University.

I want to begin from a simple but true place. It has meant the world to me to be the President of Columbia—more than you might imagine, which is what I want to try to explain by drawing on a number of personal confessions and stories. But most importantly, it has meant the world to me to have done it with all of you—with people of such special talents and good character and fun personalities. The Trustees and chairs, the members of the administration, the deans, the faculty, the students and staff, the alumni and friends of the institution: thank you to every one of you.

Before I say more about what this has meant to me, I want to begin with a few thoughts about our accomplishments. I think of them as being of two kinds: the first category is the troubles of the last two-plus decades. I think we all know that it is not easy to lead Columbia, and for that matter it is not easy for Columbia to be Columbia, given its stressed history in the second half of the last century. And certainly, the beginning quarter of this century has not been smooth sailing. I conceive of it this way: it all began and ended in silence, literally and metaphorically. The first time the city was silent was September 11th, 2001, and as is now known I was here that morning staying in a midtown hotel to meet the search committee a few blocks away. I walked with ghostly figures covered in ash, streaming up the middle of the streets from lower Manhattan. The horror and momentousness of this day deeply affected my first several years at Columbia.

Then, at the end, the city again fell silent, this time stricken by the first global pandemic in a century. Students were sent home, education continued electronically, and the rest of us retreated to our rooms. Even the medical center, which heroically led the frontline battle for all of us, was marked by a profound silence in critical care. To silence a city and a nation, the causes must be near catastrophic—and they were. But the University persevered, and collectively we summoned the best that our minds and better angels could produce, and we made it through—just as we did with lesser but still significant travails of the greatest economic collapse since the Great Depression, and with that recent fraught period in which American democracy careened towards authoritarianism.

I say all this to highlight the fact that achievements can and should include surviving disasters of which we have had our share, and that for getting us to the other side in every crisis, I am all the more grateful to have worked side by side with people of such boundless reserves of pure goodness revealed in these times of enormous stress. Now these difficult moments also provide (as Shakespeare wrote of Prince Hal's misspent youth) a foil against which the positive achievements appear all the more glittering and vivid—and the positive achievements are so many.

I like to think that a measure of whether you have done well by the people or institutions you are responsible for is whether you have given them a future to aim towards, and we at Columbia now have a future. In many respects, the Columbia of today is unrecognizable to that of the year 2000. Its diversity, its space and resources, its adventuresomeness, its preeminence in so many areas. But nearly all that we have done has been by carefully and thoughtfully discerning the essence of the institution and then building on that.

Columbia tends towards a special kind of intellectualism: cosmopolitan in the world, sophisticated, rich with ideas connected to life. Its location makes it naturally international and global in outlook, and Columbia's specific location makes it ready to engage with the gritty urbanism that produces a sense of the urgency of the real, and a respect for the teeming complexities of life. Columbia at its best does not try to escape to a bucolic environment, but rather races towards the world as it literally, really is. Because we have drawn from the essence of the University, I am confident that what has been done will not be undone, nor fade with time.

I want to finish now with what all this has meant to me. In a phrase, it has been a dream. For me this has not been a job or an interesting position, it has been the fulfillment of a dream that was undreamt, in the sense of one never expected or anticipated.

When I accepted the offer in the fall of 2001, there was an 8-month lag until I would take office. I remember thinking during that interim period, the kind of uncontrolled thought that comes to the surface of your mind and reveals something deep inside you: that I just hoped I wouldn't die before July 1. The idea was not that dying itself would be tragic, but rather that I would never be identified with this incredible, indeed, incomprehensible honor. Deep inside me this was an out-of-mind experience, and that feeling has carried me through the lows and into the highs of all these years.

I am well aware this has led me to give too much credit to being president of Columbia. At a dinner in Lincoln Center that fall of 2002, welcoming Jean and me, I observed (reflecting my state of mind I just described) how sorry I was not to have known that I would become president of Columbia because it could have helped me to get out of a lot of difficult and tight circumstances. I gave the example of how Jean and I had mistakenly decided during a little sabbatical in Japan, for the family to climb Mount Fuji as thousands of Japanese do each year, and to do so with our suitcases because we had a little vacation to follow on the other side of the mountain. But we badly misjudged the severity of the climb. We thought if the old and frail do it, so can we—with luggage. I noted in that talk in 2002 how on the way down, after the magnitude of the error had become very painfully clear, that it would have been exculpatory for me to then say, "You know, someday I'm going to be president of Columbia University." I have to say that the Japanese audiences love to hear me say that we are the only family in history to have scaled Mount Fuji carrying suitcases. However, I can now say, having tried using the president of Columbia trick multiple times since actually becoming President that it does not work as I had thought, sometimes even producing the opposite effect—demonstrating the somewhat sad fact that I seem to be more impressed by it than anyone else.

But you do have to try to understand what it's like to be me. Reinforcing my sense of exaggerated and unrealistic pride in being Columbia's president, and at the same time making me feel I have a lot to live up to in that role, I offer this little piece of evidence. Often while in London on official work and staying in a hotel near the American Embassy (the old one), at the end of an evening I would take a walk there and stand in front of the large statue of Dwight Eisenhower. The plaque read something like this: "Dwight D. Eisenhower / Born October 14,

1890 / Won World War II / Was President of Columbia / After which he became President of the United States." Now, for a person whose childhood was growing up in small towns in the West in the 1950s, being Eisenhower's successor is a bit hard to comprehend; which is to say, my state of mind about all this is a little more forgivable. Perhaps it also explains yet another side of my personality which I admit is not so innocent or merely misguided, but I have always taken a secret pleasure in hearing people say that Eisenhower was actually not a very good president of Columbia—as if, even if true, that somehow reduces the unfavorable comparison. I've also taken pleasure in hearing one of my truly gifted and wonderful predecessors, Mike Sovern, who in my mind committed the ultimate academic sin of making being a university president seem like a worthy ambition, saying of Eisenhower's speech at Mike's graduation: "For the life of me I can't remember a word of what the great man said."

The upshot of all these confessions and observations is simply this: I have not for one moment ever taken for granted being in this position, President of Columbia University in the City of New York. On the contrary, I have always felt deep inside that I had unscalable heights to strive to reach in order to fulfill the responsibilities of leading this great institution of higher learning. I think, on the whole, this has been healthy and good for me and the University. The sense of privilege and honor has been enormous, and the alignment with my own life almost perfect, even if, of course, the consequences of it all are still to be determined.

I hope you know how much I would like to acknowledge each one of you and what you did for me and for all of us together. That it is impossible to do makes it no less disappointing to me. I hope to say it personally to each of you.

It gives me great joy to recognize Jean. Again twenty-one years ago, I said that "Jean and I are so close, you cannot see any seam that divides us"—quoting Montaigne, one of my favorite authors. That was true then, and it is even more true today. Fifty-nine years ago I fell in love with a girl I saw at a dance. The merger is now complete, and it would trivialize everything to single out any influences here or contributions there. At this stage of life, cycles seem to matter in understanding the arc of one's life. And one of the most meaningful cycles begins with our arriving in New York City in the late summer of 1968 with no money, no prospects, no furniture, and life beginning in a tiny single efficiency room—fully equipped with bugs—above a bar on 104th and Broadway, and coming to Columbia. From there to this moment is astonishing.

Jean and I, like most married couples I suppose, have spent a good part of our lives working on improving the other person. With this night and this end and a new future ahead, we are ready to declare that each of us is now perfect. But to speak of perfection takes us to Lee and Carey, their wonderful spouses Jen and Ben, and our spectacular grandchildren: Cooper, Sawyer, Katelyn, Colin, and Emma. They all make life worth living and there is absolutely nothing unrealistic in Jean's and my belief that they are the ultimate source of inspiration for a good life.

Thank you for this evening. Thank you for the friendships that make this night so special. And thank you for helping us get through the hard times, all the while reaching for big dreams, and for making my own personal undreamt dreams come true. Thank you.

CHAPTER 41

COLUMBIA COLLEGE
CLASS DAY ADDRESS

Columbia University, South Lawn, May 16, 2023

In a typical commencement week at Columbia, President Bollinger would offer brief remarks at the Class Day ceremonies of the university's three undergraduate colleges: Columbia College, the Fu Foundation School of Engineering and Applied Science, and the School of General Studies, with its student body of nontraditional and mid-career students, from military veterans to former ballet dancers. While he tailored his remarks to each unique group of Columbia students, his main points remain substantially similar. Here are his final such remarks to Columbia College's 2023 graduating seniors.

I want to begin by congratulating our students, of course, and by recognizing the families and friends who are gathered here this morning. All of us appreciate how important this moment is for you, and the sacrifices and celebrations that have led to this point. We share in your joy and in the achievements of these exceptional young people. I will be speaking at length tomorrow, so I will share just a few thoughts today.

It is not possible to stand before you and not be reminded of one's own college years. I have always felt, and said, that there is nothing in life like this four-year period. Nothing. I do not mean to idealize it. For most of you it is magical; for others not so much; but for pretty much everyone, it is transformative. Especially of the mind and intellect. There is something that lasts forever in being immersed in the realm of ideas and knowledge, especially in a great research institution like Columbia.

My thought for you now is not about what you have been through and how it has changed you. It is rather to project ahead and to say something about its lasting role in our lives. I think the thing that has struck me the most about my life as I look back from where I am now is how so much of it is unexpected. Not all, by any means, and a full accounting would have to cover what has stayed the same and turned out as expected. But a lot of it has been surprising.

Let me give one example. As some of you know, my field is Constitutional Law, and the First and Fourteenth Amendments, in particular. I became engaged with this field in the era of the 1960s and 1970s, when virtually every major national issue was translated into a constitutional question. *Brown v. Board of Education* set off a torrent of civil rights decisions, laws, and policies, including Affirmative Action in higher education, all as the nation grappled with centuries of invidious discrimination against African Americans. First Amendment decisions were, in turn, shaped by this period of ferment. *New York Times v. Sullivan, Brandenburg v. Ohio*, and the Pentagon Papers, among many others seminal decisions, set the jurisprudence of the age. The year I clerked on the Supreme Court, 1972, was the year *Roe v. Wade* was decided. All these and so many other cases and issues engaged me deeply and promised a world of steady progress, as I saw it, from this profound base.

But now as I close out my career the opposite course is being charted, by a different Court, with a different jurisprudence in mind and animated by a different view of life. We saw it most dramatically a year ago with the *Dobbs* decision, and likely will see it soon with the Harvard University and University of North Carolina cases on Affirmative Action. There are many others.

To my mind it's shocking and unexpected in the arc of my life. I never would have predicted it from where I started.

Now I say all this not because I'm asking you to agree with my views of constitutional jurisprudence but rather to highlight in a way that's meaningful to me what I suspect will be true for you in ways that matter to you. The world will be altered in ways you just did not expect, sometimes, of course, for the good. But not always. It's amazing to think that the biggest world events came unexpectedly: The collapse of the Soviet Union; 9/11; the Great Recession of 2008, and of course, as you know so painfully, the COVID-19 pandemic. All these surprised people, even experts. So, will it be true in your own lives.

So, my theme is that how life unfolds, whether in big or small ways, is so often elusive to our minds. And in that elusiveness and surprise and shock the one thing you will hold dear and be your guide, and settle your mind, is the time you spent in college letting the world of ideas flow through your minds and being remade as a thinking human being. More than in any other period of life, this one is concentrated on timeless ideas and themes that cut across the ages and make you feel part of the sweep of time. This tends to have a settling effect and provides a larger perspective. Additionally, your capacity to articulate your beliefs when challenged, to engage with others who see the world differently, to adjust and renew your involvements has now been determined—and my point is that you will need it all because a lot will change and you can take nothing for granted.

So, that's my thought for this morning as we recognize your achievements and mark this moment. I very much look forward to seeing you tomorrow.

Congratulations to all of you.

CHAPTER 42

COMMENCEMENT ADDRESS

Columbia University, May 17, 2023

With his twenty-one-year tenure as president of Columbia University officially concluding on June 30, 2023, Lee C. Bollinger delivered his final address to the University community.

I t is my very great honor, indeed privilege and joy, to welcome you all here on this very special morning, in this glorious academic setting, to this magnificent occasion. I am especially sentimental today as this will be my last Commencement speech after serving more than two decades as president of Columbia University. I like to think that we are graduating together. I am sure that you and I both will hold this moment in our hearts for the rest of our lives.

On a personal note, I'm pleased to say I have a job. I now return to the life of a law professor, a career I began at more or less your age in 1973, two years after graduating from our Law School. I have loved being president of this great academic institution. By any measure I can think of, it has been a worthy way to spend my life and, most importantly, a transformative education in itself.

This transition for me is somewhat complicated (a word you will hear me say a lot this morning). I feel some elements of sadness as I leave behind colleagues, every one a dear friend, and adjust to a world in which I am increasingly unneeded. But, certainly, I am delighted to have more space and time in life for other things—perhaps the way your families felt when you went off to school. However, endings are a part of life, as this occasion so poignantly symbolizes, and I couldn't be happier that Minouche Shafik will become our next president.

So let me say, personally and on behalf of the faculty, staff, and administration, how thankful we are to each and every one of you for enriching our lives, and this appreciation extends to all who have supported you throughout your academic journey. Please take a moment to thank them as well.

———— ◆ ————

I thought a lot about what to say to you on this occasion. One naturally feels an expectation to offer thoughts as profound as this moment is in your lives. Given all that is happening in the world, you might well expect me to talk about big issues and, in particular, big threats to democracy. But it strikes me that you are already well-versed in civilization-scale problems that your generation has been tasked with solving.

What I can do, and I hope to do, is to sum up a little part of what I have learned over time contributes to a good life. I am interested in the seemingly simple matter of how to be a person in the world and what qualities to nurture and develop. I don't have a precise name for what I'm going to talk about, but, in general, it's about developing a certain disposition of openness—something frequently commented on, but little appreciated in how hard it is to achieve and sustain.

Being open-minded, whether as a society or as an individual, has many models. The place we typically start in thinking about the subject is the First Amendment and the sacred principle of freedom of speech. That is something I happen to know a little about.

But I am not turning to the First Amendment for the reason you might think—as some kind of article of faith that we all should strive to live by—in fact, quite the opposite in many respects. I understand why, in this current age, some of you may feel the First Amendment protects too many bad things, giving oxygen to the toxic forces that divide us. To that I would say, that's a legitimate debate and always has been and always will. Rather, I want to use the First Amendment as a point of reference as we set about the far more complex task of creating our own, our own personal "free speech," as it were.

This is where we decide for ourselves how to think, learn, tolerate or not, engage with others or not, including those with whom we are closest. I propose that we see life as having different ways, or layers, of trying to achieve the same thing and compare them and look at how they intersect. I see the First Amendment as a point of departure, not a destination, as it were. We are letting ourselves off the hook when we expect society to conform to standards that we know from our own lives are too unyielding to accommodate life's infinite subtleties.

But we begin with free speech and the First Amendment.

In the United States, we proudly have decided—primarily through Supreme Court cases over the last century—that the government, or the "State," should not "censor" speech except in extreme situations (for example, when it poses a serious and imminent risk of violence). This means that we must withhold imposing sanctions on speech that is racist, or antisemitic, or materially and dangerously false. We exercise this self-restraint only towards behavior we classify as "speech" (a puzzle in itself) and we embed it as a fundamental principle in the Constitution. To the questions why and to what ends we say the following:

First, we recognize that human nature is not naturally open to other beliefs and ideas. We are made for intolerance, not tolerance.

Justice Oliver Wendell Holmes, Jr., expressed this premise explicitly and succinctly in 1920, as he initiated the cascade of jurisprudence we live by today. He acknowledged: "Persecution for the expression of opinions seems to me perfectly logical. If you have no doubt of your premises or your power and want a result with all your heart you naturally express your wishes in law and sweep away the opposition. To allow opposition by speech seems to indicate that you think the speech impotent, . . . or that you do not care whole-heartedly for the result, or that you doubt either your power or your premises."

So, intolerance, or "persecution," towards other beliefs and opinions is "perfectly logical." But that's not the end of the story, Holmes says famously. We need to reject these natural impulses and aim for something higher, namely "truth." For when we realize "that time has upset many fighting faiths," then we "come to believe . . . that the ultimate good desired is better reached by free trade in ideas—that the best test of truth is the power of the thought to get itself accepted in the competition of the market, and that truth is the only ground upon which their wishes safely can be carried out."

This, as it were, has become the American creed.

And it is a wonderful and really glorious thing. But, given the equally problematic premise and the ideal, it is no wonder that each new generation must work to understand and live by this faith. And it's also odd, more intricate than this, because we do not live by this faith throughout society and, certainly not, in our own lives, even when we have the same goals in mind. Take where we are right this minute.

In the academic world, a very different framework applies in the search for truth. Here the quest is bounded by strict norms of objectivity, reason, civility, peer review, full attribution and constant skepticism applied to one's own ideas. In this realm, what I like to refer to as the Scholarly Temperament prevails, and for those who abridge the norms, the penalties (the "censorship," as it were, by another name) are severe—non-promotion, and even exclusion. As with the First Amendment commitment to free speech, the Scholarly Temperament does not come easily. It is only achieved by "education" and mental discipline.

Here, then, are two worlds I—and you—know well. They are very different in character, very different in the precepts about the permissible intellectual traits, yet both are dedicated to the discovery of truth. One is like a wilderness, and the other a manicured garden. I won't here go into how to square the two worlds in a society such as ours, nor whether they even need to be squared. My main point takes a different path.

What I want to get to is our own lives, the ones that each of us constructs day-after-day. None of us would choose personally to live according to the dictates of the First Amendment or the Scholarly Temperament. They may well be appropriate for their respective spheres, and they may be each in their own way models to turn to for guidance as we create our own. But they will not work for ordinary life, even for the same goal.

Here is where my recommendations come in. Let me say first, however, that I am not trying to solve the larger questions each of us confronts about who we will be, or what beliefs we will hold, or with what degrees of intensity and conviction. We need courage to fight for justice. That is another topic. My focus today is how we build within ourselves a disposition to be open-minded that is authentic, lasting, and ultimately a force for positive change.

So, here are some ideas I have turned to for help. I have found them useful in building my own understanding and knowledge, in feeling freer and happier, and for nurturing relationships with others. There are ten. (I say under my breath.)

The first, and in many ways the most important, recommendation is to be constantly alert to our natural impulses that lead us astray. Here you need to start where the First Amendment starts. Holmes was right—we will have our beliefs and the more strongly we hold them the more we will want to protect them from contradiction and rejection. But our impulse is even more dangerous than Holmes suggested. Not only do we want to "persecute" opposition, we also want to join with others in feeling fortified and righteous in doing so. We want to agree to agree. In other words, we need to see that our natural inclination is to be closed-minded, not open-minded. We are not born believing in free speech or openness. We have to learn to be this other way.

From there I think it's helpful to develop a conscious awareness of how little we—even experts—actually know about ourselves and our world. Human knowledge is vast, and stupendous, as this University attests, as a repository of human knowledge. But our ignorance is far greater. I love and have enormous respect for expertise, but you have to be careful not to let it be intimidating. And the best way to do that is to peer into our shared ignorance, for that is where we find our sense of shared humanity and where old and new things await our discovery.

Next, for those things we do and can know, we must always work on seeing their complexity as deeply as we can. The mind naturally simplifies things, and looks for and assumes there are answers. Sometimes there are, but more often there are choices to be made. I always tell my students to try to make the problems we study as complex as possible. And I suggest you follow the tried-and-true method of academics to ready their minds, by beginning every response by saying: "Well, it's complicated, . . . " and then go on from there.

Next, once you see the centrifugal forces against openness, and you see the path ahead, you realize this is something that happens only by continuous practice; by habit. You have to make it part of who you are, and do it over and over again. Just saying to people, "Be open" is like saying to someone, "Go play the piano." You have to work at it, build your capacities, gain agility and strength—that's why pianists do scales, and these are scales for open-mindedness.

Now, when you are in conversations with people, which is a great way to learn, you should always ask more questions than give answers. Everyone has something to teach us, something of unique interest, and your task is always to find that. Keep the proportion of questions to answers at least at 80%. Given human nature, I predict you will have no problems succeeding in this (unless you run into someone who was at this Commencement, who actually listened to what I'm saying, and who was persuaded—a vanishingly small pool of people, I realize).

Then try this: When you encounter a problem, an issue on which reasonable people disagree, imagine all the arguments you would make, until the point where no alternative seems possible. Then start all over again, imagine you are the other person and make their arguments to the same end in your mind. And THEN try to hold both arguments in your head at once. This is very hard to do.

Seven, always remember that the problems of life may be different in consequences, but are more or less equal in complexity. As your parents will no doubt agree, deciding which school to send your child to can be just as vexing as any matter of American foreign policy. Do not be dismissive of any opportunity to bear witness to the difficulties of making the "right" call under any circumstances.

Remember, too, that being open is not only a way to truth and understanding but also helps build relationships. I learned a long time ago that in marriage, family life, and friendship there is no such thing as a contract. "But we agreed" does not work when feelings change. Empathy is a branch of openness, and empathy is crucial to any relationship at any level.

Keep notes. Ask yourself, what have I learned, why didn't I understand that, and how well did I follow my own principles. Everyone from researchers to wine experts knows that by writing down your impressions you understand your experience better and have a reference point for the future.

And, finally, know that aging makes it all much easier. The older you grow the less certain you are and the more you appreciate what humans have done with curiosity. Age will help you out, making you more patient with yourself and others, and more willing to be open to the baffling but exhilarating mysteries of the world.

So, there are the ten ideas: know your bad impulses; feel our vast ignorance; work at seeing the complexity of things, not the answers; make it a habit; ask more questions than provide answers; imagine you are the person you disagree with; see complexity in ordinary life; be open and empathetic in relationships; keep notes; and let age help you out.

I've been very fortunate to have my professional life correspond to my personal life: freedom of speech, the great American university, and being a law professor and president of Columbia have all been interwoven. This has given me a mine of precious materials from which to draw, from the national to the quotidian. I love each, and I love them all together. I still do not understand all I need to, but as they intersect, I understand each better. I hope and expect you will find the same is true in your lives.

Let me return to my opening remark that this is my last Commencement address. The "commencement speech" is one of the hardest in life to give. No remarks can live up to the meaning that this has for all of you. It is a bit of a trap because when you try to close the gap the risk is that you will end up with the cliché and the banal. Enough said on that. (I only ask that you give me credit for being self-aware.) But, for sure, the commencement speech focuses the mind. And, if you're ever asked to give one, I strongly urge you to say yes—and then get out of town as quickly as possible.

My deepest congratulations to all of you, and especially to my fellow Graduates of 2023.

Lee C. Bollinger stepped down from the Columbia presidency on June 30, 2023. He currently serves as President Emeritus, the first Seth Low Professor of the University, and a professor at Columbia Law School.

NOTES

PREFACE

1. I became especially familiar with these while serving as a director on the board of the Federal Reserve Bank of New York, from January 2007 to 2012, and as chair from 2010 to 2012.

2. As a director on the board of the Washington Post Company from 2007 to 2021, I observed these closely as well.

3. See also Lee C. Bollinger and Geoffrey R. Stone, eds., *Social Media, Freedom of Speech, and the Future of Our Democracy* (New York: Oxford University Press, 2022); Lee C. Bollinger and Geoffrey R. Stone, eds., *National Security, Leaks, and Freedom of the Press: The Pentagon Papers Fifty Years On* (New York: Oxford University Press, 2021); Lee C. Bollinger and Agnès Callamard, eds., *Regardless of Frontiers: Global Freedom of Expression in a Troubled World* (New York: Columbia University Press, 2021); Lee C. Bollinger and Geoffrey R. Stone, eds., *The Free Speech Century* (New York: Oxford University Press, 2018); Lee C. Bollinger, *Uninhibited, Robust, and Wide-Open: A Free Press for a New Century* (New York: Oxford University Press, 2010; Lee C. Bollinger and Geoffrey R. Stone, eds., *Eternally Vigilant: Free Speech in the Modern Era* (Chicago: University of Chicago Press, 2001); and Lee C. Bollinger, *Images of a Free Press* (Chicago: University of Chicago Press, 1991).

4. I also co-edited a book with friend and University of Chicago Law School professor, Geoffrey R. Stone: *A Legacy of Discrimination: The Essential Constitutionality of Affirmative Action* (New York: Oxford University Press, 2023).

2. SEVEN MYTHS ABOUT AFFIRMATIVE ACTION IN UNIVERSITIES

This speech was later published as Lee C. Bollinger, "Seven Myths About Affirmative Action in Universities," *Willamette Law Review* 38 (Fall 2002): 535–547.

6. CARDOZO LECTURE ON ACADEMIC FREEDOM

1. In the two decades since this lecture, the controversy has continued and escalated, with President Bollinger expressing alarm at the rise in anti-Semitism not only at Columbia, but across many peer institutions.

2. Frederick Rudolph, *The American College and University: A History* (Athens: University of Georgia Press, 1962), 412. See also Richard Hofstadter and Walter Metzger, *The Development of Academic Freedom in the United States* (New York: Columbia University Press, 1955), 383–497.

3. Ibid., 329–34; 412–13. See also *Encyclopedia Britannica Online*, s.v. "History of Education," http://www.britannica.com/eb/article?tocId=47616. See also *Encyclopedia Britannica* entries for "university" and " University of Berlin."

4. Ellen Schrecker, *No Ivory Tower: McCarthyism and the Universities* (New York: Oxford University Press), 15. See also Thomas L. Haskell, "Justifying the Rights of Academic Freedom in the Era of 'Power/Knowledge,' " in *The Future of Academic Freedom*, ed. Louis Menand (Chicago: University of Chicago Press, 1996), 43–53.

5. Ibid., 17

6. American Association of University Presidents, *The 1915 Report on Academic Freedom and Tenure* (1915), as excerpted in Haskell, "Justifying the Rights of Academic Freedom," 58–59.

7. Hofstadter and Metzger, *The Development of Academic Freedom*, 496.

8. Hofstadter and Metzger, 495

9. Hofstadter and Metzger, 495

10. As excerpted in Robert A. McCaughey, *Stand, Columbia: A History of Columbia University in the City of New York, 1754–2004* (New York: Columbia University Press, 2003), 247.

11. Hofstadter and Metzger, *The Development of Academic Freedom*, 498

12. McCaughey, *Stand, Columbia*, 248

13. See McCaughey, *Stand, Columbia*, 245–255; and Hofstadter and Metzger, *The Development of Academic Freedom*, 499–502.

14. McCaughey, *Stand, Columbia*, 251–253

15. Ellen Schrecker, "Political Tests for Professors: Academic Freedom During the McCarthy Years," October 7, 1999. Available at http://sunsite.berkeley.edu/uchistory/archives _exhibits/loyaltyoath/symposium/schrecker.html

16. Schrecker, *No Ivory Tower*, 10.

11. GLOBALIZATION AND FREE PRESS

This lecture was published as Lee C. Bollinger, "David C. Baum Memorial Lecture 2010," *University of Illionis Law Review*, no. 3 (2011): 1011–1030.

1. See Kelly Evans, "Strong Profits. Weak Economy. Odd Couple?," *Wall Street Journal*, July 30, 2010.

2. See WORLD TRADE ORG., TRADE PROFILES 2009; WORLD TRADE ORG. WORLD TRADE DEVELOPMENTS (2009).

3. See Internet World Stats, "Internet Usage Statistics: World Internet Users and 2023 Population Stats," last accessed April 3, 2011, http://www.internetworldstats.com/stats.htm.

4. See, e.g., Orayb Najjar, "New Trends in Global Broadcasting: 'Nuestro Norte es el Sur' (Our North Is the South)," *Global Media Journal* 6 (Spring 2007).

5. ComScore Inc., "The New York Times Ranks as Top Online Newspaper According to May 2010 U.S. ComScore MMX Data," press release, June 16, 2010, https://www.comscore .com/Insights/Press-Releases/2010/6/The-New-York-Times-Ranks-as-Top-Online -Newspaper-According-to-May-2010-U.S.-comScore-Media-Metrix-Data.

6. See generally Jeffrey D. Sachs, *Common Wealth: Economics for a Crowded Planet* (New York: Penguin, 2008); and Sachs, *The End of Poverty: Economic Possibilities for Our Time* (New York: Penguin, 2005).

7. For a general discussion of this issue as well as links to other sources, see "Saving the World, Without U.S. Consumers," editorial, *New York Times*, September 25, 2009, https://archive.nytimes.com/roomfordebate.blogs.nytimes.com/2009/09/24/saving-the -world-without-us-consumers/. See also INT'L MONETARY FUND, WORLD ECON. OUTLOOK UPDATE (2010); Edmund L. Andrews, U.S. *Sees Rough*

8. See, e.g., James K. Boyce, "Green and Brown? Globalization and the Environment," *Oxford Review of Economic Policy* 20, no. 1 (2004).

9. See generally INT'L MONETARY FUND, *supra* note 7.

10. See, e.g., Joseph E. Stiglitz, *Globalization and Its Discontents* (New York: Norton, 2002), 4–22.

11. Lee C. Bollinger, *Uninhibited, Robust, and Wide-Open: A Free Press for a New Century* (New York: Oxford University Press, 2010).

12. Bollinger, *Uninhibited, Robust, and Wide-Open*, 5–6.

13. See Martin A. Lee and Norman Solomon, *Unreliable Sources: A Guide to Detecting Bias in News Media* (New York: Carol, 1991), 102–41.

14. Manuel H. Johnson, "Federal Reserve System," Library of Economics and Liberty, last visited April 3, 2011, https://www.econlib.org/library/Enc1/FederalReserveSystem.html.

15. 376 U.S. 254 (1964); J. Skelly Wright, "Defamation, Privacy, and the Public's Right to Know: A National Problem and a New Approach," *Texas Law Review* 46, no. 5 (April 1968): 630, 647n59.

16. See Debs v. United States, 249 U.S. 211 (1919); Schenck v. United States, 249 U.S. 47 (1919).

17. Eugene V. Debs ran for president on the platform of the Socialist Party of America in 1904, 1908, 1912, and 1920. He was arrested and convicted of violating the Espionage Act of 1917 following a speech in Canton, Ohio, on June 16, 1918, in which he opposed the war and urged resistance to the draft. See, generally, Ernest Freeberg, *Democracy's Prisoner: Eugene V. Debs, the Great War, and the Right to Dissent* (Cambridge, MA: Harvard University Press, 2008). He appealed to the Supreme Court of the United States, which affirmed his conviction in 1919. *Debs*, 249 U.S. at 216–17. Debs's 1920 presidential campaign took place while he was still in prison. Freeberg, *Democracy's Prisoner*, 203–14.

18. See N.Y. Times Co. v. United States, 403 U.S. 713, 714 (1971) ("We granted certiorari in these cases in which the United States seeks to enjoin the *New York Times* and the *Washington Post* from publishing the contents of a classified study entitled 'History of U. S. Decision-Making Process on Viet Nam Policy.' ").

19. See BOLLINGER, *supra* note 11, at 24–29 (noting a line of Supreme Court cases finding the press has no constitutional right of access to information).

20. See id. at 29–43 (reviewing Supreme Court precedent accepting the constitutionality of the FCC's mandate of implementing a licensing and regulatory regime for the broadcast spectrum).

21. *See id.* at 88–91 (discussing China's restrictions on speech and press).

22. See, e.g., "Change You Can Believe In? The Prime Minister Calls Frankly for Political Reform," *The Economist*, August 26, 2010, http://www.economist.com/node/16891829?story _id=16891829 (stating that Chinese prime minister "declared that economic gains could yet be lost without reforms to the political system" including " 'creat[ing] conditions for the people to criticize and supervise the government' "); Interview by Bernard Gwertzman, Consulting Editor, Council on Foreign Relations, with Nicholas D. Kristof, Columnist, The N.Y. Times (June 2, 2009), http://www.cfr.org/china/ prospects-political -change-china/p19552 ("There's a view among the 'modernists' within the Communist Party that you can't continue to reform the economy and to develop an economy unless you loosen the political controls.").

23. See, e.g., Ross Clark, "China: Perestroika, No Glasnost," opinion, *Deccan Chronicle*, February 2, 2010, http://www.deccanchronicle.com/op-ed/china-perestroika-no-glasnost-748 ("China has in some cases used authoritarianism to promote economic growth. There is a direct link between the revival of the Chinese economy this year and the presence of greater government control."); Edwin J. Feulner, "China: Economic Growth Isn't Expanding Freedoms," CNS News, August 21, 2010, http://www.cnsnews. com/commentary/article /71513 ("[W]hile China is making vast economic progress, it isn't moving for- ward on human rights.").

24. See, e.g., Universal Declaration of Human Rights, G.A. Res. 217 (III) A, U.N. Doc. A/ RES/217(III), art. 19 (Dec. 10, 1948), http://www.un.org/en/documents/udhr/ (recognizing free speech as universal human right).

25. BOLLINGER, *supra* note 11, at 113 ("In an increasingly interconnected, global society, . . . censorship anywhere can become censorship everywhere."); see also Hillary Rodham Clinton, Sec'y of State, "Remarks on Internet Freedom," Washington, D.C., January 21, 2010,   https://2009-2017.state.gov/secretary/20092013clinton/rm/2010/01/135519.htm ("In an internet-connected world, an attack on one nation's networks can be an attack on all.").

26. Clinton, "Remarks on Internet Freedom," *supra* note 25; see also "Hillary Clinton Calls on China to Probe Google Attack," BBC News, January 21, 2010, http://news.bbc.co.uk/2 /hi/americas/8472683.stm (stating that China's response to Clinton's speech was that "the row should not be linked to relations with the US"). Also, Mrs. Clinton's speech implicitly recognized that internet freedom will be taken up as a matter of foreign policy: she stated that the State Department is trying "to coordinate foreign policy in cyberspace." Clinton, "Remarks on Internet Freedom," *supra* note 25. She also stated that the United States "intend[s] to address those differences [regarding the internet between itself and China] candidly and consistently in the context of our positive, cooperative, and comprehensive relationship."

27. Cf. Feulner, "China: Economic Growth Isn't Expanding Freedoms," *supra* note 23 (discussing U.S. economic dependence on China).

28. See BOLLINGER, *supra* note 11, at 18–19 (citing *New York Times v. Sullivan* for the idea

that sovereignty rests in the people and citing Harry Kalven's idea that *Sullivan* recognized that the "[First] Amendment has a 'central meaning'—a core of protection of speech without which democracy cannot function"); *id.* at 47 (arguing that "freedom of speech and press are essential to a self-governing society"); *id.* at 46–47 (citing John Milton, John Stuart Mill, and Justice Holmes for "interest in discovering the truth" as rationale for free speech); *id.* at 50 (viewing "our extraordinary protection of freedom of speech and press as an experiment in tolerance"). See generally David A. J. Richards, "Toleration and Free Speech," *Philosophy and Public Affairs* 17, no. 4 (1988): 323–336 (discussing Bollinger's conception of free speech promoting tolerance).

29. See, e.g., China Development Research Foundation, *Eliminating Poverty Thorugh Development in China* (New York: Routledge, 2009) (assessing China's recent achievements in reducing poverty); Yeubin Xu and Nelson Chow, *Socialist Welfare in a Market Economy: Social Security Reforms in Guangzhou, China* (New York: Routledge, 2001).

30. See, e.g., Hasan Kirmanoğlu, "Political Freedom and Economic Well-Being: A Causality Analysis," ECOOMOD Annual Meeting (2003) (describing generally scholars that correlate democracy with economic development); Yang Yao, "The End of the Beijing Consensus: Can China's Model of Authoritarian Growth Survive?," *Foreign Affairs*, February 2, 2010, https://www.foreignaffairs.com/articles/china/2010-02-02/end-beijing-consensus ("[T]here is no alternative to greater democratization if the CCP wishes to encourage economic growth and maintain social stability."); see also Jakob de Haan and Clemens L. J. Siermann, "New Evidence on the Relationship Between Democracy and Economic Growth," *Public Choice* 86 (1995): 175, 193. Although de Haan and Siermann do not take a strong position that democratic rights encourage economic growth ("[W]e question the robustness of the support that many authors claim to have found for a positive relationship between democratic freedom and eco- nomic growth."), their research recognizes that "when a country seeks a high level of economic growth, it is not appropriate to adopt a policy in which democratic rights are repressed." Further, Kirmanoğlu's own empirical research did not indicate a strong correlation between political freedom and economic growth. Kirmanoğlu, "Political Freedom and Economic Well-Being," *supra* at 7. See also Bill Emmott, "Communications, Media, and Economic Development," Doha Development Forum, February 17, 2004, http://www.billemmott.com/speech. php?id=8 (arguing that although "free media is . . . an important potential servant for economic devel- opment," "we in the media should be careful with how glibly we claim that a free media is essential for development").

31. Edmund S. Phelps, "Perspectives on Economic Development," keynote lecture, EcoSoc Conference, United Nations, New York, October 8, 2007 (providing definition of "dynamism").

32. My theory seems compatible with the New Growth Theory, which is a theory recently made popular by Paul Romer that argues generally that "economic growth results from the increasing returns associated with new knowledge." Joseph Cortright, "New Growth Theory, Technology and Learning: A Practitioner's Guide," *Reviews of Economic Development Lierature and Practice*, no. 4 (2001): ii. For a more in-depth discussion of the theory, see Terry Roe and Hamid Mohtadi, "International Trade and Growth: An Overview Using the New Growth Theory," *Review of Agricultural Economics* 23, no. 2 (2001): 423, 435 (describing growth from "innovation" and growth from "imitation").

33. It seems like many economists do not think the link is quite so direct (but it is acknowl-edged in the next paragraph that there is not too much evidence right now to support this theory). See, e.g., *supra* note 30 and accompanying text (discussing economists' hesi-tation in stating that there is a robust link between democratic freedoms and economic growth).

34. Office of the High Commissioner for Human Rights, "About the Universal Declaration of Human Rights Translation Project," United Nations, last visited April 3, 2011, http://www.ohchr.org/EN/UDHR/Pages/Introduction.aspx ("Drafted by representatives with different legal and cultural backgrounds from all regions of the world, the Declaration was proclaimed by the United Nations General Assembly in Paris on 10 December 1948").

35. International Covenant on Civil and Political Rights, G.A. Res. 2200A (XXI), U.N. Doc. A/RES/2200A (XXI) (Dec. 16, 1966), http://www2.ohchr.org/English/law/ccpr.htm.

36. United Nations, "What Are Member States?," last visited April 3, 2011, http://www.un.org/ depts/dhl/unms/whatisms.shtml. ("Currently there are 192 Member States of the United Nations.")

37. Adopted by the General Assembly in 1948, the Universal Declaration of Political Rights applies to all member states of the United Nations. Universal Declaration of Human Rights, *supra* note 24 ("Whereas Member States have pledged themselves to achieve, in co-operation with the Unit- ed Nations, the promotion of universal respect for and ob-servance of human rights and fundamental freedoms. Therefore THE GENERAL AS-SEMBLY proclaims THIS UNIVERSAL DECLARATION OF HUMAN RIGHTS as a common standard of achievement for all peoples and all nations . . . both among the peoples of Member States themselves and among the peoples of territories under their jurisdiction.").

38. International Covenant on Civil and Political Rights, *opened for signature* Dec. 19, 1996, 999 U.N.T.S. 171 ("Signatories: 72. Parties: 167.").

39. International Covenant on Civil and Political Rights, *supra* note 35.

40. International Covenant on Civil and Political Rights.

41. Organization of American States, "Human Rights," last visited April 3, 2011, http://www.oas.org/en/topics/human_rights.asp (noting that the court, located in Costa Rica, spe-cializes in cases involving human rights and other issues pertaining to that topic).

42. See Mark Drajem, "Google Wants U.S. to Weigh WTO Challenge to China," Bloomberg.com, March 3, 2010, https://www.bloomberg.com/news/articles/2010-03-03/google-wants-u-s-to-weigh-challenging-china-in-wto (describing Google's push to have China's censor-ship as an unfair barrier to trade before the WTO).

43. See, e.g., Daniel W. Drezner, "A Technical Solution to a Political Problem?," *Foreign Policy*, February 4, 2010, https://foreignpolicy.com/2010/02/04/a-technical-solution-to-a-political-problem/ (blog post by Daniel Drezner, professor at the Fletcher School of Tufts University, casting doubt on using WTO procedures to bring down China's "Great Firewall").

44. See, e.g., N.Y. Times Co. v. Sullivan, 376 U.S. 254, 280 n.20 (1964) (noting that the "consen- sus of scholarly opinion" supported the Court's decision and citing such articles).

45. Jim Lobe, "Networks' Int'l News Coverage at Record Low in 2008," Inter Press Service, January 5, 2009, http://ipsnews.net/news.asp?idnews=45300.

46. See, e.g., Katharine Q. Seelye, "Drop in Ad Revenue Raises Tough Question for Newspapers," *New York Times*, March 26, 2007, https://www.nytimes.com/2007/03/26/business /media/26paper.html (describing how ad revenues began dropping even before recession).

47. Diana Saluri Russo, "Is the Foreign News Bureau Part of the Past?," *Global Journalist* (Fall 2009), 22, 24 (discussing closing of foreign bureaus and increased reliance on outsourcing); see also Reena Vadehra, "The End of an Era?," *Global Journalist* (Winter 2006), 81 (noting the closing of international bureaus even before the recession).

48. See Philip Seib, "Hegemonic No More: Western Media, the Rise of Al-Jazeera, and the Influ- ence of Diverse Voices," *International Studies Review* 7, no. 4 (2005) (discussing increasing role of Al Jazeera in in- ternational news arena); Sky Canaves, "CCTV Advertising Revenue Set to Rise," *Wall Street Journal*, November 19, 2009, http://online.wsj.com /article/SB10001424052748704204304574545251004129012.html; Dan Carlin, "CNN, BBC, Al Jazeera . . . and France 24?," Bloomberg.com, December 4, 2006, https://www .bloomberg.com/news/articles/2006-12-04/cnn-bbc-al-jazeera-dot-dot-dot-and-france-24 -businessweek-business-news-stock-market-and-financial-advice.

49. See, e.g., Jason Stverak, "The Pros and Pros of 'Citizen Journalism," *Online Journalism Review*, March 12, 2010, https://www.ojr.org/the-pros-and-pros-of-citizen-journalism/index.html (defending necessity of citi- zen journalists in increasingly online world and encouraging partnership with traditional newspapers).

50. Edward H. Clarke, "Multipart Pricing of Public Goods," *Public Choice* 11 (Fall 1971), 17 ("The free market has long been regarded as inferior to other institutional devices for making re-source allocational decisions involving public goods."); Robert W. McChesney, "Theses on Media Deregulation," *Media, Culture, and Society* 25, no. 1 (2003):125, 130 (labeling media as a public good because it is nonrivalrous, and noting its long history of regulation).

51. BOLLINGER, *supra* note 11, at 65 (describing "concentration of ownership" as a positive de- velopment). Joint operating agreements were created by the Newspaper Preservation Act of 1970, Pub. L. 91-353, 84 Stat. 466 (codified at 15 U.S.C. §§ 1801–1804 (2006)), and exempted newspapers from certain antitrust laws.

52. 47 U.S.C. § 303 (describing powers and duties of the FCC).

53. Red Lion Broad. Co., Inc. v. FCC, 395 U.S. 367, 400–01 (1969).

54. See FCC v. League of Women Voters, 468 U.S. 364, 366 (1984).

55. But see, e.g., David L. Bazelon, "FCC Regulation of the Telecommunications Press," *Duke Law Journal* (1975): 213, 226–29 (questioning "overbroad regulation of protected activity"); David L. Lange, "The Role of the Access Doctrine in the Regulation of the Mass Media: A Critical Review and Assessment," *North Carolina Law Review* 52, no. 1 (1973): 85–89 (criticizing access doctrine as putting too much trust in regulators and leading to a centrist, "American orthodoxy").

56. BOLLINGER, *supra* note 11, at 65 (describing how "concentration of ownership" in the mid- twentieth century "allowed the press to accumulate wealth which could be used to increase the staff and the level of expertise of newsrooms. Specialists with extensive educational backgrounds in law, science, economics, the arts, and other fields were hired

to report on their respective areas of know- ledge."); see also Howard Tumber, "*Journalists at Work—*Revisited," *Javnost—The Public* 13, no. 3 (2006): 57, 63 (citing 1970s scholarship beginning to recognize that contemporary journalists "undergo a lengthy period of tertiary training in their specialty and when admitted to practice normally enjoy a share in a monopoly in the performance of their work").

57. Tumber, "*Journalists at Work—*Revisited," *supra* 59n56 (describing recent "de-professionalization" of journalism, and noting "the flow of information from a proliferation of sources involving the public challenges the role of the journalists as 'experts' in the dissemination of information").

58. The Corporation for Public Broadcasting, which allocates federal appropriations for national and local public radio and TV stations, projected $420 million in federal appropriations for fiscal year 2010. CORP. FOR PUB. BROAD., FY 2010 OPERATING BUDGET (2009). The Public Broadcasting Revenue report indicates that in fiscal year 2008, another $73,000 came from federal grants and contracts, and almost $700,000 from state and local governments, which, combined with the federal appropria- tions for the Corporation for Public Broadcasting, amounts to almost $500 million. CORP. FOR PUB. BROAD., PUBLIC BROADCASTING REVENUE: FISCAL YEAR 2008 2, tbl.1 (2009).

59. The BBC's finances are more substantially supported by the British government than NPR's. In the fiscal year 2009, the BBC received £3.49 billion in license fees, which are government-supported household broadcasting fees. BRITISH BROAD. CORP., THE BBC EXECUTIVE'S REVIEW AND ASSESSMENT PART 2, at 99 (2010). The BBC also broadcasts more globally than NPR: NPR's programming reaches 27.2 million listeners "across the nation and territories," through a collection of over 900 local radio stations nationwide, while the BBC's World Service reaches 180 million listeners around the world. "NPR Stations and Public Media, NPR, last visited April 3, 2011, https://www.npr.org/about-npr/178640915/npr-stations-and-public-media, while BBC's World Service reaches 180 million listeners around the world, "A Year in Numbers [2010]," BBC World Service, last visited April 3, 2011, http://www.bbc.co.uk/worldservice/institutional/2010/06/100628_annual_review_2010_a_year_in_numbers.shtml. BBC World Service is primarily supported by a government grant of £293 million. BRITISH BROAD. CORP., *supra*, at 2.

60. Donald R. Shanor, *News From Abroad* (New York: Columbia University Press, 2003), 15 ("More than 250 [U.S.] public stations carry the BBC or Britain's Independent Television Network (ITN), an increase of 10 percent after September 11."); BBC, "A Year in Numbers [2010]," n59 (BBC World Service gained 600,000 listeners in the United States in 2010).

61. B. S. Murty, *The International Law of Propaganda: The Ideological Instrument and World Public Order* (New Haven, CT: Brill, 1989), 174n103. "Senator Karl E. Mundt, speaking on the Voice of America in 1951, stated that its strategy was to drive a wedge be- tween the people and the ruling elite of the U.S.S.R., thus restraining them from embarking upon any aggression."

62. See United States International Broadcasting Act of 1994, H.R. 2333, 103d Cong. §§ 301–309 (1994) (enacted) (establishing Radio Free Asia and consolidating U.S.-sponsored international radio programming under the International Broadcasting Bureau).

63. 22 U.S.C. § 1461(a) (2006) (prohibiting the dissemination of information in the United States by these media).
64. 22 U.S.C. § 1461(a) (2006).

12. A FREE PRESS FOR A GLOBAL SOCIETY

This lecture was later published as Lee C. Bollinger, "A Free Press for a Global Society," *Bulletin of the American Academy of Arts and Sciences* 64, no. 2 (2011): 17–21.

1.   American Academy of Arts and Sciences, "About the Academy," https://www.amacad .org/about-academy.

14. THE REAL MISMATCH

Originally published as Lee C. Bollinger, "The Real Mismatch," *Slate*, May 30, 2013, https://slate.com/news-and-politics/2013/05/supreme-court-and-affirmative-action-dont -make-schools-trade-race-for-class.html.

15. TO MOVE FORWARD, WE MUST LOOK BACK

Originally published as Lee C. Bollinger, "To Move Forward, We Must Look Back," *Chronicle of Higher Education*, June 27, 2013, https://www.chronicle.com/article/to-move -forward-we-must-look-back/.

16. SIXTY YEARS LATER, WE NEED A NEW *BROWN*

Originally published as Lee C. Bollinger, "Sixty Years Later, We Need a New *Brown*," *New Yorker*, May 16, 2014, https://www.newyorker.com/news/news-desk/sixty-years-later-we -need-a-new-brown.

18. HOW TO FREE SPEECH: AMERICANS ONLY FIGURED OUT FREE SPEECH FIFTY YEARS AGO. HERE'S HOW THE WORLD CAN FOLLOW OUR LEAD

Originally published as Lee C. Bollinger, "Americans Only Figured Out Free Speech Fifty Years Ago. Here's How the World Can Follow Our Lead," opinion, *Washington Post*, February 12, 2015, https://www.washingtonpost.com/opinions/in-america-freedom-of -speech-hasnt-been-around-as-long-as-you-think/2015/02/12/3a2bec88-b0e8-11e4-886b -c22184f27c35_story.html.

19. WHAT ONCE WAS LOST MUST NOW BE FOUND: REDISCOVERING AN AFFIRMATIVE ACTION JURISPRUDENCE INFORMED BY THE REALITY OF RACE IN AMERICA

Published as Lee C. Bollinger, "What Once Was Lost Must Now Be Found: Rediscovering an Affirmative Action Jurisprudence Informed by the Reality of Race in America,"

Harvard Law Review 129, no. 6 (April 2016), https://harvardlawreview.org/forum/vol
-129/what-once-was-lost-must-now-be-found-rediscovering-an-affirmative-action
-jurisprudence-informed-by-the-reality-of-race-in-america/.

21. AFFIRMATIVE ACTION ISN'T JUST A LEGAL ISSUE. IT'S ALSO A HISTORICAL ONE.

Originally published as Lee C. Bollinger, "Affirmative Action Isn't Just a Legal Issue. It's
Also a Historical One.," opinion, *New York Times*, June 24, 2016, https://www.nytimes.com
/2016/06/25/opinion/affirmative-action-isnt-just-a-legal-issue-its-also-a-historical-one
.html.

22. THE NO-CENSORSHIP APPROACH TO LIFE

Originally published as Lee C. Bollinger, "The No-Censorship Approach to Life," *Chronicle of Higher Education*, September 18, 2016, https://www.chronicle.com/article/the-no
-censorship-approach-to-life/.

1. Knight Foundation, "Free Speech on Campus: A Survey of U.S. College Students and U.S.
    Adults," Arpil 4, 2016, https://knightfoundation.org/reports/free-speech-campus/.

28. THE FREE SPEECH CENTURY: A RETROSPECTIVE AND A GUIDE, PART 1: ONE HUNDRED YEARS OF FREE SPEECH

Published in Mark Matheson, ed., *The Tanner Lectures on Human Values*, vol. 38 (Salt Lake
City: University of Utah Press, 2020).

1. Sterling M. McMurrin, ed., *The Tanner Lectures on Human Values*, vol. 1, 1980 (Cambridge:
    Cambridge University Press, 2011).
2. Lee C. Bollinger, "Freedom of Press and Public Access: Toward a Theory of Partial Regu-
    lation of the Mass Media," *Michigan Law Review* 75, no. 1 (1976).
3. Lee C. Bollinger, *The Tolerant Society: Freedom of Speech and Extremist Speech in America*
    (New York: Oxford University Press, 1986).
4. Lee C. Bollinger and Geoffrey R. Stone, eds., *The Free Speech Century* (New York: Oxford
    University Press, 2018).
5. U.S. CONST. amend. I.
6. *Schenck v. United States*, 249 U.S. 47 (1919); *Debs v. United States*, 249 U.S. 211 (1919); *Frohwerk
    v. United States*, 249 U.S. 204 (1919).
7. In a representative case, the Court of Appeals for the Ninth Circuit upheld a conviction
    under the Espionage Act of an author who mailed a book suggesting that patriotism was
    an idea created by Satan. Since the work had the "natural and probably tendency" of pro-
    ducing actions that violated the Espionage Act, the First Amendment did not protect
    this speech. *Shaffer v. United States*, 255 F. 886, 887 (1919).
8. *Schenck*, 249 U.S. at 52.
9. *Debs*, 249 U.S. at 212.
10. *Abrams v. United States*, 250 U.S. 616, 630 (1919 (Holmes, J., dissenting).

11. 274 U.S. 357 (1927).

12. 274 U.S. 357 (1927) at 375 (Brandeis, J. dissenting).

13. 274 U.S. 357 (1927) at 376.

14. 274 U.S. 357 (1927) at 377.

15. *Dennis v. United States*, 341 U.S. 494 (1951).

16. *New York Times Co. v. Sullivan*, 376 U.S. 254 (1964).

17. *Cohen v. California*, 403 U.S. 15 (1971).

18. *Brandenburg v. Ohio*, 395 U.S. 444 (1969).

19. *New York Times Co. v. United States*, 403 U.S. 713 (1971); *United States v. Washington Post Co.*, 403 U.S. 713 (1971).

20. *Red Lion Broadcasting Co. v. FCC*, 395 U.S. 367 (1969).

21. *Miami Herald Publishing Co. v. Tornillo*, 418 U.S. 241 (1974).

22. See *Shaffer*, 255 F. 886 (1919).

23. See *Masses Publishing Co. v. Patten*, 244 F. 535 (1917).

24. *Noto v. United States*, 367 U.S. 290, 297–98 (1961).

25. *Dennis*, 341 U.S. at 510.

26. *Brandenburg*, 395 U.S. at 447.

27. See, e.g., *Chaplinsky v. New Hampshire*, 315 U.S. 568, 572 (1942) (identifying several categories of speech that did not receive full constitutional protection: "the lewd and obscene, the profane, the libelous, and the insulting or 'fighting' words those which by their very utterance inflict injury or tend to incite an immediate breach of the peace").

28. See *United States v. O'Brien*, 391 U.S. 367, 376 (1968) (rejecting the idea that a "limitless variety of conduct can be labeled 'speech' whenever the person engaging in the conduct intends thereby to express an idea").

29. See *Police Dep't of City of Chicago v. Mosley*, 408 U.S. 92, 95 (1972) ("[A]bove all else, the First Amendment means that government has no power to restrict expression because of its message, its ideas, its subject matter, or its content.").

30. See *O'Brien*, 391 U.S. at 381–82 (upholding a statute prohibiting the burning of draft cards because the governmental interest was in running a draft efficiently, not stopping antiwar protests).

31. See, e.g., *Central Hudson Gas v. Public Service Commission of New York*, 447 U.S. 557, 563 (1980) ("The Constitution . . . accords a lesser protection to commercial speech than to other constitutionally guaranteed expression."); *Pickering v. Bd. of Ed. of Twp. High Sch. Dist. 205, Will Cty., Illinois*, 391 U.S. 563, 568 (1968) (noting a need to strike a balance between public employees' speech rights and government's need to provide public services efficiently).

32. *Hague v. CIO*, 307 U.S. 496 (1939).

33. *Press-Enter. Co. v. Superior Court of California for Riverside Cty.*, 478 U.S. 1 (1986).

34. The Radio Act of 1927 created the Federal Radio Commission. In 1934, the law was repealed with the passage of the Communications Act of 1934, which created the Federal Communications Commission (FCC). 47 U.S.C. § 151 et seq.

35. 395 U.S. 367 (1969).

36. 418 U.S. 241 (1974).

37. *Red Lion*, 395 U.S. at 394.

38. *In Re Complaint of Syracuse Peace Council against Television Station WTVH Syracuse, New York*, 2 F.C.C. Rcd. 5043 (1987).

39. 403 U.S. 713 (1971).

40. See, e.g., *United States v. Aguilar*, 515 U.S. 593 ("As to one who voluntarily assumed a duty of confidentiality, governmental restrictions on disclosure are not subject to the same stringent standards that would apply to efforts to impose restrictions on unwilling members of the public.").

41. Cf. *Landmark Communications, Inc. v. Virginia*, 435 U.S. 829 (1978) (holding that news media could publish truthful information regarding confidential judicial inquiry proceedings that had been leaked); *Bartnick v. Vopper*, 532 U.S. 514 (2001) (refusing to punish a media outlet that published tapes that were obtained by a third party in violation of wiretapping laws).

42. David E. Pozen offers a more thorough exploration of this enforcement regime in "The Leaky Leviathan: Why Government Condemns and Condones Unlawful Disclosures of Information," *Harvard Law Review* 127, no. 2 (2013).

43. See, e.g., *Terminiello v. Chicago*, 337 U.S. 1, 4 ("A function of free speech under our system of government is to invite dispute.").

44. Alexander Meiklejohn, *Free Speech and Its Relation to Self-Government* (New York: Harper & Brothers, 1948).

29. THE FREE SPEECH CENTURY: A RETROSPECTIVE AND A GUIDE, PART 2: THE NEXT HUNDRED YEARS—A GLOBAL PUBLIC FORUM

Published in Mark Matheson, ed., *The Tanner Lectures on Human Values*, vol. 38 (Salt Lake City: University of Utah Press, 2020).

1. See, for example, Catharine A. MacKinnon, "The First Amendment: An Equality Reading," in *The Free Speech Century*, ed. Lee C. Bollinger and Geoffrey R. Stone (New York: Oxford University Press), 140.

2. John Stuart Mill, *On Liberty* (London: Longman, Roberts, & Green, 1869).

3. Donald J. Trump, "Press Conference after Charlottesville Violence," August 15, 2017, available at CSPAN, https://www.c-span.org/video/?432633-1/president-trump-news-conference?.

4. *N.Y. Times Co. v. United States*, 403 US 713 (1971).

5. David Strauss, "Keeping Secrets," in *The Free Speech Century*, supra 123n1.

6. Glenn Kessler et al., "President Trump Has Made More Than 5,000 False or Misleading Claims," *Washington Post*, September 13, 2018, https://www.washingtonpost.com/politics/2018/09/13/president-trump-has-made-more-than-false-or-misleading-claims/?utm_term=.fe33ofe7ce34.

7. Tim Wu, "Is the First Amendment Obsolete?," in *The Free Speech Century*, supra 272n1.

8. Fred Schauer, "Every Possible Use of Language?," in *The Free Speech Century*, supra 272n1.

9. *Debs v. United States*, 249 U.S. 211 (1919).

10. *Dennis v. United States*, 341 U.S. 494 (1951).

11. *Knight First Amendment Institute v. Donald J. Trump*, 302 F.Supp. 3d 541 (SDNY 2018).

12. Emily Bell, "The Unintentional Press: How Technology Companies Fail as Publishers," in *The Free Speech Century*, supra 235n1; Monika Bickert, "Defining the Boundaries of

Free Speech on Social Media," in *The Free Speech Century*, *supra* 254n1; Wu, "Is the First Amendment Obsolete?," *supra* note 7.

13. Communications Act of 1934, 47 U.S.C. § 151 et seq. (1996).

14. Tim Cook, chief executive officer, Apple Inc., "Keynote Address," 40th International Conference of Data Privacy and Privacy Commission, Brussels, Belgium, October 24, 2018.

15. Communications Decency Act of 1996 § 230, 477 U.S.C. § 230 (1996).

16. G.A. res. 217A (III), U.N. Doc A/810 at 71 (1948).

17. Dec. 16, 1966, S. Treaty Doc. No. 95-20, 6 I.L.M. 368 (1967), 999 U.N.T.S. 171.

18. American Convention on Human Rights, Nov. 21, 1969, 1144 U.N.T.S. 143.

19. 376 U.S. 254 (1964).

20. See Claire Cain Miller, "Google Has No Plans to Rethink Video Status," *New York Times*, September 14, 2012, https://www.nytimes.com/2012/09/15/world/middleeast/google-wont -rethink-anti-islam-videos-status.html. See also *Garcia v. Google, Inc.*, 786 F.3d 733 (9th Cir. 2015) (rejecting claim of unwitting actress featured in the trailer seeking preliminary injunction requiring Google to remove the fim from its platforms).

21. 561 U.S. 1 (2010).

22. 561 U.S. 1 (2010) at 33–37.

23. 52 U.S.C. § 30121.

24. 22 U.S.C. § 611 et seq.

25. See, e.g., 18 U.S.C. § 1030 .

26. *Trump v. Hawaii*, 585 U.S. (2018).

27. Brief of Colleges and Universities et al. as Amici Curiae Supporting Respondents, *Trump v. Hawaii* (March 30, 2018) (No. 17–965).

28. See Ana Swanson and Keith Bradsher, "White House Considers Restricting Chinese Researchers Over Espionage Fears," *New York Times*, April 30, 2018, https://www.nytimes .com/2018/04/30/us/politics/trump- china-researchers-espionage.html.

29. See Sewell Chan, "14 Million Visitors to U.S. Face Social Media Screening," *New York Times*, March 30, 2018, https://www.nytimes.com/2018/03/30/world/americas/travelers-visa -social-media.html.

30. Sarah Cleveland, "Hate Speech at Home and Abroad," in *The Free Speech Century*, *supra* 210n1.

31. Tom Ginsburg, "Freedom of Expression from Abroad: The State of Play," in *The Free Speech Century*, *supra* 193n1.

32. Global Freedom of Expression, Columbia University, "Case Law," last accessed December 14, 2018, https://globalfreedomofexpression.columbia.edu/cases/ (last visited Dec. 14, 2018).

33. Global Freedom of Expression, Columbia University, "Okuta v. Attorney General," last accessed December 14, 2018, https://globalfreedomofexpression.columbia.edu/cases/okuta -v-attorney-general/.

34. Global Freedom of Expression, Columbia University, "Primedia Broadcasting v. Speaker of the National Assembly," last accessed December 14, 2018, https://globalfreedomofexpression .columbia.edu/cases/primedia-broadcasting-v-speaker-national- assembly-2/.

35. Global Freedom of Expression, Columbia University, "Alestra v. Mexican Institute of Industrial Property," last accessed December 14, 2018, https://globalfreedomofexpression .columbia.edu/cases/alestra-v-mexican-institute-industrial-property/.

36. Global Freedom of Expression, Columbia University, "Korea Communications Standards Commission v. Martyn Williams," last accessed December 14, 2018, https://globalfree domofexpression.columbia.edu/cases/korea-communications-standards- commission-v -martyn-williams/.

37. Global Freedom of Expression, Columbia University, "Felix v. Gangadharan," last accessed December 14, 2018, https://globalfreedomofexpression.columbia.edu/cases/felix-v -gangadharan/.

38. Global Freedom of Expression, Columbia University, "Softić v. Montenegro (Constitutional Court)," https://globalfreedomofexpression.columbia.edu/cases/softic-v-montenegro/.

39. Procuradoria-Geral da República, " 'O ensino não se reveste apenas do caráter informa-tivo, mas de formação de ideias,' defende Raquel Dodge no STF," press release, Brasilia, last accessed December 14, 2018, http://www.mpf.mp.br/pgr/noticias-pgr/201c0- ensino-nao-se -reveste-apenas-do-carater-informativo-mas-de-formacao-de-ideia201d-defende-raquel - dodge-no-stf/.

30. HOW THE U.S. COULD PROSECUTE JAMAL KHASHOGGI'S KILLERS

Originally published as Lee C. Bollinger, "How the U.S. Could Prosecute Jamal Khashog-gi's Killers," opinion, *Washington Post*, March 31, 2019, https://www.washingtonpost.com /opinions/how-the-us-could-prosecute-jamal-khashoggis-killers/2019/03/31/1f8a7f4c -5180-11e9-88a1-ed346f0ec94f_story.html.

OTHER BOOKS BY LEE C. BOLLINGER

Eternally Vigilant: Free Speech in the Modern Era. Edited with Geoffrey Stone. Chicago: University of Chicago Press, 2001.

The Free Speech Century. Edited with Geoffrey Stone. New York: Oxford University Press, 2018.

Images of a Free Press. Chicago: University of Chicago Press, 1991.

A Legacy of Discrimination: The Essential Constitutionality of Affirmative Action. With Geoffrey Stone. New York: Oxford University Press, 2023.

Money, Politics, and the First Amendment: Fifty Years of Supreme Court Decisions on Campaign Finance Reforms. Edited with Geoffrey Stone. New York: Oxford University Press, 2025.

National Security, Leaks, and Freedom of the Press: The Pentagon Papers Fifty Years On. Edited with Geoffrey Stone. New York: Oxford University Press, 2021.

Regardless of Frontiers: Global Freedom of Expression in a Troubled World. Edited with Agnès Callamard. New York: Columbia University Press, 2021.

Roe v. Dobbs: The Past, Present, and Future of a Constitutional Right to Abortion. Edited with Geoffrey Stone. New York: Oxford University Press, 2024.

Social Media, Freedom of Speech, and the Future of our Democracy. Edited with Geoffrey Stone. New York: Oxford University Press, 2022.

The Tolerant Society: Freedom of Speech and Extremist Speech in America. Oxford: Clarendon Press, 1986.

Uninhibited, Robust, and Wide-Open: A Free Press for a New Century. New York: Oxford University Press, 2010.

INDEX